Michael's Guide
London

Yael Gilboa

MICHAEL'S GUIDE SERIES INCLUDES:

MICHAEL'S GUIDE ARGENTINA, CHILE, PARAGUAY
& URUGUAY
MICHAEL'S GUIDE BOLIVIA & PERU
MICHAEL'S GUIDE ECUADOR, COLOMBIA & VENEZUELA
MICHAEL'S GUIDE BRAZIL
MICHAEL'S GUIDE SOUTH AMERICA (Continental)

MICHAEL'S GUIDE NEW YORK CITY
MICHAEL'S GUIDE CALIFORNIA
MICHAEL'S GUIDE NORTHERN CALIFORNIA
MICHAEL'S GUIDE SOUTHERN CALIFORNIA

MICHAEL'S GUIDE SWITZERLAND
MICHAEL'S GUIDE SCOTLAND
MICHAEL'S GUIDE LONDON
MICHAEL'S GUIDE PARIS
MICHAEL'S GUIDE AMSTERDAM
MICHAEL'S GUIDE BRUSSELS & ANTWERP
MICHAEL'S GUIDE FRANKFURT
MICHAEL'S GUIDE MADRID
MICHAEL'S GUIDE JERUSALEM
MICHAEL'S GUIDE EASTERN TURKEY
MICHAEL'S GUIDE WESTERN TURKEY
MICHAEL'S GUIDE CYPRUS

MICHAEL'S GUIDE
London

By
Yael Gilboa

Series editor
Michael Shichor

*I*NBAL
Travel Information Ltd.

Inbal Travel Information Ltd.
P.O.Box 39090 Tel Aviv Israel 61390

©1989 edition
All rights reserved

No part of this publication may be reproduced, stored in a retrieval system. or transmitted in any form or by any means, electronic, mechanical, photocopying, recording or otherwise, without the prior written permission of the publishers.

ISBN 965-288-029-9

Graphic design: Orly Kaltboim
Cover photo: BTA
Photographs: T.I.B
Typesetting: Inbal Travel Info. Ltd.
Plates, printing & binding: Havatzelet Press

Distributors:
U.S. & Canada: Hunter Publishing Inc., 300 Raritan Center Parkway, Edison, New Jersey 08818; **U.K.**: Kuperard (London) Ltd., 30 Cliff Rd., London NW1 9AG; **Australia**: Rex Publications, 413 Pacific Highway, Arparmon, N.S. Wales 2064; **Belgium**: Geocart, Breedstra 108, 2700 Sint-Niklaas; **Bolivia**: Los Amigos del Libro, Casilla 450, Cochabamba; **Denmark and Finland**: Scanvik Books aps, Store Kongensgade 59 A, DK-1264 Copenhagen, K. Denmark; **France**: MA Editions, 6 rue Emile Dubois 75014 Paris; **Netherlands**: Nilsson & Lamm bv., Pampuslaan 212-214, 1382 JS Weesp-Nederland.

CONTENTS

Preface   **9**
Using this Guide   **11**

INTRODUCTION 13

Part One — An Overview   **13**
2000 Years of History (13), Landmarks in London's History (17), London Topography (18), Climate (20), Architecture — Periods and Styles (21), The City — The Business and Finance Center (23), The Royal Family (24), British Rulers from 1066 (25), Development of the Regime (26), British Society (27)

Part Two — Setting Out   **28**
When to Come and How Long to Stay (28), Holidays and Vacation Days (28), Documents (29), Customs (29), Insurance (30), How Much Will It Cost? (30), Clothing (31)

Part Three — Practical Information   **32**
How to Get There (32), Transportation in London (34), Accommodations (37), Services for the Disabled (41), Tourist Information (41), Important Tips for Getting Around (42)

LONDON 47

Getting to Know the City   **47**
Bus Tours (47), Water Tours (48), Walking Tours (48)

London Area by Area   **50**
The City of London — The Ancient Heart	50
The Inns of Court — The Halls of Justice	67
Adelphi and Covent Garden — The World of Dickens and the World of Theater	75
Whitehall and Westminster — Stronghold of the Regime	83
St.James's and Buckingham Palace — The Royal District	95

Mayfair — The Life of the Aristocracy	105
Soho — Bohemian Chic	112
Bloomsbury — The Home of Writers and Poets	120
Oxford Street and St. Marylebone — A Shopping Paradise	125
Regent's Park — The First Garden Suburb	130
Hyde Park and Kensington Gardens — Oasis in the City	134
Knightsbridge and Kensington — Shops and Museums	140
Chelsea — A Fashionable Address	145
Southwark — The City South of the Thames	151
The East End — An Immigrant's Haven, a Seaman's History	161
Hampstead — An Artist's Retreat	169
Greenwich — A Different Time	176
Kew Gardens and Richmond — From the Finest of Parks to the Finest of Villages	183
Hampton Court — Majestic Estate of the Kings	189
Windsor and Eton College — A Royal Retreat	194
London Under the Night Lights	200

An Umbrella for Two   **203**

London for Children   **204**

In the Lap of Nature — Parks and Gardens   **207**

"MUSTS" 213

Excursions   **217**

MAKING THE MOST OF YOUR STAY 224

Wining and Dining (224), Culture and Entertainment (233), Sports (239), Filling the Basket — Where to Shop for What (242), Important Addresses and Phone Numbers (251)

INDEX 253

NOTES 259

TABLE OF MAPS

OUR LONDON WALKS	inside front cover
THE CITY OF LONDON	51
TOWER OF LONDON	59
THE INNS OF COURT	70
ADELPHI AND COVENT GARDEN	78
WHITEHALL AND WESTMINSTER	86
WESTMINSTER ABBEY	90
THE ROYAL DISTRICT	98
MAYFAIR	106
SOHO	114
BLOOMSBURY	122
OXFORD STREET AND ST. MARYLEBONE	126
REGENT'S PARK	131
HYDE PARK AND KENSINGTON GARDENS	135
KNIGHTSBRIDGE AND KENSINGTON	142
CHELSEA	146
SOUTHWARK	154
THE EAST END	162
HAMPSTEAD	170
GREENWICH	178
KEW GARDENS	186
RICHMOND	187
HAMPTON COURT	190
WINDSOR AND ETON COLLEGE	195
LONDON UNDER THE NIGHT LIGHTS	202
THE LONDON UNDERGROUND	inside back cover

Preface

London is more than another destination in the modern tourist's itinerary; it is a prime visiting sight with tremendous appeal. The capital of the United Kingdom is not only Big Ben and the British Museum, but far beyond that. London is the Englishman, the theater, the department stores, the parks, the weather, the Houses of Parliament, the musical events, the Changing of the Guard, and more — it is one of the most diverse and dynamic cities in the world, and a world center of culture, entertainment, business, and shopping. It is a city that will intrigue and thrill any visitor.

As such, we have prepared a highly detailed and comprehensive guide book, catered to suit the needs of the traveler who is truely eager to get to know the city intimately. Whether a first time or frequent visitor, you will find that the guide offers a wealth of information and insights in a thorough, enriching, and enjoyable manner, to allow you to better appreciate London's sights, flavors, and people while saving time and money.

Much effort has been put into making the book. A team of London's experts and lovers has researched, compiled, organized, and verified the material.

I would like to thank Yael Gilboa, who wrote the guide, Amir Shichor and Eliezer Zaks who expanded the information and the entire team at Inbal Travel Information (1983) Ltd.

We all hope that your love for London will bloom during your visit and that your trip will remain a most fulfilling memory for days to come.

Michael Shichor

TO TRAVEL AROUND BRITAIN — FIRST GET TO THE CENTER

BRITISH TRAVEL CENTRE
12 Regent Street, Piccadilly Circus, London
Telephone: 01-730 3400

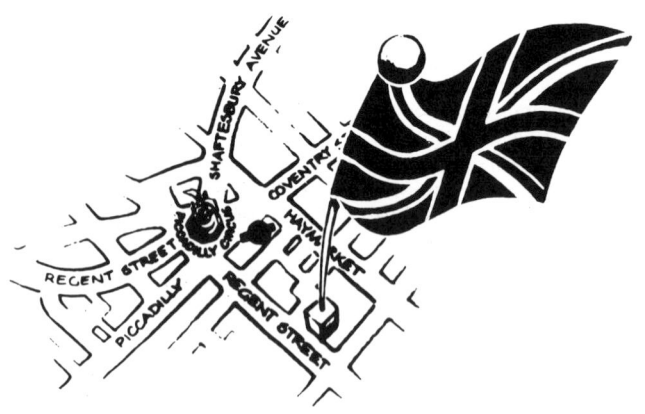

Free 'All Britain'
tourist information service

Reservations and Tickets for: Rail ★ Air
★ Car ★ Coach and Sightseeing tours
★ Foreign Exchange ★ Theatre ★ Travel books
and gifts ★ Accommodation
Open 7 days a week, Monday to Friday 9am-6.30pm
Saturday and Sunday 10am-4pm

 Over 700 Tourist Information Centres
at your service

Using this Guide

The facts contained in this Guide are meant to help you find your way around London, and to assure that you see the most, with maximum savings of money, time, and effort.

The basic guideline in all "MICHAEL'S GUIDE" publications is to provide practical information about a city, followed by an overview of sights and areas organized into walking tours.

The Introduction should be read carefully, as it supplies important details that will help you make the appropriate decisions and arrangements for your trip. Reviewing the material thoroughly will allow you to feel familiar and comfortable with London upon arrival.

The tour routes, laid out geographically, lead the visitor up and down London's streets, offering a survey of the sights and calling attention to those details that deepen one's familiarity with the city. The maps that accompany the tour routes have been specially prepared, and show the visitor exactly how to reach the sights and attractions discussed in the itineraries.

Following the tour routes, we have included a selection of excursions to places easily accessible within a few hours of London. Each of these excursions makes for a very pleasant day trip out of the city.

A concise list of "Musts" follows, describing those sights without which a visit to London is not complete.

Since London is a magnet for lovers of fine culture and entertainment, shopping, and good food, we have devoted special chapters to making the most of your stay in the city. Here you will find a broad range of possibilities to suit your interests, schedule, and budget.

To further facilitate use of this Guide, we have included a detailed index at the back of the book.

During your visit you will have many fascinating experiences. We have therefore left several blank pages at the back of the Guide. These are for you to jot down your observations, thoughts, and reactions along the way.

A rule of thumb when traveling, especially to a dynamic city like London, should be to consult local sources for opening hours, telephone numbers, and the like. Although we have made every effort to confirm that information is current, changes do occur and travelers may find that certian details are out of date. For this we apologize in advance.

In order to be as up-to-date as possible, assistance would be appreciated from those of you who have enjoyed the information contained in this Guide. For this purpose we have included a short questionnaire at the end of the Guide, and will be most grateful to those who complete it and send it to us. A **complimentary copy** of the new edition will be forwarded to those of you who take the time, and whose contribution will appear in the up-dated version.

Have a pleasant and exciting trip — Bon Voyage!

INTRODUCTION

Part One — An Overview

2000 Years of History

Under the concrete sea of the City of London lie the remains of a small Roman colony — the nucleus from which developed the great metropolis of London.

In 54 B.C. the Roman general Julius Caesar invaded the British Isles, which were inhabited by the Celts. The Romans failed to stabilize their hold, and in 43 A.D., during the period of Emperor Augustus, the Roman army invaded yet again. A short time after the second invasion, the Romans established the colony of Londinium — a Latinized Celtic name. Its strategic location off the bank of the river Thames made the colony a successful merchant's center.

Not long after its establishment, Londinium was sacked by the Iceni Queen Boadicea in 61 A.D. Her armies pillaged the city and massacred the inhabitants before they were defeated.

London was rebuilt by the Romans and grew rapidly. In the second century it was surrounded by a wall, and for the next thousand years the "Square Mile" comprised the main section of the city.

Under Roman rule in the fourth century, London became the most significant commercial center in southern England, and in 368 it received the title "Augusta" or Imperial.

Little is known about the period between the collapse of the Roman Empire in the fifth century and the Saxon occupation of the city. A bishop was dispatched to London at the beginning of the seventh century, although the major see was established in Canterbury, to the south. In the eighth century the English monk and historian, Saint Bede, described London as a thriving commercial center in his history of England.

In 836 Britain was invaded by the Scandinavian Vikings, called Danes by the British. The Danes settled in the eastern part of the island, in an area called Danelaw. They also captured London and terrorized its inhabitants. Some fifty years later, in 886, they were chased out of the city by the Saxons. The Saxons were led by King Alfred the Great — a title he earned after ridding London of the Danish oppression and subsequently developing the city.

The Danish threats, however, continued for the next 150 years or

INTRODUCTION

so, and in 1016 their king, Canute, was recognized as a ruler of all England. His death was followed by unrest, but it ended when Edward the Confessor was elected king in London in 1042. By this time London was already the largest city in England. Edward was the first king to leave the boundries of the City of London when he established a new center for government, west of the City, in Westminster.

Edward was educated in Normandy, which accounts for the substantial Norman influence of his rule. He died with no heir, but William, the Duke of Normandy demanded the Crown, claiming that Edward promised him his throne. The Londoners, who had already crowned Harold and were opposed to Norman rule, protested. They were defeated by William in the Battle of Hastings in 1066, and were forced to accept William the Conqueror as their king.

William stabilized his regime by granting a charter to the citizens of London in which he recognized their laws. In return they accepted him as sole secular authority. William brought a new spirit to the structure of the state and society. He allowed the citizens many rights, expressing a willingness to compromise. He ordered a survey that recorded and analyzed information on the holdings of the feudal lords, national resources, and population — the Domesday Book. He initiated the construction of a chain of strongholds to protect his Kingdom. The most famous of these is the White Tower, the earliest section of the Tower of London, which still stands today.

The citizens of the City of London utilized the rights granted to them. In 1135, after the death of Henry I, they chose a king, crowning Stephan. At the end of the century Londoners elected their own Lord Mayor, a privilege they still enjoy. Even today the English monarch must obtain the Lord Mayor's permission before making an official visit inside the City's boundries. The City's affairs were managed by the Corporation of London, the first city council to be established in the Kingdom.

The residents of London in the Middle Ages relentlessly demonstrated their independence. Two of their dignitaries are mentioned as those assigned to enforce the Magna Carta, the historical charter issued by King John in 1215 that granted fundamental freedoms to the church, nobles, and subjects. In 1265 they supported Simon de Monfort in his struggle against Henry III over the nobility's involvment in ruling the kingdom, thus aiding the establishment of the first parliament in the world. During the Peasant's Revolt in 1381, Londoners came to the aid of peasants who wanted to advance their rights by abolishing discriminating laws. Although Londoners did help them occupy the city, the revolt failed.

The activities of the guilds and the church during medieval times

INTRODUCTION

brought London a flourishing economy. The great monastic orders that established themselves in London accumulated considerable assets and developed the city by building great churches, including the awesome Gothic St. Paul's Cathedral, at the time the largest in Europe. The wooden London Bridge was reconstructed with stone during this period, thereby bolstering the development of commerce with the areas south of the river.

The sixteenth century saw the rise of the Tudors, who brought great changes to the kingdom and to London. The Crown increased its power at the expense of the merchants and the guilds. The feudal system was almost completely abolished and England became a naval power, whose embrace extended across the oceans.

Henry VIII had a dispute with the papacy over the issue of his divorce from Catherine of Aragon; in 1534 he established the Reformation in England through the Act of Supremacy, making the king head of the English church. The monasteries were closed and their land claimed by the Crown. Henry also began the construction of new palaces, including St. James's, Hampton Court, and Whitehall, which was never completed.

When the monasteries' lands were made available for sale, Londoners started to settle outside the City walls. During the reign of Queen Elizabeth I, the nobility also began moving out of the City, westward along the Strand on the road to Westminster. The queen tried to prevent this migration with a special decree issued in 1562 that prohibited construction within three miles of the City, but to no avail. By the end of the century the population of London had tripled and comprised a fifth of England's population.

The seventeenth century witnessed a series of catalytic events. King Charles I refused Parliament's demand to participate in church and military matters and the nomination of ministers. He attempted to arrest five of his opponents in the Parliament, ignoring their immunity. The five escaped to the City, raised an army, and, with the support of Londoners, declared war against the king. The civil war that erupted in 1642 continued until 1648 and ended with the deposition of the king. In January 1649 Charles was tried and beheaded.

England was declared a Commonwealth under the rule of Lord Protector Oliver Cromwell. After the death of Cromwell, civil rule failed to stabilize, and the reinstatement of the monarchy seemed the only feasible solution. In 1660 Charles II entered London followed by celebrating masses.

The Restoration, as Charles II's crowning is called, was followed almost immediately by two disasters. In 1665 the Great Plague infested the city, killing one-sixth of the population. A year later, in 1666, the Great Fire erupted, destroying eighty percent of the

INTRODUCTION

City in four days. A reconstruciton program started immediately at the initiative of the City fathers and the architect Sir Christopher Wren, who rebuilt most of the City's churches, among them St. Paul's Cathedral. The new buildings were constructed with bricks, not wood. The ancient pathways were preserved, and to this day the City has no wide boulevards or squares such those found in the western neighborhoods.

The Restoration also meant the revival of the nobility's political and economic standing. Two parties were founded at that time: the Tory party, which supported the divine origin of the king's supreme authority, and the rival Whig party, which demanded that the foremost authority be held by the Parliament.

The split was based on the political fear of an enforced return of Catholicism to England under influence of the French monarchy. For this reason the opponents of the Catholic King James II called in Prince William of Orange, ruler of Holland and the husband of Mary, James's Protestant daughter. William consented and in 1689 landed on the shores of England, claiming the throne without any bloodshed, an event called the "Glorious Revolution." William and Mary were crowned together as joint monarchs.

Eighteenth century England produced great political and commercial achievements. The aristrocracy continued intensive construction in the western neighborhoods, and Westminster soon outgrew the City in size. The wall that had surrounded the City since the Roman era was almost completely demolished. Slums sprung up next to the mansions, increasing the crime rate in those areas.

In the nineteenth century the British Empire's influence overseas grew. London continued to develop, annexing many villages, and the metropolitan area was enlarged. The London port grew to be the largest in the world.

Victorian London was a city of contrasts. On the one hand the industrial revolution brought thousands of workers to the city — stretching slum areas to the east and north of the City, and south of the river — pushing the crime rate up even further. Charles Dickens, the talented nineteenth-century novelist, vividly illustrates this period of London's history in his writings.

On the other hand, there was a marked improvement in the amount and quality of public service in the city: a police force was established to maintain public order and fight crime; gas street lights were installed; an extensive sewage system was constructed; new bridges were erected; mass transportation services were set into motion, including the underground train; more parks were opened to the public; museums opened; and new schools were added to serve the educational system.

INTRODUCTION

In the middle of the century London held the Great Exhibiton, for which the Crystal Palace was erected in Hyde Park. Toward the end of the century the Londoners were terrorized by the brutal murders of Jack the Ripper, who was never caught. In 1897 Queen Victoria celebrated 60 years on throne at her Diamond Jubilee.

The twentieth century and two world wars brought the decline of the Empire. The city's government became more centralized, and legislation was introduced to Parliament concerning the welfare of London. In 1932 the "Green Belt" was established around the city in an effort to prevent its expansion. In 1939 London reached a peak size; its population amounted to more than 8.5 million citizens.

Many Londoners still remember the trauma of the Blitz of 1940-41. For weeks on end the German air-force bombed the city, causing immense destruction in many areas. Towards the end of the war the Germans attacked with "Flying Bombs," new missiles that they developed during the war, threatening the population yet again. After the war an extensive rebuilding and reconstruction effort evolved in the city's damaged areas. In the City, the rebuilding continued for many years and only ended quite recently.

The Greater London Council (GLC) was established in 1965 to deal with the problems of the London metropolitan area and to incorporate the planning, development, and provision of municipal services under one roof. The prime minister dissolved the GLC in 1986; some say this happened because of the significant amount of political power the GLC had accumulated. Today London is governed by 33 local councils.

Landmarks in London's History

43 — Londinium colony is founded.
200 — Wall is constructed around the City.
836 — Viking invasion.
1066 — Norman conquest and crowning of William I.
1191 — First Lord Mayor of London is elected.
1215 — Magna Carta is signed by King John.
1269 — Westminster Abbey is dedicated.
1290 — Jews are expelled from England.
1301 — Road barrier is erected at Temple Bar to prevent the monarch from entering the City without the Lord Mayor's permission.
1348 — The Black Death takes the lives of half the city's population.
1381 — Peasants' Revolt, the rebellion attempting to end feudalism led by Wat Tyler, who was killed.
1461 — Beginning of the House of York period.
1483 — Child King Edward V is imprisoned and ostensibly murdered in the Tower of London.

INTRODUCTION

1485 — Beginning of the Tudor period.
1533 — The Reformation, in which monasteries are closed.
1562 — Queen Elizabeth I prohibits construction within a distance of three miles from the City.
1637 — Hyde Park becomes first park open to the public.
1649 — Charles I is executed. Commonwealth is established by Oliver Cromwell.
1660 — Restoration of the monarchy.
1665 — The Great Plague kills some 100,000 of the city's population.
1666 — The Great Fire destroys most of the area of the City.
1675 — Reconstruction of St. Paul's Cathedral is begun by Sir Christopher Wren.
1694 — The Bank of England is founded.
1714 — Beginning of the House of Hanover period.
1733 — Fleet River is covered and becomes a street.
1801 — First census indicates population of 1,117,290.
1832 — The National Gallery is founded.
1834 — Westminster Palace burns down.
1836 — First railway opens in London.
1843 — First tunnel under the Thames is built.
1851 — The Great Exhibition is held at the Crystal Palace, Hyde Park.
1852 — The Victoria and Albert Museum is founded.
1863 — First underground railroad line, the Metropolitan, opens.
1901 — Beginning of the House of Saxe-Coburg period.
1910 — Beginning of the House of Windsor period.
1932 — Green Belt is established around the urban area.
1939 — London population reaches record size of 8,615,050.
1940 — The Blitz. German air raids destroy a large part of the City and the East End.
1965 — Greater London Council is established.
1986 — The Greater London Council is dissolved.

London Topography

The Romans who founded the Londinium colony in the middle of the first century A.D. did not choose a particularly fertile area. The Thames River basin, surrounded by limestone hills, is built of tertiary layers created by glacial and river erosion. The clay earth is heavy and marshy and almost impossible to cultivate. This farmer's curse, however, was the builder's blessing; the same clay provided many generations with excellent construction material, used to produce the red bricks that are typical of the London suburbs.

Why did the Romans settle in the center of a swamp? The answer lies in the Thames River. Some 65 kilometers from the mouth of the

INTRODUCTION

Thames at the North Sea, just before the river makes a huge turn (around the Isle of Dogs), two sedimentary rubble hills were created on the northern bank. The tide of the North Sea reached this point and even farther west, enabling passage of boats inland; with this artery for transport, Londinium quickly became southern England's major trade center. Two small rivers, the Fleet and the Walbrook, crossed the city and emptied into the Thames, which made it possible for small boats to enter the city as well. These rivers still flow, but they are now underground, covered by streets. The marshy quality of the soil has not changed, and London is sinking at a rate of about 30 centimeters a century.

The North Sea tides, which brought economic and commercial prosperity up until the end of the nineteenth century, also caused vast damage by frequently flooding the city. A complex engineering project resulted in the Thames Barrier, which has protected London from this danger since 1982. Over hundreds of years the river became increasingly polluted, the end product of the constant dumping of London's sewage into the Thames. The problem was reduced in the 1860s when an extensive sewage system that ran parallel to the river was installed. Current laws concerning industrial emissions and advanced purification systems have gone a long way toward sanitizing the river, although the situation is still problematic.

The actions of reigning monarchs also took part in shaping London's landscape. The kings and queens of England, who did not like to mingle with their subjects, built the Westminster and Whitehall Palaces upstream, moving the center of the government westward. Some of the monarchs tried to limit expansion of the City, and even issued royal decrees forbidding construction within a considerable radius from the City walls, but the growth persisted.

The major thrust of development began after the Great Fire in 1666, which had destroyed a large part of the City, and gained momentum during the following century. In the second half of the eighteenth century, the aristocracy developed the areas in the West, such as the Mayfair, St. James, Soho, St. Marylebone, and Bloomsbury districts. The poor settled to the east of the City, in the East End and south of the river.

In the nineteenth century the northern suburbs developed, as did additional areas south of the river. Great changes took place in the land by the Thames. Once a sewage system had been installed and the water cleaned, embankments were built along the river. The development of trade in the British Empire necessitated the establishment of wharves, anchorages, and warehouses on the lengthy shores; the Port of London became the largest in the world. But the fall of the Empire during the first half of the twentieth century, combined with the construction of giant merchant ships too large

INTRODUCTION

for the port brought its decline and its docks were finally closed in the 1960s. This wide area is now an attraction for entrepreneurs and speculators, who view it as a spot for future residential and commercial development of the city. The shipping center itself was moved east, closer to the mouth of the Thames, in Tilbury.

The Greater London Council (GLC) played a significant role in shaping the landscape of the metropolis, until its abrogation in 1986. The 33 local councils that now govern London allow the city to take form without a master plan, subject to the political, economic, and cultural whims of its population.

Today's Greater London is a collection of villages and towns that comprise an area of some 1600 square kilometers (610 square miles). The core is Central London, consisting mainly of the City and Westminster. Surrounding this core is Inner London, an area that grew until World War I. Outer London, the exterior ring, developed during this century. It is bordered by the Green Belt, the rural district that was legally designated to prevent further expansion of the city. In fact, the urban region is contained not only in size: migration to rural areas continues, and the city's population is now smaller than it was during World War II.

Climate

The British climate is famous for its unpredictability. A standard daily forecast from the meteorological service usually includes grey skies, scattered showers and temporary clearing, with rain again the following day. The most stable thing about the weather is its instability.

The continual rainfall, which has no regard for season, is part of a relatively mild climate. Although the British Isles lie at the same latitude as colder countries such as Holland and Denmark, the residents here enjoy the benefits of the warm sea current from the Gulf of Mexico. Even after its long journey across the Atlantic, the current is still strong enough to warm the western coast of the British Isles considerably. The eastern shore, which is closer to London, is colder, as it is chilled by the icy North Sea.

Although England is cold in the winter, it is seldom freezing, and the light snow that occasionally falls in London rarely sticks. In the summer thunderstorms and heavier rainfall can be expected.

For many years, most commonly during the winter, the combination of high humidity and air pollution created a thick smog called "pea soup," a phenomenon that made London notorious for its eerie, vision-reducing aura. However, strict enforcement of environmental quality laws has minimized the air pollution level in the city, and

INTRODUCTION

the heavy fog has been relegated to history, and to the scenery of Sherlock Holmes stories.

Architecture — Periods and Styles

It seems that the channel separating the British Isles and the European continent was no barrier to the influence of European artistic and architectural styles on local construction, although most of the great architects who built London were local residents. The major trends in British art, however, did not always coincide with nor necessarily suit European taste.

Londinium was a typical Roman colony, and like other colonies it had a basilica, a temple to the gods, villas, and bathhouses. The British laws for preservation, which strictly protect structures from the last few centuries, failed to ensure preservation of most of the Roman remnants that were uncovered in the City. Part of the wall and the Temple of Mithras are the only remains that, due to public pressure, were preserved and restored close to where they were found.

The Saxon style of architecture is shrouded in mystery. The Saxons built mainly with wood, and, because of constant dampness and fires, little has survived of their buildings. The oldest structures in the city date back to the Norman period, the most famous being the White Tower of the Tower of London. The Norman Conquest resulted in the construction of large fortresses and an augmentation of Romanesque architecture. England boasts some of the most splendid creations of this school, which has left its impression in huge churches with large arcades and vaulted roofs. A small sampling of this style can be seen in London in the Temple Church, in the Church of St. Bartholomew the Great, and in the White Tower prayer chapel. Larger and more impressive Romanesque churches can be found in other parts of England.

The architecture of the Middle Ages reached its peak of development during the Gothic period. The Gothic style began in the late twelfth century and it remained prominent until the sixteenth century. Typical features include pointed arches, elongated windows, protruding ribs, and flying buttresses. Of the Gothic churches that have survived in London, the most famous is Westminster Abbey. Next to it stands Westminster Hall, part of the Westminster Palace that burned down in the nineteenth century. Another example is the Southwark Cathedral, the largest Gothic structure in London.

The Gothic school of architecture influenced the buildings of the Tudor period. These were characterized by the widespread use of wood rafters, turrets, and sharply sloping roofs. The private buildings in London were made primarily of wood, most of which

INTRODUCTION

were destroyed in the Great Fire of 1666. The most impressive Tudor-style building in the London area is Hampton Court Palace.

The end of the sixteenth century is characterized by the classical influences of the Italian Renaissance. Architect Inigo Jones built the Banqueting House in Whitehall and the Queen's Palace in Greenwich according to the theories of the Italian Andrea Palladio, who in 1570 published a treatise on the principles of classical architecture. John Webb, a pupil of Jones, also contributed to some of the buildings in Greenwich.

During the early seventeenth century the Jacobean style of elaborately carved wood and molded plaster was popular. This style can be seen in some of London's older pubs. In the mid-1600s many of the City's churches that burned in the Great Fire were being restored. The architect Sir Christopher Wren, influenced by the Baroque style, was responsible for much of the restoration. His finest creation is undoubtedly St. Paul's Cathedral, with its huge Baroque dome. Wren also built the Royal Hospitals in Chelsea and Greenwich, as well as wings of the palaces at Hampton Court and Kensington. Other famous Baroque architects were Nicholas Hawksmoor, Thomas Archer, and James Gibbs.

In the eighteenth century there was a reaction against the Baroque influence and a return to simplicity and the classical principles of Palladio. Queen-Anne period architecture manifests none of the Baroque ornamentation and is characterized by clean, elegant lines. Richard Boyle, Earl of Burlington, helped lead the return to Palladian principles, followed by John Wood and his son, also named John. The neoclassical style reached its peak with Robert Adam, who built the Adelphi in London, and Sir William Chambers who built Somerset House.

Nineteenth-century English Regency architecture is characterized on the one hand by progress, and on the other by a search for roots. The classical revival is seen in the design of Regent Street in London, by John Nash. He transformed the neoclassical into something more flowing and picturesque. His long terrace houses were inhabited mainly by the wealthy. The Gothic revival was led by Augustus Pugin and Sir Charles Barry, evident in the Houses of Parliament, and by Sir George Gilbert Scott, who designed the Albert Memorial. The Tudor revival is represented in Lincoln's Inn. On the other hand, the use of modern materials led to the exploration of new styles. Crystal Palace, built in honor of the Great Exhibition, was constructed of iron and glass, so that it could be dismantled and moved. Modern materials such as concrete, steel, and glass were used mainly for bridges, train stations, factories, and the like. Private construction was dominated by the Victorian style, still typical of many London neighborhoods.

INTRODUCTION

In the present century London's growth and development have been extremely rapid. In the new suburbs, relatively low buildings were raised, each with an adjacent yard. The buildings were functional, built of red bricks, without the typical Victorian curves. Only after the Second World War, when the Germans destroyed many of the existing building, was wide-spread public construction allowed in the City of London. One project, the large Barbican complex, is controversial not only because of its questionable esthetic value but also in terms of its practicality. The skyscrapers have created a new and interesting horizon for the City, but no functional modern planning is visible in the street. London, it appears, is still chained to its historical and architectural past.

The City —
The Business and Finance Center

The financial trade center that developed in the City of London, the ancient core of the city, plays an important role in international economy today. During the last century the economic activity of the Empire was centered in London, and, even after its fall, many financial institutions continued to function there. Today almost every self-respecting international bank has a commercial branch in the City. The banks played a significant role in the renovation of the City after the Second World War devastation.

In October 1986 London became the financial nerve center of the world with an event known as the Big Bang. This event, the deregulation of the influential, yet relaxed London Stock Exchange, threw the system into the fast-paced, complex, and highly competative world of electronic international finance. The effects of the Big Bang were felt by crowds of brokers who were replaced by flickering screens. Updated information shown on the screens simplified trade in international shares and at the same time tremendously increased the turnover of transactions. Negotiated commission rates, international computer link-up networks, and independent off-the-floor trading, also a result of the Big Bang, lured international investors to the City, who were already attracted to the lucrative Eurodollar market.

An important advantage of the City's finance market stems from its geographic location. Trade starts in London just before it closes in the Far East, and closes after trade has begun in New York. Therefore investors in London can constantly be on top of the international market.

In the City there is also an exchange for future merchandise, the London International Financial Futures Exchange (LIFFE) at the Royal Exchange, where prices are set by verbal agreement. Here

INTRODUCTION

the festivity of specualtion integrates with the festivity of colors created by the jackets worn by representatives of the various institutions.

The Royal Family

"We are not a family," King George VI once declared, "We are a firm." These words, proclaimed more than fifty years ago, stand true to this day.

The Royal Family is the most important and central asset in the life of the British nation. Queen Elizabeth II of Windsor, in addition to being one of the wealthiest women in the world, has a well-established family tree. Its roots go back to the sixth century, to Cedrick, king of the conquering Saxons, through Alfred the Great and William the Conquerer. She is also related by blood and by marriage to most European royalty; even her husband, Prince Phillip, is a distant cousin.

The continued rule of the British monarchs was broken only once, for a decade starting in 1649, when the Commonwealth was declared and later governed by Oliver Cromwell.

The scepter of rule is always passed to the eldest son or to his descendants. If there is no son, the oldest daughter takes the crown, and it is passed on to her descendants. The next heir to the throne is Prince Charles of Wales, followed by his eldest son.

The queen heads the Anglican Church, and she is the supreme ruler of the United Kingdom and of what remains of the British Empire. Her official title is "Elizabeth the Second, by the Grace of God of the United Kingdom of Great Britain and Northern Ireland and of Her Other Realms and Territories, Queen, Head of the Commonwealth, Defender of the Faith." In many of the former Crown colonies, including some full democracies such as Canada and Australia, the queen is still the official head of state, and is represented there by the High Commissioner.

The British adore their queen and they strictly preserve the ceremonies and manners that maintain her status as head of the nation. Although Britons sometimes explain their devotion by pointing out the great importance of the Royal Family as a tourist attraction, there is no doubt that the members of the Royal Family have a no less important a social role.

Modern mass media also helps reinforce the status of the Royal Family. Journalists are aware of the family's power and take advantage of its activities. The crowning of Queen Elizabeth II, in 1952, was the first such ceremony ever to be broadcast on television, direct to millions of viewers. This was also the first time

INTRODUCTION

that all subjects of the British monarchy could watch the ancient, mysterious, and exclusive ceremony, which until then had been restricted to royalty and heads of state. The trend of including the public reached a climax in the coverage of the splendid wedding of Prince Charles and Lady Diana Spencer, which was transformed into an international media celebration.

British Rulers from 1066

William I: 1066-1087
William II: 1087-1100
Henry I: 1100-1135
Stephen: 1135-1154
Henry II: 1154-1189
Richard I: 1189-1199
John: 1199-1216
Henry III: 1216-1272
Edward I: 1272-1307
Edward II: 1307-1327
Edward III: 1327-1377
Richard II: 1377-1399
Henry IV: 1399-1413
Henry V: 1413-1422
Henry VI: 1422-1461, 1470-1471
Edward IV: 1461-1470, 1471-1483
Edward V: 1483
Richard III: 1483-1485
Henry VII: 1485-1509
Henry VIII: 1509-1547
Edward VI: 1547-1553
Lady Jane Grey: 1553
Mary I: 1553-1558
Elizabeth I: 1558-1603
James I: 1603-1625
Charles I: 1625-1649
Commonwealth declared: 1649
Oliver Cromwell, Lord Protector: 1653-1658
Richard Cromwell, Lord Protector: 1658-1659
Charles II: 1660-1685
James II: 1685-1688
William III: 1689-1702
  together with
Mary II: 1689-1694
Anne: 1702-1714
George I: 1714-1727
George II: 1727-1760
George III: 1760-1820
George IV: 1820-1830

INTRODUCTION

William IV: 1830-1837
Victoria: 1837-1901
Edward VII: 1901-1910
George V: 1910-1936
Edward VIII: 1936
George VI: 1936-1952
Elizabeth II: 1952-

Development of the Regime

The regime in England is known as a legal monarchy, that is, although the king or queen is the supreme ruler of the land, laws are determined by a national assembly, the Parliament. This kind of government is the result of a process of nearly one thousand years. An important milestone in its development was the famous signature of the Magna Carta by King John. In this document the nobility demanded liberties that would protect them against the monarchy.

The Parliament was first convened in 1265 by Simon de Montfort, and was actually forced upon King Henry III. Initially, it met infrequently; it was only during the reign of King Henry VIII that a regular schedule of sessions was set. The power accumulated by this body was sometimes a hindrance to the sovereigns of England. The struggle between the monarchy and the Parliament came to a head in the seventeenth century, under King Charles I, and resulted in the English Civil War. Charles I was defeated — and executed — and the Parliament ruled without a king for a decade. When a monarch was again throned, the balance of power was more even.

The Parliament is composed of three separate bodies: the monarch; the House of Lords, in which only people who have inherited or received titles are represented; and the House of Commons, consisting of representatives of the parties, chosen in general elections. England has no written constitution, so the Parliament may legislate on various issues as it sees fit. The British view this as a great advantage because legislation can suit the spirit of the times, without the restrictions of a basic constitution. The Parliament meets annually; the session is opened by the queen with an impressive traditional ceremony held in the House of Lords. Members of the House of Commons are invited to attend.

Elections are held in Britain at least every five years. The queen appoints the head of the largest faction in the House of Commons to set up a government, and it is the government that determines the domestic and foreign policy of the state. The queen's role is mainly representative and her real influence on government policy is minimal.

INTRODUCTION

British Society

The British are almost unmatched in their social stratification. The differences in social standing are clear and expressed in almost everything, from titles to dress and manners. A person's background can be identified on the basis of his accent — Oxford, Scottish, Welsh, North London, East London, Cockney, public school, etc.

Until the First World War the nobility constituted the elite of English society. In many families, vast land assets were passed from one generation to the next. Royal titles were often attached to their names, such as Duke, Marquis, Earl, Viscount, Baron, and Baronet. The landed aristrocracy declined after the war, while the middle class grew, setting the tone for economic and cultural life. The working class remained in the same position as before.

Although the aristocracy did lose their assets, many British to this day proudly bear their family coat of arms. These date back to the Middle Ages when symbols were drawn on the knights' armor in order to distinguish among them.

London of the 1980s is full of foreigners — immigrants from Europe and the West Indies, India, Pakistan, and Arab nations — a great mixture of races, religions, and languages that gives the city a special cosmopolitan feeling. The presence of immigrants in recent years has at times been a point of contention for the local English, depending on the economic situation, although it has also made them more tolerant.

INTRODUCTION

Part Two — Setting Out

When to Come and How Long to Stay

Come to London whenever you can and stay as long as possible. The spread of tourism and the rise in trade bring more and more people each year, and each year London becomes increasingly dynamic and noisy. Once summer was the "season," when the aristocracy would move from the rural areas to their city residences in order to spend time at the theater, the opera, and at social gatherings. Today there is less distinction among the seasons, and each month has advantages benefitting a visit.

Tourism is still relatively heavier during the summer months; at this time the competition for hotels and the crowds at tourist sights and activities are greatest. For culture-lovers, the height of theater activity, festivals, and musical events is in the summer.

It rains all year round, although the summer is rainier than the winter. The winter is cold, although advantages to visiting in January are the end-of-the-season sales and large discounts after Christmas.

The most beautiful time of the year is the spring: the city is full of flowers from around Easter until the end of May. The beauty of the English springtime has been expressed by many poets.

London is a city of discoveries. The more you investigate, the more charming, unique spots you will find. It is best to plan your first visit for at least a week to ten days. After that, the desire to stay longer will come naturally.

Holidays and Vacation Days

Some Britons claim that they have more vacation days than work days; a few of these are religious holidays, and the rest are civil holidays, known as bank holidays, which usually fall on Monday, making a long weekend. Various tourist facilities and places of interest are closed on these holidays.

January 1	New Year's Day (if it falls on Sunday, it is celebrated on Monday)
April (date changes)	Good Friday
	Easter Monday
First Monday of May	May Day Bank Holiday

INTRODUCTION

Last Monday of May	Spring Bank Holiday
Last Monday of August	Summer Bank Holiday
December 25	Christmas
December 26	Boxing Day

On Saturdays most shops are open, some banks remain open half a day, and government offices are closed. They are also closed on Sundays, as are banks and most shops.

On Christmas most banks, government offices, shops, department stores, museums, and historic sites are closed. Some are also closed on other holidays — you should check ahead of time. If you intend to travel to Scotland or Northern Ireland, it is worthwhile checking their holidays and vacation days as well.

Documents

Foreigners need a valid passport or other official documents that confirm national identity in order to enter the United Kingdom as a tourist. In most cases citizens of the European Common Market countries and the United States of America do not need a visa for entry. Citizens of the Commonwealth countries are required to obtain entry certificates at their local consulates, in place of a visa.

Before going through passport control, you must fill out a landing card. The entry permit stamped in your passport will include a time limit for your stay (up to 6 months), as well as additional restrictions, such as the right to work.

In order to extend your stay you should apply, before the permit expires, to the Deputy Minister of the Interior, Immigration and Nationals Section, Lunar House, Wellesley St., Croydon (Tel. 686-0688).

If you want to drive a vehicle, be sure to obtain an international drivers' license or a valid license with an identifying photograph that is recognized outside your own country.

An international student card is an advantage. It entitles the carrier to discounts at various tourist sights and sometimes on performance and concert tickets.

Customs

British law requires tourists entering the country to declare any products over the amount that is exempt from tax and customs, any product that is prohibited or restricted for import, and all items intended to be left or sold in Britain.

INTRODUCTION

You are not required to declare your personal possessions (unless you intend to stay in Britain over 12 months), nor tax-exempt items that were purchased outside of the Common Market, such as the following:

Tobacco: 200 cigarettes or 100 cigarillos or 50 cigars or 250 grams tobacco

Alcohol: 1 liter of a beverage containing more than 22% alcohol, or 2 liters of a beverage contianing less than 22% alcohol, in addition to 2 liters table wine

It is forbidden to bring counterfeit coins or bills, flick knives, or pornographic material of any type into England. Products requiring a license include medicine, regulated drugs, arms, radio and telephone equipment, plants, and animals.

Strict laws concerning pets require that they be left in quarantine for a long period — 35 days for birds and 6 months for animals. Consequently, it is best that they be left at home.

Insurance

The health services in Britain are highly developed. Free treatment is extended only to citizens of the Common Market, and to citizens of countries that have a reciprocal medical agreement with Britain. Visitors who are not in this category are treated gratis at the emergency wards in Nationl Health Service hospitals, but hospitalization is at your expense — and it is expensive! Therefore it is wise to arrange medical insurance in your home country (in the hope that you will not need it). It is also worthwhile to insure your personal belongings against loss or theft, as such incidents occasionally occur.

How Much Will It Cost?

It is up to you! Set a budget according to your means, as the channels for spending in London are endless — theater, music, clothes, restaurants (not necessarily in that order), and more.

For the struggling student, it is recommended to budget at least £25 per day, in order to enjoy the city's treasures as you should. From this point on, the expenses only increase. The average cost in a moderate-priced hotel ranges from £40 to £80, and to this you should add meals out, sightseeing, entertainment, and shopping. The prices in the prestigious hotels are sky-high, as they are in the fine restaurants.

In other words, your trip to London should be budgeted according to your ability, aspirations, and, naturally, the length of your stay.

INTRODUCTION

Clothing

Whatever season you come to London you should take a light raincoat, as it rains often throughout the year. In fact, some say the trademark of the Englishman is an umbrella.

The most pleasant months are spring and fall, when the weather is comfortable and ideal for touring. You should have a light jacket or coat because evenings — in the summer as well — can be cool. In winter, you should be prepared for the possibility of cold days, although the temperature rarely drops below freezing, and bring sweaters and warmer clothing.

Men are advised to include a jacket and tie in their travel wardrobe, and women should take a good outfit. Formal dress is part of being British, and it is customary to dress accordingly for the theater and events such as the Ascot horse races.

INTRODUCTION

Part Three — Practical Information

How to Get There
England is an island and can be reached only by sea or by air.

By Air
Two major international airports serve London: Heathrow and Gatwick. International flights also land at two smaller London airports, Luton and Stansted; the latter is the third in size in London.

In Greater London, in the Docklands area, there is a small airport that opened in November 1987. Catering primarily to businesspersons, the **London City Airport** services flights to and from Paris, Brussels, Amsterdam, and Jersey, in the Channel Islands. Tel. 474-5555.

The British have made an effort to ensure convenient transportation from the airports to the center of their capital city.

Heathrow Airport: Tel. 759-4321. Heathrow is the airport closest to central London. Four passenger terminals currently serve Heathrow. If you expect someone to meet you, you should enquire in advance at which terminal you will land.

If you have rented a car, take Great West Road (A-4) or Motorway M-4.

Taxis are widely available but are the most expensive way to get to central London; the price is approximately £20, plus a tip. The trip can take from 40 to 80 minutes.

The quickest and most inexpensive way to get from Heathrow to London is by the underground (subway), which runs daily every 5-10 minutes from 5:30am to midnight, 6am to 11pm on Sundays. Take the Piccadilly Line, and you will be in the center of London within 40 minutes. Tickets cost about £1.70.

Special bus lines: The *Airbus*, lines A1 and A2, leaves from each terminal at Heathrow and stops at all major hotel areas in central London. It operates seven days a week, from 6am to 10pm. Tickets are about £4.00 and the trip takes 50 to 80 minutes.

The *Airliner* service, a minibus with eight seats, also travels to the center of town.

INTRODUCTION

The *Flightline 767* offers service between all four terminals at Heathrow and stations at Victoria, Kensington, and Knightsbridge, in approximately an hour. Coaches leave daily every half hour, hourly during the winter.

Two bus lines connect the airports. *Speedlink* travels between Heathrow and Gatwick every 20 minutes during the day and hourly in the evening. Travel time is 50 minutes. *Jetlink 747* runs between Gatwick, Heathrow, and Luton. Connections between Gatwick and Heathrow run every 30 minutes during the day and hourly in the evening.

Gatwick Airport: Tel. 668-4211 or (0293) 28822. Slightly farther from London than Heathrow, it serves mainly international and national charter flights.

If you have rented a car, take Motorway A-23.

Taxis cost approximately £20 plus a tip, and the ride takes about an hour.

The fastest and cheapest way to get from Gatwick to London is by train, the British Rail Gatwick Express, to Victoria Station in London. Trains leave every 15 minutes from 5:30am to 11pm, and once an hour after that. The trip takes about 30 minutes and costs approximately £5.00. A through ticket can also be purchased, allowing the traveler to transfer directly from the train to the underground at Victoria Staion. Cost ranges from £5.50 to £6.70, depending on the final destination.

There are also buses, *Green Line* and *Flightline 777*, to Victoria Station. Tickets are approximately £6.00.

Luton Airport: Tel. (0582) 36061. Situated north of London, it also serves mainly charter flights.

If you have rented a car, take Motorway M-1.

Trains leave an average of twice an hour for St. Pancras Station in London.

Stansted Airport: Tel. (0279) 502380. The third London international airport (mainly for charter flights), it is also situated north of the city.

If you have rented a car, take Motorway M-11.

A train to Liverpool Street Station in London runs regularly from Bishop's Stortford; you can get to this station from the airport by taxi or bus. The trip takes approximately 45 minutes.

By Sea

Britain is still not connected to the European continent, although the spectacular Channel tunnel project, which will create a land bridge

INTRODUCTION

between Europe and the British Isles, has already been approved. In the meantime, numerous ferry lines link almost all shores of northern Europe to British ports, where you can get a train to London. The shortest route is between Calais on the French coast and Dover on the British coast, and from there by train to London.

The ferry is the most inexpensive means for reaching England by sea — and the slowest. The hovercraft is faster and more comfortable, but more expensive as well. Tickets for both can be purchased at travel agencies in the various European capitals, or before boarding at the port.

There is also a regular train service between London and the European capitals, via special direct train-ferry connections to and from Victoria Station. Details are available at the station, or from British Tourist Authority offices.

Transportation in London

London Transport operates all the underground train and bus services in the British capital. Free pocket maps of all the transportation services are available at the Travel Information Centres run by the company and in all underground stations. The Centres are located in the underground stations at Victoria, Piccadilly Circus, Oxford Circus, St. James's Park, King's Cross, Charing Cross, Euston, and Heathrow Central, as well as at the arrival areas of all the Heathrow terminals and at the Victoria British Rail station. Information is also available 24 hours a day by calling 222-1234.

If you plan to travel frequently by public transportation, you can save a lot of money by buying one of the tickets for unlimited travel by bus and underground. Purchased according to zones, these are very economical. It is worthwhile getting a ticket that includes the zone of your hotel as well as the Central Zone.

Travelcard entitles you to unlimited travel on all buses and most of the underground trains throughout Greater London, for a period of one, three, four, or seven days, or for a month. To make the purchase, you need a passport picture. Three- and four-day tickets are not available in Britain, and must be purchased from your travel agent before you come.

Capitalcard entitles you to unlimited travel on British Rail trains, as well as the underground and buses in all areas of Greater London. It can be purchased for a period of one day, one week, one month, or more.

INTRODUCTION

Buses

The red double-decker buses operated by London Transport is as much a trademark of London as Buckingham Palace. The buses go almost everywhere, and prices vary according to the distance of the trip. On the double-decker buses serving the busier areas tickets are purchased from a conductor; otherwise, purchase the ticket directly from the driver. Climb up to the top deck (where, by the way, smoking is allowed) and enjoy the sights of London.

Single-decker Red Arrow buses are express buses, with limited stops. For these you must prepare the exact fare before boarding, and give it to the driver or put it into the automatic fare box.

Buses do not automatically stop at every station. At stations marked with a REQUEST sign, you must wave your hand to signal the driver to stop.

To check a bus's destination, before boarding look at the sign posted in front of the bus.

The *Night Owl* bus service operates from around midnight until 6am on some of the routes of the daily buses.

The Underground or Tube

The underground train, popularly called the Tube, is also operated by London Transport. There are nine lines and two short secondary lines, each marked on the map in a different color. The trains leave every few minutes between 5:30am and midnight (on Sundays and holidays from 7:30am until close to midnight).

Every underground station is clearly marked with the name of the line and the final destination of the train, as well as the stations en route. In each car you will find a diagram of the route, but you are advised to use your own map.

If you have not purchased one of the multi-ride ticket cards, you should prepare small change to buy your ticket from a ticket machine. Do not throw the ticket away — you must present it to a collector when you leave the train at your desired destination.

It is strongly advised that you avoid traveling on the Tube during rush hour, between 8:30 and 9:30 in the morning, and between 4:30 and 6:30 in the afternoon. At these times the trip, however short, turns into an exhausting experience.

Taxis

London cabbies are well-known for their efficiency and perhaps also for their wild driving. To get a license, Black Cab drivers must pass a strict test of their familiarity with the streets of Greater London.

INTRODUCTION

Thousands of taxis serve the traveling public. These too have become a symbol of London, with their black, rounded shape that has hardly changed over the decades. The special design enables the passenger to enter the taxi easily, almost standing up. The taxis have room for five passengers. Next to the driver is a special place for baggage.

When a taxi is available, the sign TAXI or FOR HIRE is lit in yellow on its front. Taxis can also be ordered from a station (check in the phone book), or through a radiophone network. The telephone numbers of the major radiophone networks are 286-4848, 286-0286, and 272-3030.

Fare rates change according to the day of the week, the time of the day, the destination, and the number of passengers. The price table is exhibited in the passenger cabin. Currently there are regular additions to the price: 20p per person and 10p for every piece of luggage placed next to the driver. After 8pm, add 40p to the price of the trip; from midnight until 6am, and on weekends, add 60p. On Christmas and New Year's Eve, add £2 from midnight until the morning.

Drivers reserve the right to refuse to travel more than 10 kilometers, or more than 32 kilometers from Heathrow Airport.

You should give the driver a tip.

Car Rental

In England the driver sits on the right side of the car and drives on the left side of the street. This makes driving difficult for those not accustomed to it. In the city you have to be doubly careful not to leave your lane and not to run over innocent tourists who are used to looking left rather than right when crossing the street.

In the center of London there is almost always heavy traffic, and it is very difficult to find parking. Therefore it is not advised to rent a car if you intend to stay in London only.

If you want to travel outside of the city with the convenience of a car, do not let the driving differences intimidate you. On the contrary, rent a car and enjoy the countryside. The terms for rental vary among companies. Most firms require a minimum age of between 21 and 25 for rental. They also require that the custumor have a driver's license that has been valid for at least one year.

Car Hire Centre operates a free information and reservations service from more than 400 rental stations throughout Britain. The center is open Monday through Friday, throughout the year. Summer

INTRODUCTION

hours are 9am-5:30pm; winter hours are 9am-5pm. It is located at 23 Swallow St., Piccadilly Circus, London W1R (tel. 734-7661).

It is worthwhile to find out about renting while you are still in your home country. In most cases, if you reserve ahead of time the price may be less expensive, and you can be assured of a waiting car, even at the height of the season.

Limousine Services

For those who like to travel in style, London offers limousine services, usually a Rolls Royce or a Bentley. Some hotels have their own limousines available for their guests. You can also hire one from an agency. Particularly recommended is *Chase Executive and Chauffeur Services Ltd.*, 2 Archway Close, London N19 (tel. 263-9499).

Bicycles

London does not pretend to be a university city like Oxford, and therefore it does not have many bicycle riders. Nevertheless, if you want to ride a bike, especially for touring in parks, you will be able to rent one.

There are several bike rental companies in central London, including the following:

Bell Street Bikes: 73 Bell St., NW1. Tel. 724-0456. Edgware Road underground station.
Dial-a-Bike: 18 Gillingham St., SW1. Tel. 828-4040. Victoria underground station.
Rent-a-Bike: Kensington Student Center, 38 Kensington Church St., W8. Tel. 937-6089. Kensington High Street underground station.

Water Transit

A new water taxi service recently began operating on the Thames. The *Thames Line Riverbus* runs between Chelsea Harbour and Greenland Piers, with stops at other piers along the way. It offers a scenic alternative to the traffic of downtown London for commuting between tourist areas. Boats leave the piers every 15 minutes Mon.-Fri. 7am-10pm, and every half hour Sat. and Sun. 10am-6pm.

Thames Line: The Old Mill, Creek Rd., East Molesey, Surrey KT8 9NG. Tel. 941-5454.

Accommodations

One of the biggest problems facing the tourist is the question of where to stay. Greater London offers a wide selection of

*I*NTRODUCTION

accommodations for tourists, from exclusive hotels to bed-and-breakfast rooms at lower prices. Nevertheless, there are not enough rooms for the number of tourists, especially during the height of the summer season. Finding a place to stay can be a challenge, and the prices are high, often with less than adequate service.

British law requires that all hotels and guest houses with more than four rooms display a rate chart, showing the price of accommodation per night and stating whether the price includes meals, value-added tax (VAT) and service charge. The rate for a room usually includes breakfast, either British or Continental.

It is strongly advised that you come to London with hotel reservations in hand. If you do come to London without a place to stay, go to the Tourist Information Centre at Heathrow or at Victoria Station, and they will help you.

Agencies for Reserving Accommodations

The companies that operate room rental agencies in the airports are private and, based on our experience, extremely unreliable. The prices of the rooms in the hotels these agencies recommend are high, and the location is not always what they promise. Try to avoid using their services as much as possible, and turn instead to the official authorities.

Hotels

In the following list we have tried to name the hotels that we estimate as being especially suitable according to their location, prices, services, etc. Naturally they are only a small portion of a very wide selection. Less expensive accommodations can often be found in outer London, but do not let the lower prices mislead you. London is a very large city, and travel from the outskirts to the main sights in the center can be both expensive and time-consuming.

The hotels recommended here are divided into four categories, by rate for a room for two. All are located as close as possible to the center of London, and near convenient transportation to the major tourist sights.

Luxury (£120 and above)

Le Meridien Piccadilly: Piccadilly, W1. Tel. 734-8000. Extremely expensive (£150-£200 per night). Excellent location near Piccadilly Circus. Very modern with all the conveniences, including a charming health club. Especially recommended for businesspersons and those who enjoy luxury.

The Ritz: Piccadilly, W1. Tel. 493-8181. One of the best-known hotels in town, with a famous tea parlour that is frequented by

INTRODUCTION

the jet set. Good location, near the center and bordering Green Park.

Claridge's: Brook St., W1. Tel. 629-8860. Quiet splendor of bygone days. Old-fashioned service according to the dictums of proper etiquette, which is sometimes oppressive.

The Savoy: The Strand, WC2. Tel. 836-4343. A hotel with a long tradition. Near the City. Good location for businesspersons.

London Hilton: 22 Park Lane, W1. Tel. 493-3000. Overlooking Hyde Park; within walking distance from Oxford St. Modern American style.

Sheraton Park Tower Hotel: 101 Knightsbridge, SW1. Tel. 235-8050. A bit far from the center. Close to the shopping area in Knightsbridge, and within walking distance from Hyde Park.

Athenaeum Hotel: 116 Piccadilly, W1. Tel. 499-3464. A luxurious hotel, although not as well known as others in this category. A very good location.

Grosvenor House: Park Lane, W1. Tel. 499-6363. A long-standing luxurious hotel. Very British. A good location overlooking Hyde Park.

Expensive (£80 and above)

Berners Ramada Hotel: Berners St., W1. Tel. 636-1629. Excellent central location, off Oxford St. Good food. Professional and friendly service. Elegant lobby but small rooms. Recommended.

The Cumberland: Marble Arch, W1. Tel. 262-1234. Excellent location in the busy junction of Marble Arch. Some rooms overlook Hyde Park.

Holiday Inn Marble Arch: 134 George St., W1. Tel. 723-1277. Excellent location. A wide range of services.

Kenilworth Hotel: Great Russell St., WC1. Tel. 637-3477. Good location, near the British Museum and within walking distance of Oxford St.

The Selfridge Hotel: Orchard St., W1. Tel. 408-2080. Excellent location, on the corner of Oxford St. A luxurious hotel. Very comfortable. Ideal for shopping. Has a nice restaurant and coffee shop.

Moderate (£40 and above)

Mount Royal Hotel: Bryanston St., W1. Tel. 629-8040. Excellent location by Marble Arch. A huge hotel, no intimacy, with hundreds of rooms, most of which are basic and dated.

The Regent Palace Hotel: Piccadilly Circus, W1. Tel. 734-7000. A huge hotel with approximately 1,000 rooms. An excellent location in Piccadilly Circus. The rooms are basic but the prices are attractive considering the location. Recommended.

Swiss Cottage Hotel: 4 Adamson Rd., NW3. Tel. 722-2281. A charming and intimate hotel, far from the center.

INTRODUCTION

Kingsley Hotel: Bloomsbury Way, WC1. Tel. 242-5881. A very good location, close to the British Museum and within walking distance of Oxford St. A wide range of services.
Central Park Hotel: Queensborough Terrace, W2. Tel. 229-2424. A medium-size hotel, within walking distance of Marble Arch, overlooking Hyde Park.
Savoy Court: Granville Place, W1. Tel. 408-0130. Excellent location. A small basic hotel. Very small rooms. Not a first choice.
London Embassy Hotel: 150 Bayswater Rd., W2. Tel. 229-1212. On the far end of Hyde Park. Recommended for its services. An underground station close by.
The Strand Palace: Strand, WC2. Tel. 836-3080. A very good location next to Covent Garden. A huge hotel with a wide range of services. Recommended.

Inexpensive (less than £40)

There is a wide selection of inexpensive hotels, and the differences between them concerning comfort and service are considerable. Therefore we have recommended hotels in this category according to their location. It is advisable to have a look at the room you are renting before you commit yourself.

Apollo Hotel: 12-22 Lexham Gardens, W8. Tel. 373-3236.
Atlas Hotel: 24-30 Lexham Gardens, W8. Tel. 373-7873.
Beaver Hotel: 57 Philbeach Gardens, SW5. Tel. 373-4553.
Caring Hotel: 24 Craven Hill Gardens, W2. Tel. 262-8708.
Chesham House Hotel: 64-66 Ebury St., SW1. Tel. 730-8513.
Concord Hotel: 155 Cromwell Rd., SW5. Tel. 370-4151.
Crichton Hotel: 36 Bedford Place, WC1B. Tel. 637-3955.
Gresham Hotel: 36 Bloomsbury St., WC1B. Tel. 636-4888.
Royal Norfolk Hotel: 25 London St., W2. Tel. 402-5221.
Terstan Hotel: 29-31 Nevern Sq., SW5. Tel. 373-5368.
Warwick House Hotel: 6-8 Norfolk Sq., W2. Tel. 723-3386.

In the area surrounding the Bloomsbury neighborhood, there is a wide selection of small hotels, offering modest and inexpensive rooms. To get there, take the underground to Tottenham Court Rd., Holborn, Goodge St., or Russel Square stations.

Particularly popular are the bed-and-breakfast rooms in private homes. The Tourist Information Centre will refer you to accommodations in whatever location you request, but it is advised to be careful that you are not sent anywhere very far from the center that is not near an underground station.

Apartment Hotels

Another kind of accommodation in London, especially recommended for families, is in an apartment hotel. These offer

INTRODUCTION

all facilities, including kitchens. In most cases you will be required to pay in advance. It is best to reserve an apartment through a travel agent abroad. If you choose this option once you are in London, you can contact the following agencies:

A. Abel Property Services Ltd.: 4 Shephard St., W1. Tel. 499-7971/2.
Aston's Budget Studios: 39 Rosary Gardens, SW7. Tel. 370-0797 or 730-1100.
Plaza Estates: 29-31 Edgware Rd., Marble Arch, W2. Tel. 724-3100.

Youth Hostels

In London there are five youth hostels. Three of them are close to the center.

Holland House: Holland Park, W8. Tel. 937-0748, Holland Park underground station.
London Youth Hostel: 36 Carter Lane, EC4. Tel. 236-4965. Situated in the heart of the City. Blackfriars underground station.
Earl's Court: 38 Bolton Gardens, SW5. Tel. 373-7083. Located a bit far from the center. Earl's Court underground station.

Services for the Disabled

Awareness of the special needs of the disabled is steadily increasing in Britain. Most hotels, restaurants, theaters, and public buildings are equipped with facilities for the disabled, but, unfortunately, not all are. This is particularly true with regard to facilities for wheelchairs. For updated information, see the publication *Britain for the Disabled*, available from the British Tourist Authority. *Access in London*, a guide for the disabled, is available in most bookstores. A special telephone service, *Arts Line* (388-2227/8), will provide you with information about cultural activities available for the disabled.

Tourist Information

When planning your trip to London from abroad, there are several valuable sources of information. In most major cities in Europe, and in several major cities in North America, there are branches of the British Tourist Authority (BTA). Information packets can be requested by phone or mail.

Australia: Midland House, 4th Floor, 171 Clarendon St., Sydney, NSW 2000. Tel. (612) 298627.
Canada: 94 Cumberland St., Suite 600, Toronto, Ontario M5R 3N3. Tel. (416) 925-6326.
U.S.A.: 40 West 57 St., 3rd Floor, New York, NY 10019. Tel. (212) 581-4700.
John Hancock Center, Suite 3320, 875 N. Michigan Ave., Chicago, IL 60611. Tel. (312) 787-0490.
World Trade Center, 350 S. Figueroa St., Suite 450, Los Angeles,

INTRODUCTION

CA 90071. Tel. (213) 628-3525.
Cedar Maple Plaza, Suite 210, Cedar Springs Rd., Dallas, TX 75201. Tel. (214) 720-4040.

British embassies and consulates, although not specializing in tourist information, can provide some literature if there is no access to a tourist office nearby.

Once you arrive in London, the city's abundance of everything, from hotels and tour companies to stores and money exchange offices, might confuse even the most experienced traveler. In order to help unravel the confusing possiblities, the London Tourist Board (LTB) has established Tourist Information Centres that provide information on any needed service: accommodations, restaurants, banks, etc. In addition, they offer maps, brochures, and even guidebooks and films. Centres can be found at the following locations:

Victoria Station Forecourt: Main Centre. Open Easter-Nov., daily 9am-10:30pm; Nov.-Easter, Mon.-Sat. 9am-7pm, Sun. 9am-5pm.
Harrods: Knightsbridge, SW1. Open during store hours.
Heathrow: Terminals 1, 2, 3, underground station concourse. Open daily 9am-6pm.
Selfridges: Oxford St., W1. Open during store hours.
Tower of London: West Gate, EC3. Open April-Oct., daily 10am-6pm.
City of London Information Centre: St. Paul's Churchyard, EC4. Open daily, summer 10am-4pm, until 2:30pm in winter.

The LTB also operates *London Information*, a phone service, available Mon.-Fri. 9am-6pm. Tel. 730-3488.

Written enquires can be sent to the LTB: Correspondence Assistant, Distribution Department, London Tourist Board, 26 Grosvenor Gardens, London SW1W 0DU.

The British Tourist Authority also offers tourist information for travel in London and the rest of England as well. The main office, the British Travel Centre, is located a few steps from Piccadilly Circus at 12 Regent Street, SW1. (Open Mon.-Fri. 9am-6:30pm, Sat. 9am-5pm. Telephone hours daily and on Sun. 10am-4pm. Tel. 730-3400.) The experienced and courteous staff is very helpful and will answer questions on any subject.

Important Tips for Getting Around

Currency and Exchange

The British unit of currency is the pound sterling (£), which is divided into 100 pence (p). The bills currently in circulation are £5, £10, £20, and £50. Coins are issued in values of 1p, 2p, 5p, 10p, 20p, 50p, and £1.

INTRODUCTION

British law does not limit the amount of money or traveler's checks, in any currency, that a tourist is permitted to bring into the country.

Credit cards of major international firms are accepted in Britain, and are widely accepted at tourist sites. One can also use them to obtain currency from banks or automatic-teller machines.

Traveler's checks marked in pound sterling values can be cashed in almost all banks, hotels, and department stores, with no fee charged.

Foreign currency can be exchanged at most banks. When the banks are closed, you can exchange money in the offices of the major travel agencies, in the currency exchange offices of the large department stores, with the cashiers at major hotels, or in independent currency exchange agencies. You should check the exchange rate and fees before making your transaction — usually such offices charge a high commission.

VAT and Retail Export

In Britain there is a 15% value-added tax (VAT) on most products and services.

The British program for retail export entitles the tourist to an exemption from VAT on purchase of goods (not including services such as hotels, restaurants, and car rental). Not all stores are willing to cooperate with this program; some will not provide the appropriate document, or will require you to make a minimum purchase (usually £50). To get a VAT rebate, the tourist must obtain a proof of purchase from the store and verify that the products purchased are being taken out of the country by showing them to a customs official at the airport. The official signs a form, which you then should send back to the place of purchase; the money will be returned by mail to your home. In case of a credit-card purchase, the money will be credited to your account.

Communications

Telephones

The red color, evidently a British favorite, is used not only on their buses, but on the royal mailboxes and public phone booths as well. Unfortunately, British Telecom decided to replace these phone booths, some of which date back to the beginning of the century, with modern booths, painted yellow. Thanks to the fuss made by various institutions for preservation, some 200 of the old-style phone booths were maintained. The rest were sold off — some have been converted into shower stalls in Texas.

Older, rotary-dial public pay phones take 10p coins; more modern, push-button phones take other coins as well, up to £1. Telephones

INTRODUCTION

that can be operated with Phonecards are presently being installed in several locations. This green-colored card entitles the carrier to make calls for a set number of meter units and can be obtained at post offices and at some stores. In airports and other tourist areas, there are telephones that can be operated with a credit card. These phones are clearly marked with pictures of the credit cards.

From most of the modern phones one can make direct-dial international calls. After inserting the appropriate amount of money, a credit card, or a phonecard, dial first 010, then the international code of your country, and then the area code plus the phone number.

The area code for London is 01.

Post Offices
Post offices are open Monday through Friday from 9am to 5:30pm, and on Saturday from 9:30am to 1pm. The post office in Trafalgar Square is open Monday through Saturday from 8am to 8pm, and on Sunday and public holidays from 10am to 5pm. This post office also has a *post restante* service, where mail is kept for one month. The address is Post Restante, Trafalgar Square PO, London WC2N 4OL (tel. 930-9580).

Stamps are sold only in post offices and in stamp machines outside the post offices.

Banks

Banks are open Monday through Friday from 9:30am to 3pm. They are closed on Saturday and Sunday and on public holidays, with the exception of a few branches that are open on Saturday morning.

In each of the major London airports, Heathrow and Gatwick, there is a bank open 24 hours a day.

Stores

Normal shopping hours in London are Monday through Saturday from 9am to 5:30pm. Stores are closed on Sunday. Some stores in the West End are closed on Saturday afternoon as well.

A long shopping day is held on Wednesday in Knightsbridge and Chelsea, and on Thursday in the West End and on Kensington High Street. Some tourist shops and open-air markets are also open on Sunday.

Tipping

Tipping is a well-accepted institution, and there are a few basic guidelines to follow.

INTRODUCTION

It is generally accepted to tip porters 20p per suitcase.

In hotels a tip of 50p to £1 is usually expected for each suitcase. The room service waiter should be tipped a similar amount (although not for serving breakfast).

In restaurants, it is generally accepted to add 10%-15% to the total bill (if the proprietor has not done so already).

Taxi drivers also expect a tip of 10%-15% of the fare, but no less than 20p.

At the hairdressers, one usually gives 50p to the person who cuts your hair, and 50p to the assistant who washes your hair.

In the theater, movie theater, and garages, tips are not usually given.

Drink and Be Merry

The public house is a British institution almost as old as royalty. Once a decent woman did not dare show her face in the male world of a pub, but times have changed and women also come alone to drink and eat in pubs. In London there are hundreds of pubs, some very old with long, interesting histories. No tour of London is complete without a visit to one of these.

Pubs in London are open Monday through Saturday from 10am to 11pm. On Sunday and holidays the hours are from noon to 3pm and from 7pm to 10:30pm, so that people can attend church without having to miss the fun at their neighborhood pub.

Wine bars are equally popular eating and drinking establishments. "Off-license" shops usually sell bottles of wine and hard liquor throughout the day, including during hours when the pubs are closed, but not for consumption on the spot. Not every restaurant has a license for serving wine.

Hard liquor is sold only to those over age 18. Children from age 14 may enter pubs if accompanied by an adult, but they are served soft drinks only.

Public Rest Rooms

To our great fortune, the British lawmakers took our basic human needs into consideration and required public rest rooms in all British Rail train stations, in some of the public parks, in underground stations, in department stores, in pubs, and in restaurants (including fast-food enterprises). In most places the facilities are clean and well kept, and you usually do not have to pay to use them.

INTRODUCTION

Measurements, Electricity, and Time

Measurements
Britons are gradually switching to the metric system. While distances are still measured in miles and feet, many other units are given in metric figures. Below is a conversion table which may be useful.

Weight:	28.35 grams	1 ounce
	453 grams	1 pound
	1 kilogram	2.2 pounds
Volume:	0.47 liters	1 pint
	1 liter	approximately 1 quart
	3.79 liters	1 gallon
Distance:	2.54 centimeters	1 inch
	30.5 centimeters	1 foot
	1 meter	approximately 1 yard
	1 kilometer	0.628 miles
	1.6 kilometers	1 mile

As in the rest of Europe, what would be the American first floor is called the ground floor, and the next one up is the first floor.

Clothing and Shoe Sizes
London offers a variety of clothing and shoes of high quality at reasonable prices. The sizing system in England differs from that of continental Europe and America; the following table should help you buy the right garment.

Clothing
English:	6	8	10	12	14	16	18	20	22
	28	30	32	34	36	38	40	42	44
Continental:	34	36	38	40	42	44	46	48	50
United States:	4	6	8	10	12	14	16	18	20

Shoes
English:	3	3.5	4	4.5	5	5.5	6	6.5	7	7.5	8	8.5
Continental:	35	36	37	37	38	38	39	40	40	41	41	42
United States:	4.5	5	5.5	6	6.5	7	7.5	8	8.5	9	9.5	10

Electricity
The electric power grid in England operates at 240 volts AC.

Time
London is in Greenwich Mean Time during the winter. During the summer it adheres to European Summer Time, GMT + 1 hour.

*L*ONDON

Getting to Know the City

Organized Tours of London

An endless variety of tours are offered in London, from seeing the sights by bus, to sailing on the Thames, to exploring hidden alleyways by foot. Whether you choose to concentrate on traditional tourist sights or prefer more specialized ventures, you will find many companies offering you their services.

Bus Tours

For tourists who want to catch all the major sightseeing spots in the city without wearing out their legs, an introductory bus tour at the beginning of your visit to London is highly recommended. The *Original London Transport Sightseeing Tour*, organized by London Transport, leaves from Haymarket (near Trocadero), Marble Arch, Baker Street, and Victoria Station, once every half hour. The tour lasts about an hour and a half and is led by an English-speaking guide; it is sometimes narrated in other languages. The tour includes more than 25 kilometers of sightseeing. For more information, call London Transport at 222-1234.

The yellow *Culture Bus* circles the city every 30 minutes, stopping at 37 stations where you can get off and on for an entire day. This allows you to visit all the sights of your choice at the cost of a single ticket. The main office is at 87 London Road, Southend, SS1 1PP. Tel. 0702-355711 for further information.

There are numerous other private touring companies that offer a selection of tours lasting from a few hours to a few days. Prices can be high, but the tours offer you the opportunity to get to know the city within a short time. These tours are available in many different languages, and it is worth checking the schedule in advance.

Some companies with worthwhile tours include the following:
Tragical History Tours Ltd.: Business Center, 1 Bromley Lane, Chiselhurst, Kent BR7 6LH. Tel. 857-1545 or 467-3318. Tours following ghostly and tragic historical figures, specializing in "the sinister side of London."
Evan Evans Tours Ltd.: 27 Cockspur St., Trafalgar Sq., SW1. Tel. 839-6415. A variety of sightseeing tours, including tours of up to eight nights.

LONDON

National Express: 13 Regent St., SW1Y. Tel. 437-4208. Tours in London and all around the country.

Water Tours

The Thames River
Complement your visit to London with a leisurely cruise on the Thames, viewing the sights along its banks. Several companies offer boat services, with boats leaving from the following piers:

Charing Cross Pier: Boats to the Tower of London, Greenwich, and the Thames Barrier.
Westminster Pier: Boats downstream to the Tower of London and Greenwich; upstream to Kew Gardens, Richmond, and Hampton Court.

Call Riverboat Information for details, tel. 730-4812.

Canals
Two canals cross London, the Grand Union Canal and Regent's Canal. A Waterbus operates on Regent's Canal; it leaves Camden Lock via the London Zoo, to Little Venice. There are also several floating restaurants on the canal, where you can spend a romantic evening to the sound of music. Check with any Tourist Information Centre for details. Two companies specialize in canal trips:

Jason's Trip: Opposite 60 Bloomfield Road, Little Venice, W9. Tel. 286-3428.
London Waterbus Company: Camden Lock, NW1. Tel. 482-2323 or 482-2550.

Walking Tours
London is famous for its walking tours. Although we focus on fairly detailed walking tours in this book, various London companies may offer you itineraries on special subjects. Choices range from following the footsteps of Sherlock Holmes to a review of Jack the Ripper's trail, to a tour of pubs (with proper drinking), to visiting homes with a ghostly history.

Major Companies
Citisights of London: 102a Albion Rd., N16. Tel. 241-0323 or 359-2715. History and archaeology.
City Walks: 9/11 Kensington High St., W8 5NP. Tel. 937-4281. Literary and historical walks.
Discovering London: 11 Pennyfields, Warley, Brentwood, Essex, CM14 5JP. Tel. (0277) 213704. A variety of special-interest tours.
Guided Walks of London: 32 Grovelands Rd., N13 4RH. Tel. 882-3414. Political, literary, and other specialized walks.

*L*ONDON

The Londonder Pub Walks: 3 Springfield Ave., Muswell Hill, N10 3SU. Tel. 883-2656.

London Walks: 139 Conway Rd., Southgate, N14. Tel. 882-2763. Emphasizes the "hidden and unusual."

Company brochures can usually be found in the Tourist Information Centre at Victoria Station.

*L*ONDON

London Area by Area

The City of London — The Ancient Heart

This tour will lead you through the heart of hearts of London — the City. In this area, the most ancient in town, you will encounter sights covering a range of different periods, from two-thousand-year-old Roman remains to an ultra-modern stock exchange that has just been completed. The sights vary in style as well: churches, commercial centers, financial institutions, etc. We recommend this tour for weekdays as it is quiet here on weekends, and many of the sights are closed on Sundays.

Begin the tour at the **Blackfriars train station**. *Blackfriar* refers to the black-robed Dominican monks who lived in the area from 1276 until their monastery, like many others, was closed during the Reformation in the sixteenth century; the name remained. At the train station exit turn left. On the corner of New Bridge Street is a unique structure; the statue of a black-robed monk represents its name, *Blackfriar Pub*. Art-Nouveau decorations make the interior particularly impressive.

Across from the station, parallel to the train tracks, is Blackfriars Lane, site of the grand **Apothecaries Hall,** founded in 1670. The livery companies or professional unions in the City inherited the position of the guilds of the Middle Ages. Ninety-six are currently in operation, and many are located in old, charming buildings. Visits, however, must be arranged in advance.

In the lane under the train bridge there is also a cabaret restaurant, called *Shakespeare Tavern*, and next to it an Italian restaurant, *Angelo's* (open for lunch only on weekdays).

Turn back and descend in the direction of **Blackfriars Bridge**, whose foundations were first laid in 1760. In 1865 the original bridge was replaced with the stone and steel structure you see today. The few pillars in the water are left over from its extension at the beginning of the century, to accommodate the electric train track. Until 1875, its operators charged pedestrians a crossing tax. The bridge is parallel to the Blackfriars Railway Bridge. Take the steps down to the walkway. Between the two bridges, where the Fleet River empties into the Thames, a Roman ship was discovered in the 1960s, with a load of stones apparently intended for constructing the second-century city wall.

Turn left and you will come to an area called Puddle Dock, now the site of one of the only theaters within the City, the **Mermaid**. While the theater is quite modern, the site itself is historic. Some

THE CITY OF LONDON

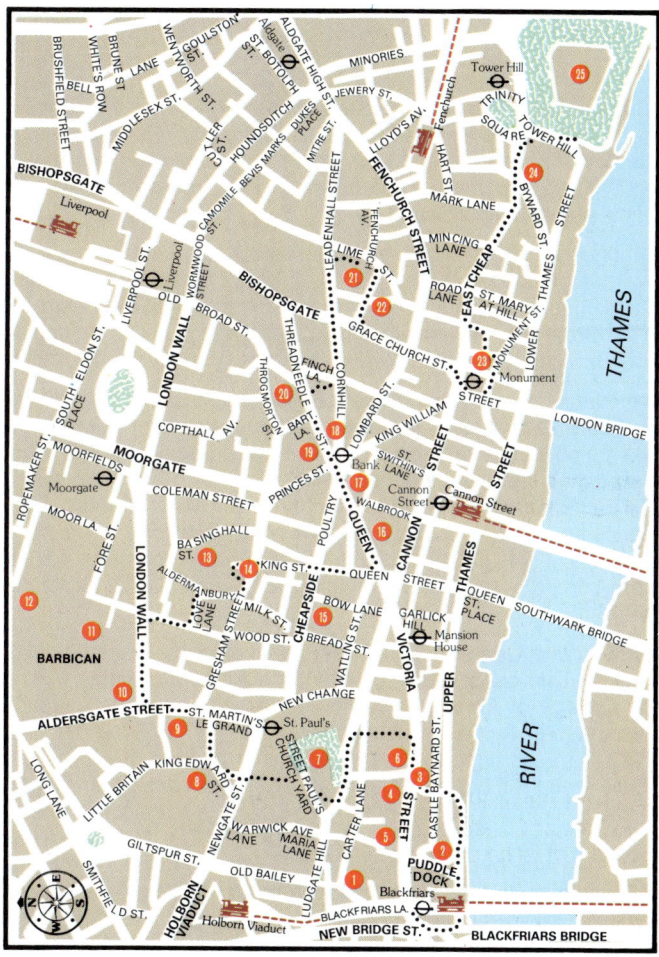

Index
1. Apothecaries Hall
2. Mermaid Theatre
3. St. Benet's
4. Faraday Building
5. St. Andrew-by-the-Wardrobe
6. College of Arms
7. St. Paul's Cathedral
8. National Postal Museum
9. St. Botolph-without-Aldersgate
10. Museum of London
11. Barbican Centre for Arts and Conferences
12. St. Giles Cripplegate
13. Guildhall
14. St. Lawrence Jewry
15. St. Mary-le-Bow
16. Temple of Mithras
17. Mansion House
18. Royal Exchange
19. Bank of England
20. London Stock Exchange
21. Lloyd's of London
22. Leadenhall Market
23. The Monument
24. All Hallows-by-the-Tower
25. Tower of London

LONDON

900 years ago the *Baynard Castle* was built here on the banks of the river. It burned down and was rebuilt and expanded a few times. Henry VII turned it into a palace, where Lady Jane Grey was staying when she first learned of her crowning. The Great Fire of 1666 put a final end to the building.

Continue along the river, and after about 50 meters go up the overpass to Queen Victoria Street, towards **St. Benet's**, a church redesigned by Sir Christopher Wren after the original was destroyed in the Great Fire. The architect Inigo Jones was buried in the original church. Today the church serves the Welsh community of London.

Were it not for the large **Faraday Building** opposite, you could see St. Paul's Cathedral in its full glory from here. After this building was completed, a prohibition was introduced against construction higher than four stories in this area, so as not to bar the profile of the cathedral from the direction of the river. West of the building stands another church, **St. Andrew-by-the-Wardrobe**. As its name suggests, it was situated next to the royal wardrobe building. Both were burned in the Great Fire; this church was also renovated by Wren.

Further down Queen Victoria Street you approach a modest building from the late seventeenth century, with gilded iron gates. This is the **College of Arms**. (Open Mon.-Fri. 10am-4pm. Free entrance. Evening tours for small groups can be arranged for a fee. Tel. 248-2762.) In accordance with a royal charter of 1484, the College is solely responsible for the approval, registration, design, and award of coats of arms. The members of the College are appointed directly by the Crown, on recommendation by the Earl Marshal, a title that is passed by inheritance to the Dukes of Norfolk. The British still continue to regard this anachronistic institution with utmost seriousness. Inside, in the entrance hall, there is an exhibit of the pillow on which the monarchs of England sit when being crowned.

After the College, turn left onto Peter's Hill Lane, and go up the stairs. Opposite you towers the huge dome of St. Paul's Cathedral. Before going there, you can visit the City of London Information Centre to get updated information on the events of the day. Information on special services and happenings can be obtained by calling the church or through the city's newspapers or at the church's Chapter House notice board.

St. Paul's Cathedral is the largest, most impressive, and most famous church in the City. (Open daily 7:30am-6pm, until 5pm in winter. Tel. 248-2705.) As early as the year 604 a wooden church stood at the top of Ludgate Hill. In the eleventh century it burned down and the Normans built a stone church in its place. Renovations and expansions transformed the old St. Paul's into the largest Gothic church in Britain. In 1315, a tower with a steeple was

LONDON

added, estimated to be about 149 meters (489 feet) high, the highest that had ever been built on a church. The steeple's height, however, was its downfall; in 1561 it was razed to the ground when it was hit by lightning, and it was never reconstructed. A century later the Great Fire sent the entire cathedral up in flames, and when the flames died all that remained were huge, blackened ruins.

The present cathedral is a magnificent creation of the architect Sir Christopher Wren. A few months before the Great Fire, Wren presented his plans for the reconstruction and renovation of the run-down Gothic church, but its total destruction presented him with a greater challenge — to design a huge, new cathedral, a fitting symbol of the capital of the kingdom. In 1673 Wren presented his plan for the building, which is based on the design of the traditional cross. Work began in November of that year and was completed in less than four decades, with considerable alterations and deviations from the original plan. The budget went sky-high, but the result is maginficent. Above the basically classic structure, harmoniously integrated, rises the second largest dome in Europe. In the winter of 1940, when the air raids bombarded the City, a unit of fire fighters was assigned to the building to prevent its destruction. The image of the persistent dome over the clouds of fire and smoke has come to symbolize the heroic standing of the residents of London.

The front of the cathedral faces west. On either side are Baroque bell towers. In the tower on the right is a clock and a huge 17-ton bell whose ring echoes every day at 1pm. In the small church courtyard there is a statue of Queen Anne.

Enter the church, walk through the nave, and stop beneath the central dome, which rises 66.5 meters (218 feet) above your head. Here you will feel dwarfed by the enormous dimensions of the church. Look at the choir stalls. The domes that decorate the ceiling above are covered with beautiful nineteenth-century mosaics; the organ, decorated with carvings by the sculptor Grinling Gibbons, was originally ordered by Wren. Return to the northwest corner. In the **Chapel of All Souls** is a monument in memory of Lord Kitchener. Further on, on the right, is a large monument dedicated to the Duke of Wellington, in honor of his glorious victory over Napoleon in the Battle of Waterloo in 1815.

Go into the **Ambulatory**. (Open Mon.-Fri. 10am-4:15pm. Entrance fee). The lovely wrought-iron gates, handmade by Huguenot Jean Tijou, separate the Ambulatory from the choir. The large altar on the right is made of Sicilian marble; it replaced the former altar which was destroyed in the bombing. The apse on the left serves as a memorial chapel for the American soldiers who were stationed in England and lost their lives during the war. Further on is the **Lady**

The magnificent St. Paul's Cathedral

Chapel, where there is a statue of the Virgin Mary. Past it you come to a marble effigy of the greatest of the English metaphysical poets, John Donne.

Leave the Ambulatory and go down into the **Crypt**, the final resting place for many of the designers of British culture. (Open the same hours as the Ambulatory. Entrance fee.) Buried here, among others, are Wren, the artists Joshua Reynolds and J.M.W. Turner, musical collaborators Gilbert and Sullivan, the poet and artist William Blake, the Duke of Wellington, Florence Nightingale, and the Admiral Lord Nelson. Further on there is a model of Wren's original design of the cathedral.

The exquisite interior of St. Paul's Cathedral

Return to the main hall and ascend the many steps to the **Whispering Gallery**. (Open same hours as the Ambulatory. Entrance fee.) The gallery surrounds the interior dome, and the fantastic acoustics make it possible to hear even a whisper uttered on its opposite side. From the gallery you can look closely at the frescoes on the dome, which recount the life of St. Paul the apostle. Continue up and step out onto the balcony that surrounds the dome on the outside. The breathtaking view of the City, in all directions, is worth the climb.

Before leaving the cathedral, note the picture on the southern wall, *The Light of the World*, by the Pre-Raphaelite artist Holman Hunt.

*L*ONDON

After your tour of the cathedral, you can refresh yourself with food and drink in Paternoster Square, which lies to the north. Cross the square and go out to Newgate Street. Exactly opposite, on the other side of the street, stands a single, fragile-looking tower. This is all that was left of Wren's **Christ Church** after the air raids of December 1940.

Cross Newgate Street to King Edward Street. The **National Postal Museum**, which portrays the history of the British postal system, is located here. (Open Mon.-Thur. 10am-4:30pm, Fri. 10am-4pm. Free entrance. Tel. 432-3851.) An impressive exhibit of pictures and British stamps from the Victorian period and onward, and a collection of stamps of the nations of the world are displayed.

Bear right on Angel Street, then turn left on Aldersgate Street. You will pass **St. Ann and St. Agnes Church** and then come to **St. Botolph-without-Aldersgate**. The church, dedicated to the patron saint of travelers, is an impressive example of late eighteenth-century Baroque architecture. Its Corinthian wooden pillars, which support the rich plaster ceiling, and the windows adorned with pictures are among the few beautiful remnants that survived the war without damage.

At this stage in your tour, when you reach London Wall, you will have arrived at the City's great project of renewal. The controversial **Barbican** complex is built on an area of 60 acres that was severely damaged during the war. The complex includes a huge network of residential buildings for some 6,000 people, a man-made lake, a medieval church, schools, an arts center, and a museum, all connected by concrete bridges and overpasses.

On the corner facing you is the **Museum of London**, which exhibits the history of the city. (Open Tues.-Sat. 10am-6pm, Sun. 2-6pm. Free etrance. Tel. 600-3699.) Exhibits include archeological finds from excavations in the City, models of the Whitehall Palace designed for King Henry VIII and the Gothic St. Paul's Cathedral before the Great Fire, a sound-and-light experience of the Great Fire, and — most impressive of all — the golden carriage of the Lord Mayor, built in 1757 and still used in the annual November Lord Mayor's Show.

When you leave the museum, continue to the left down London Wall a few meters until you come to the remains of a **Roman fortress**, which was probably constructed at this site at the end of the first century A.D., and was integrated into the city wall at the end of the second century. The ancient wall was repaired and rebuilt several times during the Middle Ages, until the fifteenth century. When the city expanded it was neglected and almost completely destroyed. These remains are the little that is left.

LONDON

If you have time, or if you wish to hear some afternoon music, or see an interesting exhibit, pay a visit to the **Barbican Centre for Arts and Conferences**. Follow the route marked on the sidewalk. On the way you will pass **St. Giles Cripplegate**, a church with sections dating to the sixteenth century. The church, which stood outside the City gates, survived the Great Fire, but it was hit during World War II. Past the church is a man-made lake, and after that is the crescent-shaped building of the Centre. Situated there today are the Royal Shakespeare Company and the London Symphony Orchestra. There is also a hall for changing exhibitions, a public library, cinemas, a good, inexpensive restaurant, and other facilities.

Return to London Wall and turn south onto Wood Street, where you will see more remains of the City wall. The tower standing in the middle of the street is called **St. Alban**. Turn left on Love Lane, then right on Aldermanbury towards Gresham Street, and you will come to a handsome Gothic building, **Guildhall**. This is the seat of the City Corporation of London and its most important secular building. (Open Mon.-Fri. 10am-5pm. Free entrance. Tel. 606-3030.) There is not a more attractive medieval-style building in the whole City. Built originally around the 16th century, Guildhall was damaged badly in the Great Fire and rebuilt. Only parts of the foundation remain. The impressive facade was added in 1789, and above is the coat of arms of the City of London.

Inside, the City Corporation of London convenes in the **Great Hall**. It was badly damaged in 1940 and was beautifully renovated by Sir Giles Scott in the 1950s. Take particular note of the impressive wooden statues of the mythological **Gog and Magog**. Ask for directions to the medieval **crypt** of Guildhall. After being severely damaged in the Great Fire, it was closed for many generations. Only in the last twenty years have its vaults been reconstructed and the area reopened to the public.

From inside the building you can also reach the **Guildhall Library**. (Open same hours as the Guildhall.) The library was founded around 1423, and it currently contains over a hundred thousand books and publications. Here you will also find the **Clock Museum**, which houses a beautiful collection of clocks and watches donated by the Worshipful Company of Clockmakers, established in 1528. (Open Mon.-Sat. 9:30am-5pm. Print Room closed Sat. Free entrance. Tel. 606-3030.)

Bordering the Guildhall courtyard is **St. Lawrence Jewry**. This is the official church of the City Corporation, which was also redesigned by Sir Christopher Wren. The name Jewry refers to the residential area of the Jews of London during the Middle Ages, before they were expelled from England in 1290.

Walk down King Street until you reach **Cheapside**, one of oldest

*L*ONDON

The imposing White Tower of the Tower of London

streets in the City and one-time location of the flourishing open market of medieval London (*ceap* was Old English for "barter" or "bargain"). On your right, standing high, is the handsome steepled tower of **St. Mary-le-Bow**, the most beautiful — and also the most expensive — of the church steeples built by Wren. The long architectural history of the church dates back to the Saxon period. Norman bows (contributing to the name) and Wren's extensive reconstruction after the Great Fire, as well as further renovation this century after the Blitz, are also part of its history. The bells of the church are famous; anyone born within hearing distance of them is traditionally considered a true Cockney.

Continue south, back to Queen Victoria Street. Opposite are the remains of the **Temple of Mithras**, one of the few Roman sites in the City found worthy of preservation — after public pressure. The mysterious ritual of the god Mithras was held in Londinium in the second century A.D., and was particularly popular among the legionnaires of the Roman army. The remains of the sanctuary had been situated on the banks of the Walbrook river, close to this location. They were uncoverd in 1954 and were moved here so that Bucklesbury House could be built in its place.

*L*ONDON

TOWER OF LONDON

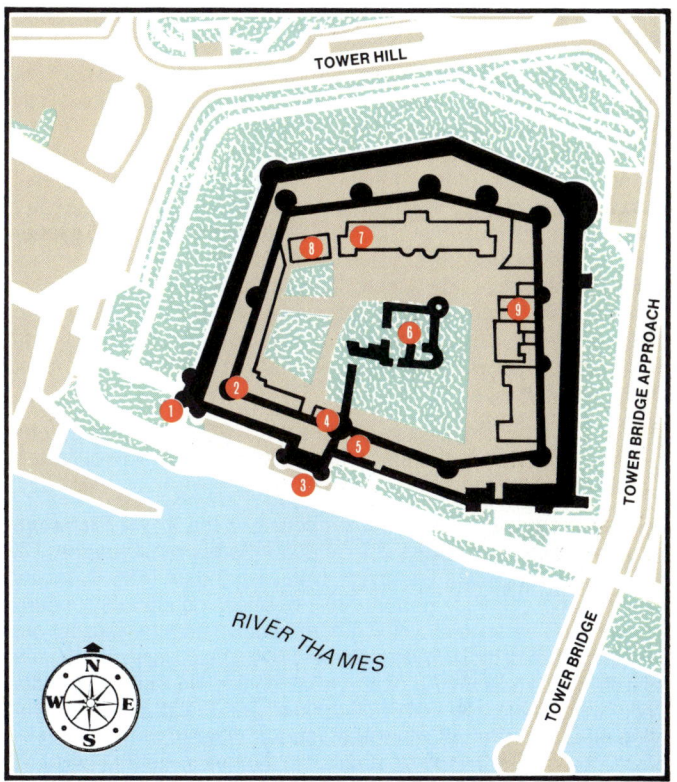

Index
1. Byward Tower
2. Bell Tower
3. Traitor's Gate
4. Bloody Tower
5. Wakefield Tower
6. White Tower
7. Jewel House
8. Chapel of St. Peter-ad-Vincula
9. Royal Fusiliers Museum

This area of the City abounds in pubs full of old English atmosphere, such as *Ye Olde Watling*, *Ye Old Wine Shades*, *Williamson's*, and others. Some of them date as far back as the period prior to the Great Fire. At 39 Queen Victoria Street you will find *Sweetings*, an old London fish restaurant, which is open for lunch only. The

*L*ONDON

restaurant was established in 1830 and has been at this location since 1906. It has preserved the furniture and atmosphere of the period of King Edward VII.

Past the restaurant is a major intersection where for a moment you may think you have landed in the agora of an ancient Greek city. Three impressive neoclassical buildings frame the square. To your right stands **Mansion House**, the official residence of the Lord Mayor during his year in office. (Open to groups only, by arrangement. Free entrance. Tel. 626-2500.) The building, which was dedicated in 1753, has the facade of a Corinthian temple. Inside, the **Egyptian Hall** is used for banquets and balls. A beautiful ceiling adorns the **Long Parlour** and embroidered Victorian tapestries add to the list of ornaments. Every year on the second Saturday of November, after the election of the new Lord Mayor of the City, the colorful Lord Mayor's Show starts from this building and continues along the streets of the City.

In back of this building hides another church, **St. Stephen Walbrook**. Its dome is similar to that of St. Paul's, and it is considered one of Wren's best works.

The second building bordering the square is the **Royal Exchange**. (Visitors' gallery open Mon.-Fri. 11:30am-2pm. Free entrance. Tel. 623-0444.) The Royal Exchange was founded in 1566 to enable the city's merchants to perform their business comfortably under a single roof. The original building burned down and the present one was constructed by Sir William Tite in 1844. The building now serves as a place for business in future merchandise, housing the London International Financial Futures Exchange (LIFFE). It is here that the price is set for the cup of coffee you will drink from next month's crop. The activity inside is a sight to see, not simply because of what the participants are doing, as much as because of the colorful jackets that the officials and company representatives wear as they make their transactions.

On the other side of the street stands a third building, the most massive and formidable of all. This is the **Bank of England**, established in 1694 and nationalized in 1946. (Open Mon.-Fri. 9:30am-3pm. Tel. 601-4444.) The building was designed in 1788 and completed in 1833 by architect Sir John Soane. In the course of twentieth century renovations and expansion, only the impressive facade Soane designed has been preserved. The absence of windows on the lower floors is for security purposes — the old reserves of the United Kingdom are buried deep in the cellar.

On Threadneedle Street (named for the Merchant Tailors, whose Guildhall is located here), to the right, you will approach a number of specialty shops that serve the businessmen of the City during their lunch break. Tobacco and cigars can be purchased at *J. Redford*

LONDON

& Co., pipes at *G. Nazer*, fancy umbrellas at *Carter's Umbrellas*, high-priced men's shoes at *Church's*, gold-plated pens at *Pencraft*, and hand-made chocolates at *Bendicks*.

You can now visit the **London Stock Exchange**. (Visitors' gallery open Mon.-Fri. 9:45am-3:15pm. Free entrance. Tel. 588-2355.) In October 1986 the London Stock Exchange underwent a revolution that the media called the Big Bang. In addition to various policy changes, sophisticated computerization of the entire exchange simplified the process of trading international stocks.

The London Stock Exchange now aspires to be the largest exchange in the world. The 1987 daily transactions were valued at over 4 billion pounds sterling. In the Exchange you will find information pamphlets and a short explanatory film. Highly recommended for those interested in this field.

Turn now to Cornhill Street. On the right-hand corner stands a bright blue water pump, a remnant of the eighteenth century. The Gothic tower rising opposite you belongs to **St. Michael's Church**.

Further down, Cornhill Street becomes Leadenhall Street, the location of the most interesting modern building to be erected in the City in recent years: the new home for **Lloyd's of London**. (Visitors' gallery open Mon.-Fri. 10am-2:30pm. Free entrance. Tel. 623-7100.) All that remains of the original structure that was built in 1928 is a white stone facade, somewhat humbled by the mass of nickel and glass rising around it. If the structure reminds you of the Georges Pompidou Centre in Paris, it may be because both were designed by architect Richard Rogers. The visitors' gallery displays a small exhibit on the development of the insurance business. Particularly interesting are some of the "unusual risk" insurance claims such as Marlene Dietrich's legs, Elizabeth Taylor's violet eyes, and the life and welfare of the Loch Ness Monster.

Located in a Victorian structure behind Lloyd's is one of the most charming food markets in London, **Leadenhall Market**. Today the market consists mainly of wine stores and delicatessens, and you can order a fancy picnic hamper full of everything your heart desires, for an indulgent weekend outdoors.

Gracechurch Street leads you towards the oldest, busiest, and best-known bridge of the City, **London Bridge**. This bridge has a long history, and we can only speculate as to how much the City's development was affected by its existence. The Romans were the first to build a wooden bridge at this spot, and wooden bridges appeared here in one form or another for no less than a thousand years. During the late twelfth to early thirteenth centuries, the first stone bridge was constructed on a chain of pillars sunk into the bottom of the river. This bridge was almost like a dam;

Yeoman — Guardians of the fortress complex

The Tower Bridge spanning the Thames

the river current slowed down so much that in the cold winter days the water iced over and became a huge skating rink. The gradual deterioration of the bridge over hundreds of years finally warranted a replacement. The old London Bridge was taken down and in 1831 construction was completed of a new, granite bridge, designed by John Rennie. Over a century later, this bridge proved to be too narrow to hold modern vehicles. In the late 1960s the London Bridge was sold for nearly $2.5 million to an American corporation. It was dismantled stone by stone and reassembled in the heart of Arizona. The wide bridge you now see was constructed in its place in 1973.

In this area, on the night of 2 September 1666, a fire broke out in a small bakery on Pudding Lane and quickly spread out of control. For four days and nights the fire raged, burning down most of the City of that time. In memory of the Great Fire, Wren erected the **Monument**, a large column some 70 meters (202 feet) high, with a golden

LONDON

flame at the top. (Open April-Sept., Mon.-Fri. 9am-6pm, Sat. and Sun. 2-6pm.; Oct.-March, Mon.-Sat. 9am-2pm and 3-4pm. Entrance fee. Tel. 626-2717.) 311 circular stairs lead you to the observation deck where you will discover a panoramic view of the City. To the south winds the river; to the west rises St. Paul's Cathedral; to the north you see the skyscrapers of the City, topped by Westminster Tower, the highest office building in Europe; and to the east is the Tower of London.

On your way to the Tower of London, the last stop on this tour, walk down Eastcheap Street. At No. 23 you will find an ornate building that looks something like a Persian harem. In the distance you will see a pointed turret. This belongs to **All Hallows-by-the-Tower**, a church that displays a bit from each page of London's history. Founded by the Saxons in the seventh century, the church was expanded by the Normans, and later renovated time and time again. Like many other buildings, it was badly damaged in the war. It was subsequently rebuilt, and in 1958 a modern steeple was added. Inside the church is a Brass Rubbing Centre with magnificent medieval pictures (tel. 481-2928 for details). The church also boasts one of the finest font covers in London, carved by Grinling Gibbons. In the crypt there are some Roman remains.

Between the church and the Tower of London is **Tower Hill**, a former site for executions; a small garden now indicates the spot. London's masses used to gather here to watch and cheer as the condemned were led to the scaffold, many of them directly from the Tower. The wealthy among them would bribe the executioner to sharpen his axe, so that the event would end smoothly and quickly, in a single blow.

The **Tower of London** is the most important and most famous of the kingdom's citadels. (Open March-Oct., Mon.-Sat. 9:30am-5pm, Sun. 2-5pm; Nov.-Feb., Mon.-Sat. 9:30am-4pm, closed Sun. Entrance fee. Tel. 709-0765.) It was first built in the eleventh century, of wood and bricks, by William the Conqueror, in order to secure his hold on the City. The citadel was soon replaced by a solid stone structure, which became known as the White Tower. The following century Richard the Lion-Hearted began expanding the fortifications, a project that was completed in the thirteenth century, and the Tower became an impenetrable fortress.

From a royal home to the kingdom's treasury, from a prison to a museum — at no time did the Tower of London cease to serve a central role in the history of the City. Within its walls are woven intrigues of conflict, scheming, and rebellion, and through its halls the cries of the tortured and the murdered have echoed.

A modern concrete bridge has replaced the wooden drawbridge that connected the **Byward Tower** to the front gate. Wherever you

LONDON

turn, you will encounter one of the 39 Yeomen Warders wearing blue or red uniforms of the Tudor period. They are in charge of guarding the site and guiding visitors. Every night at 9:40 the guards perform the Ceremony of the Keys, in which they lock the Tower gates. This ceremony has been held nightly for 700 years without a break, even during the Blitz of World War II. (Tickets to the ceremony can be obtained free of charge by sending a written request, along with a self-addressed, stamped envelope, to: The Resident Governor, HM Tower of London.)

Walk in between the double walls. Directly across the entrance is the **Bell Tower**, which rings twice a day. To the right is **Traitor's Gate**, which used to be the main entrance from the direction of the river. At the entrance to the courtyard is **Bloody Tower**, where, according to rumor, the infant King Edward V and his brother the Duke of York were murdered in the fifteenth century. Next to it is **Wakefield Tower**, where the crown jewels were once kept. The pale, dominant structure in the center of the courtyard is the famous **White Tower**. Inside is the **Chapel of St. John**, the most outstanding example of Norman architecture in London. There is also an exhibition of one of the world's finest collections of medieval weapons and armor. Close to the end of the exhibit is a small sign, marking the place where a terrorist bomb exploded in 1974, injuring numerous visitors.

The **Jewel House** opposite holds the main attraction for many of the Tower's visitors: the Crown Jewels. (Closed Sun. and for the entire month of February. Additional entrance fee.) On the ground floor is a display of plates, medals, maces, coronation robes, and the royal order's insignia. In the basement are the jewels and crowns of the royalty, including the crown of King Edward — used for coronations only and first worn by Charles II in 1660 — the crown designed for Queen Vicotria's coronation, and many more.

Next to this building is the **Chapel of St. Peter-ad-Vincula** (St. Peter in chains), where many of those who died in the Tower are buried, including the body of the beheaded Thomas More and the two queens of Henry VIII who were accused of treason, Anne Boleyn and Catherine Howard. These two, along with seven other "privileged" prisoners were put to death on the small lawn in front of the church, in order to avoid the humility of a public execution.

In other buildings in the Tower you will find the **Royal Fusiliers Museum**, the guards' quarters, a tower in which instruments of torture are shown, and more. Notice the huge black clipped-wing crows in the yard. They are part of the Tower landscape, and legend has it that as long as they continue to live at the site, the Tower will continue to stand.

LONDON

Other Sights in the Area

John Wesley's Chapel and House, where John Wesley, an eighteenth-century priest and the founder of Methodism, was born, lived, and died. It mainly contains Wesley's personal belongings. (47 City Road. Open Mon.-Sat. 10am-4pm. Free entrance. The chapel is open daily, and for prayer on Sun. Tel. 253-2262.)

*L*_ONDON_

The Inns of Court — The Halls of Justice

If you suddenly find yourself strolling down tranquil paths where it seems as though time has ceased, right in the backyard of the hustle and bustle of the city, you will know that you have come upon one of the London **Inns of Court**. Up until the eighteenth century, these inns were small campuses for law students. The students lived and studied here until receiving their degrees, and maintained contact with the inn even after they had become jurists and lawyers.

Four such inns were established in London. Each is an independent institution, directed by a group of senior judges and jurists, called benchers. Once a year each group elects a treasurer from among its graduates; many of the famous people in English history have served in this position. Today, because of their high price, many of the rooms in the inns are rented to successful lawyers and barristers. But traditions are still preserved. To this day, every law student is accepted to one of the inns and remains in contact with it after receiving his degree. The relations between the students and the graduates are maintained through banquets held several times a year.

You should tour the inns during the week, not on the weekend, since they are closed then. Start from the **Chancery Lane underground station**. Opposite the station is an interesting building, **Staple Inn**, one of the nine Inns of the Chancery, which until the seventeenth century housed students before they moved on to the Inns of Court and completed their training in law.

Turn west and at the first lane turn right, toward the Gatehouse of **Gray's Inn**. (Open Mon.-Thur. 9am-6:50pm, Fri. 9am-5:50pm. Free entrance. Tours can be arranged in advance. Tel. 405-8164.) This inn is mentioned in writings dating as early as the fourteenth century. Its name comes from the Greys of Wilton, a family of lords whose residence was located here. In the center of the southern square stands a statue of the British philosopher Francis Bacon, who was treasurer of the inn in the seventeenth century. In the **Hall**, which was built in the late sixteenth century, Shakespeare first presented *The Comedy of Errors*. The Hall and the adjacent chapel, as well as the other buildings in the square, were severely damaged in World War II, requiring substantial restoration. Pass the Hall and turn left. On your right is Gray's Inn. The private garden is open to the public in the summer at lunchtime only.

Return to Holburn Street and continue to Chancery Lane. Down the

LONDON

street, at No. 53, you can drop in at the *London Silver Vaults*, where antique silver is exhibited and sold.

Across the street enter the courtyard of **Lincoln's Inn**. (Open Mon.-Fri. 9am-6pm. Free entrance; guided tours available for a fee. Tel. 405-1393.) The inn has existed since the thirteenth century, but the first written reference is dated to 1422. Turn toward the **Chapel**, which was constructed in the early seventeenth century. (Open Mon.-Fri. noon-2:30pm.) Beneath the Chapel is an open undercroft, a sort of basement, which once served as a meeting place for members of the law community, and more recently was used as a shelter from the German air raids in World War II. The passageway opens onto the yard, where there are gas lamps still in use. The yard is flanked on the right by the **Old Hall**, a handsome brick building from the late fifteenth century.

Cross the large square to the gatehouse facing you. The two buildings on the right, the **Library** and the **New Hall**, were built in the nineteenth century in a neo-Tudor style. At that time two men with great influence on international politics studied at this inn: Benjamin Disraeli and William Gladstone, the rival prime ministers.

Leave the inn grounds to **Lincoln's Inn Fields**. Huge plane trees, which have somehow managed to survive London's air pollution, shade this square, which is one of the largest in central London. The square was designed by the architect Inigo Jones. The tranquil atmosphere here hides a rather violent history. In the sixteenth century a number of public executions took place in the square. Some of the victims were quartered, and their parts were displayed in various areas of the city, as a warning to all.

At the northern and western edges of the square were buildings that were also designed by Jones, but it seems that only one of these remains. Before leaving the square it is worth visiting **Sir John Soane's Museum**. (Open Tues.-Sat. 10am-5pm. Free entrance. Tel. 405-2107.) Soane was a neoclassical architect and an enthusiastic collector, who willed his home to be a national museum. Among the attractions here are an Egyptian sarcophagus and several paintings by Hogarth, including the *Rake's Progress* series.

In the southern part of the square is a large building, the **Royal College of Surgeons**. It once housed the largest medical museum in the world, but this was almost completely destroyed in World War II. In order to arrange a visit to see what is left of the John Hunter collection, write to the Hunterian Museum, Royal College of Surgeons, Lincoln's Inn Fields, WC2, or call tel. 405-3474.

As you leave the square, you will see a small souvenir shop at 14 Portsmouth Street, which claims to be the oldest in London. It carries the same name as the Dickens book, *The Old Curiosity Shop*.

*L*ONDON

Continue heading southeast to Carey Street. On your right is the back of the Royal Courts of Justice. On your left stands an old pub, *The Seven Stars*, which was established in 1644, and has always attracted lawyers. Past the pub, at No. 56, is the silversmith *Woodhouse & Son*, which opened in 1690. In the eighteenth century English gentlemen used to purchase silver mousetraps here to present as gifts to their wives and lovers, so that they could protect their powdered hair and wigs. Further down the street you will come to Wildy's Passage, named for the second-hand law bookstore located there.

At the end of Carey Street, on Chancery Lane, you will see the **Public Record Office**, the institution that houses all the country's official documents. The building, designed in the Tudor style in the mid-1800s, also houses a museum. (Open Mon.-Fri. 10am-5pm. Free entrance. Tel. 876-3444.) The exhibit includes, among other documents, William the Conqueror's eleventh-century land survey, the Domesday Book.

Turn right on Bell Yard and follow it to Fleet Street. Opposite you will see *The Wig & Pen Club*, a pub established in 1625. In the center of the street, to the west, the **Temple Bar Monument** marks the border of the City of London. On it stands a griffin, the symbol of the City. At this spot there used to be a barrier with metal spikes, on which the heads of those who had been charged with treason were displayed — a cordial welcome for people approaching the City gates. Today the Lord Mayor receives the monarch here on official visits to the City. The quaint, multi-towered, neo-Gothic building on the right, which was built in the nineteenth century, houses the **Royal Courts of Justice**.

St. Clement Danes Church is located on the traffic island to your right as you cross the street. A church was first constructed on this site in the ninth century; the current building was designed by Sir Christopher Wren, although after the World War II bombings extensive restoration was required. It was rebuilt and converted into a memorial church for the Royal Air Force. The ceremony of distributing lemons and oranges to children at the end of March is thought to originate from a church tax once excised on boats carrying these fruits down the Thames. The tradition has been immortalized, as have the church bells, in the famous children's song:

> "Oranges and lemons," say the bells of St. Clement's,
> "You owe me five farthings," say the bells of St. Martin's,
> "When will you pay me?" say the bells of Old Bailey,
> "When I am rich," say the bells of Shoreditch.

Before turning onto Devereaux Lane, take a look at *Mr. Toby's Carving Room*, the pub on your right, and *Twinings*, the 1706 shop

THE INNS OF COURT

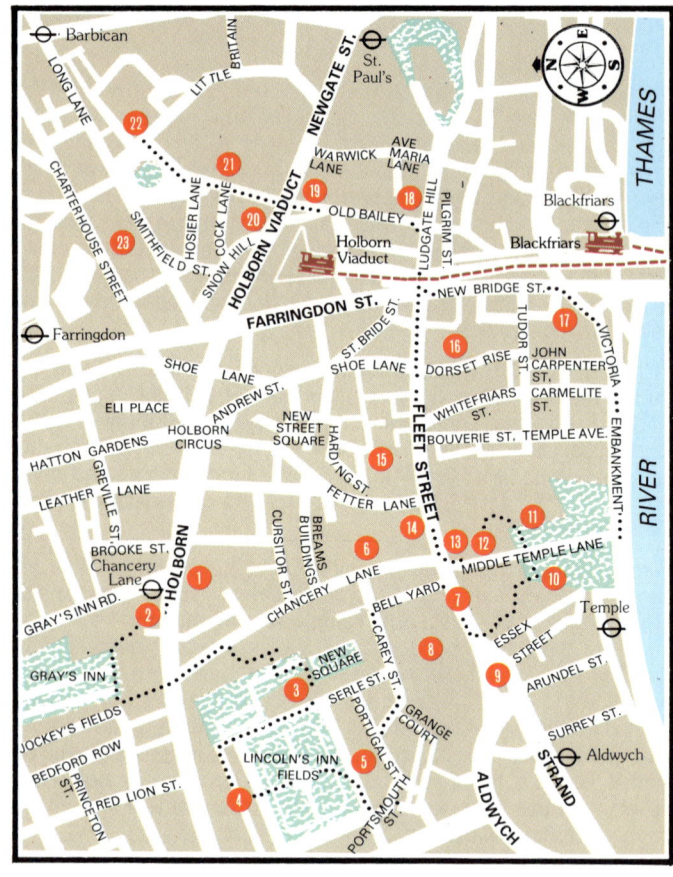

Index
1. Staple Inn
2. Gray's Inn
3. Lincoln's Inn
4. Sir John Soane's Museum
5. Royal College of Surgeons
6. Public Record Office
7. Temple Bar Monument
8. Royal Courts of Justice
9. St. Clement Danes Church
10. Middle Temple
11. Inner Temple
12. Temple Church
13. Prince Henry's Room
14. St. Dunstan-in-the-West Church
15. Dr. Johnson's House
16. St. Bride's Church
17. Unilever House, Sion College
18. St. Martin-within-Ludgate
19. Central Criminal Court — Old Bailey
20. St. Sepulchre-without-Newgate
21. St. Bartholomew's Hospital
22. St. Bartholomew the Great
23. Smithfield Central Market

*L*ONDON

Exploring Lincoln's Inn Fields in the rain

which is thought to be the most narrow in London and is best known for its famous tea. In the lane is a pub of the same name, generally visited by people who frequent the courts. Go through the gate; on your left you will see the Thames glistening in the distance. You are now in the yard of **Middle Temple**, the third of the Inns of Court. (Open Mon.-Fri. 10am-4pm, until 3pm in August. Tel. 353-4355.) The hall south of the yard was built in the days of Elizabeth I, and recently underwent extensive renovations after suffering severe damage in the war. It is said that Shakespeare first presented *Twelfth Night* here, long before it was shown to the public.

Continue eastward and go into the last inn of the tour, **Inner Temple**. (Entrance to buildings by advance arrangement only. Tel. 353-8462.) On your right is the inn's beautiful garden, with an impressive metal gate (closed to the public). On your left are the hall and the library; go around them and you will come to the church that serves both the Temple inns.

Temple Church was built by the Knights of the Templar Order in 1185, in Norman Romanesque style. (Open daily 10am-4pm, closed August and September. Free entrance. Tel. 353-1736.) This is one of five round churches existing in England, and is one of the few structures built in the Middle Ages that has survived within London.

*L*ONDON

The Great Fire of 1666, which burned down most of the city, stopped just short of this church.

Pass the church and turn right onto **Fleet Street**, named for the Fleet River, which used to flow here. The river, which had become a polluted health hazard, was covered by the present street, turning it into a covered sewer that still flows underground. The street became famous for the river of ink that flowed in the large newspaper buildings set along it.

Another building that escaped the flames of the Great Fire is at No. 17, **Prince Henry's Room**. Inside is a collection of letters and belongings of Samuel Pepys, the diarist who lived and worked in London in the seventeenth century, documenting the dramatic events of that time in his diaries. The first floor is decorated with an original Jacobean plaster ceiling. (Open Mon.-Fri. 1:45-5pm, Sat. until 4:30pm. Free entrance. Tel. 353-7323.)

Fleet Street is also famous for its many pubs. These are particularly active in the evening, during the working hours of the daily newspapers. One of these is *Cock Tavern*, at No. 22, which maintains the atmosphere of a past era, like many of the others. Opposite stands **St. Dunstan-in-the-West Church**. Notice its front and the clock tower, which was built in gratitude for the church's escape from the Great Fire. The present building was erected by John Shaw in 1833. The tower was restored after suffering damage in World War II.

Continue walking east on Fleet Street. No. 47 houses *El Vino* wine bar, whose owners still abide by the etiquette of wine-serving and specialize in port wine, the popular Victorian upper-class drink. At the point where the street winds, the dome of St. Paul's Cathedral suddenly reveals itself in the distance. If it is now lunch time, turn into Wine Office Court, where there is an old pub and restaurant that was rebuilt in 1667 (after the Great Fire, of course), oddly named *Ye Olde Cheshire Cheese*. Inside you will be given high quality English food, and you can see the chair where Dr. Samuel Johnson, the eighteenth-century lexicographer, used to sit. To see **Dr. Johnson's House**, continue down the lane and turn left to 17 Gough Square. Johnson lived in this house from 1749 to 1759, and it is here that he compiled his famous dictionary. (Open Mon.-Sat. 11am-5:30pm, in the winter until 5pm. Entrance fee. Tel. 353-3745.)

Return to Fleet Street. To the south, in the direction of the river, is Whitefriars Street, named after the Carmelite order that dwelled here until the Reformation. Located in this area are the buildings of some of the major newspapers, such as *The Daily Express* and *The Daily Telegraph*.

A little further down the street, between the lanes that lead to the river, you can see the delicate steeple of **St. Bride's Church**, the tallest of Wren's steeples. The steeple served as the inspiration for the wedding cake that a local baker prepared for his daughter, and this began a tradition that has continued to this day. Samuel Pepys was christened in this church. It was almost completely destroyed in World War II and was virtually built anew. The excavations of its basement and the modest exhibit of the development of printing on Fleet Street are worth a visit.

From this point, you have a choice of two alternate routes.

Route A

If you are tired, turn right onto New Bridge Street, toward the river. At the western corner, in front of Blackfriars Bridge, is **Unilever House**, a huge, impressive building that was recently renovated. In back of it on the right is the neo-Gothic **Sion College**, which was designed in 1886 by Arthur Blomfield. Victoria Embankment along the Thames, with its wrought-iron benches and lampposts, was completed in 1870, narrowing the river considerably. A few ships are now tied to the platform. Follow the Embankment to the **Temple underground station**.

Route B

Cross Ludgate Circus. On the opposite side of the intersection, to the right, *Bridewell Prison* used to stand. Originally this was a Norman castle in which the monarchs of England occasionally resided. Henry VIII and his queen, Catherine, were the last of the Royal Family to live there. In 1556 Edward VI donated it to the City, which used the castle as a prison for disreputable women and indigents. To the left of the intersection there also used to be a prison, the *Fleet Prison*, which was then on the bank of the river. The prison primarily served debtors, who were then exiled overseas. Many of their descendants are now the pillars of society in former British colonies.

On top of Ludgate Hill is **St. Martin-within-Ludgate**, which was also renovated by Wren in 1687. In the church there is seventeenth-century woodwork well worth a peek. Turn left on Old Bailey and walk a few meters to the *Reader's Digest Shop*, on the right. Further on you will find the **Central Criminal Court**, known as **Old Bailey**, London's famous criminal court. Cases are heard in this massive building that was erected to replace Newgate Prison; the trials are open to the public. Enter through the visitors' gate.

Continue north. On your left stands **St. Sepulchre-without-Newgate**, on Holburn Viaduct. The largest parish church in the City, it originally stood outside the City walls. The handsome Gothic tower was

LONDON

erected in the fifteenth century, and one of its bells was sounded when the prisoners of Newgate were led to the scaffold. (These are "the bells of Old Bailey," referred to in the children's song quoted earlier.) Inside the church is a splendid gilded organ built in 1671. In back of the church is Cock Lane, probably so named because of the chickens raised here for cockfights in the Middle Ages. Another kind of entertainment this neighborhood was known for during that period was prostitution; since it was outside the walls, what went on here could not harm the morality of the City.

Continue north on Giltspur Street toward **St. Bartholomew's Hospital**, nicknamed St. Bart's. This hospital was founded in 1123 by an Augustinian monk. Above the entrance, which was erected in 1702, is the only statue in London of King Henry VIII. Go into the yard and turn left toward the Great Hall, built in the eighteenth century. The hall became famous for its huge wall mural, painted by Hogarth in 1737, depicting the miracle of Jesus at the Bethesda Pool.

Leave the hospital grounds and turn right. In the Middle Ages the nobility used to gather in this area, called Smithfield, to watch the knights participate in tournaments. In a later period the crowds gathered here again, but this time to view the more macabre sight of public executions.

Bear right on West Smithfield, where you can visit one of the most impressive churches in London, **St. Bartholomew the Great**. Rahere, the same Augustinian monk who built the hospital, founded the church in 1123. Go through the thirteenth-century gate and enter what is left of the enormous church that once stood here. The structure preserves the beauty of Norman architecture, with its massive pillars and crossing arches. Take a look at the northern part of the church, where there is an unusual and impressive effigy of Rahere from the fifteenth century. Back on the street, you will see a huge structure covering about 10 acres. This is the **Smithfield Central Market**, built in the nineteenth century, when it was the largest market for meat in the world. In light of the relative sterility in which trade is done today, you have to use your imagination to picture the filth that Oliver Twist faced when he came here to steal. Complete the tour up the street at the **Barbican underground station**.

*L*ONDON

Adelphi and Covent Garden — The World of Dickens and the World of Theater

The prolific nineteenth-century author Charles Dickens was well acquainted with the area covered in this tour. His stories are full of the characters he met, the places he visited, and the varied experiences he had here.

Start the tour at the **Embankment underground station**. Turn right and exit to the Victoria Embankment, which was reclaimed from the Thames River in the nineteenth century in order to build a promenade and gardens. On the riverbank is Charing Cross Pier, where you can take a boat to Greenwich and to the Thames Barrier.

Some 200 meters to the northeast is **Cleopatra's Needle**, an Egyptian obelisk made of pinkish granite. It is one of a pair of obelisks erected by Pharoah Thotmes III in Heliopolis, circa 1500 B.C. This obelisk was presented as a gift to England by Mohammed Ali in 1819, but it took over 60 years to arrive. Cleopatra's Needle was placed in this location in 1878, in memory of Admiral Nelson and General Abercrombie. The United States received its twin, now standing in Central Park, New York.

Return to the underground station and walk north to Villiers Street. Turn right into the **Victoria Embankment Gardens**. Located here is **York Water Gate**, a massive seventeenth-century stone gate. The gate marked the private entrance to the now-demolished *York House*, where Francis Bacon was born in 1561. The Water Gate was installed by the next occupant, George Villiers, then Duke of Buckingham. A colorful character, Villiers earned progressively higher titles of nobility at an astounding rate from King James I, at the same time accumulating influence that was sometimes equal to that of the king himself. Notice that the front of the Gate faces the garden, which was planted where the river once ran.

Follow the steps by the Water Gate. On the lane to your left there is a nondescript door. This door leads to *Gordon's Wine Bar*, popular among members of the high society, whose presence is announced by the accent they acquire at prestigious boarding schools. Continue to Buckingham Street. On both sides are handsome buildings from the seventeenth and eighteenth centuries. From 1679 to 1688 No. 12 was the home of Samuel Pepys, whose diaries depict the dramatic events of the London of his time, including the execution of King Charles I and the Great Fire. In the entrance to No. 18 there is a hollow cone structure, once used for extinguishing oil torches. Before streetlights were introduced, the well-to-do used to rent the services of a boy with a torch to light their way in the dark, and to protect them from robbers. More than once the boy would suddenly put out the lamp and attack his unlucky customer.

Turn right onto John Adam Street, and you will come to the **Adelphi**, mentioned in several of Dickens's stories. The Adelphi was the ambitious proposal of the Scottish Adam brothers, Robert and James (*adelphoi* means "brothers" in Greek). In 1768 they designed an elegant residential neighborhood on the area sloping down to the Thames. Because of the difficult topography, they had to build on a network of underground supporting arches, which Dickens's hero David Copperfield may have liked, but which actually made the venture extremely expensive and almost led the brothers to bankruptcy. In 1773 Parliament approved a lottery to help them raise the funds necessary to complete the project. Londoners, who loved a gamble, paid £50 for the opportunity to win a house.

Many of the attractive terrace houses of the Adelphi were torn down in 1936 in order to undertake another ambitious project, the construction of the York House office building. One of the most noteworthy houses that remains, located at 8 John Adam Street, is the **Royal Society of Arts**, which was founded in 1754 to promote the arts and trade. No less impressive is the building on the eastern corner of the street, 7 Adam Street. Its proportional measurements and decorative pilasters are in keeping with the principles of classical architecture.

From John Adam Street turn left on Adam Street to the **Strand**, the ancient route connecting the City to Westminster. For many years this road was lined with the palaces and mansions of the nobility, most of which were demolished, and the rest serve as public and commercial buildings. To this day the Strand is used as a central thoroughfare in London, and it is packed with traffic at all hours.

Cross the road opposite the **Adelphi Theatre**, turn left and then right to Bedford Street, the location of many publishing houses in the nineteenth century. A remnant of these can be found on the corner of Maiden Lane, site of *The Lady*, a women's magazine founded in 1885. Written for the woman who considers herself a "lady," with all its implications, the magazine still maintains an aristocratic character, with ads seeking servants and governesses, and articles dealing with the typical pastimes of women of leisure.

Turn right onto Maiden Lane toward No. 26, where the famous English painter J.M.W. Turner was born and lived. On the right

*L*ONDON

you will find the back entrance of the Adelphi Theater. Across the street, at No. 35, is the veteran **Rule's Restaurant**, founded in 1798 and still serving traditional English cuisine. Notice the worn brass sign hanging by the entrance. Rumor has it that when King Edward VII was Prince of Wales he would dine here discreetly with his lover, actress Lillie Langtry. Today's clientele also include members of the Royal Family.

Turn right onto Southampton Street, go back to the Strand, and turn left. On the other side of the street, at No. 100 is another old restaurant, *Simpson's-in-the-Strand*, established in 1848; it too specializes in traditional English cooking.

The gold statue of a prince on the same side of the street marks the entrance to the **Savoy Theatre**, built in 1881 for presentation of Gilbert and Sullivan operas. A hotel of the same name was built close to the theater. Both buildings were designed by Richard D'Oyly Carte. On the same block, to the east, is the **Savoy Chapel**, built in the early 1500s on the grounds of the medieval Savoy Palace.

Continue eastward along the Strand. On the corner of Lancaster Place, which leads to Waterloo Bridge, is the enormous and impressive **Somerset House**. The Palladian-style building was designed by Sir William Chambers. Construction began in the late 1770s on unfinished foundations built by Lord Protector Somerset in 1547; he was executed before he could complete his palace. The building currently houses government offices. The fabulous art collection of the **Courtauld Institute Galleries** is expected to be moved here from Bloomsbury in August 1989, and will be exhibited in the wing facing the Strand (see "Bloomsbury — The Home of Writers and Poets").

Further down the Strand is the attractive **St. Mary-le-Strand**, a church built by James Gibbs in 1714. It is most appreciated for its delicate spire and impressive plaster decorations.

Turn left, continue toward Aldwych, a crescent-shaped street, and make an immediate left onto Catherine Street. At No. 25 is a good Indian restaurant called *Taste of India*. The right side of the street is dominated by the **Theatre Royal, Drury Lane**, which has an attractive colonnade on the outside. This is the fourth building to be constructed on this site; it dates back to 1812 and was built by Benjamin Wyatt. This theater, more than any other, is responsible for the reputation of the area as the stronghold of actors and playwrights. Many famous actors began their careers here during the last three hundred years.

Turn left on Russell Street, which intersects Bow Street to your right and Wellington Street to your left. At 41 Wellington Street is *Penhaligon's*, a perfume and cosmetics shop that dates back to

*L*ONDON

ADELPHI AND COVENT GARDEN

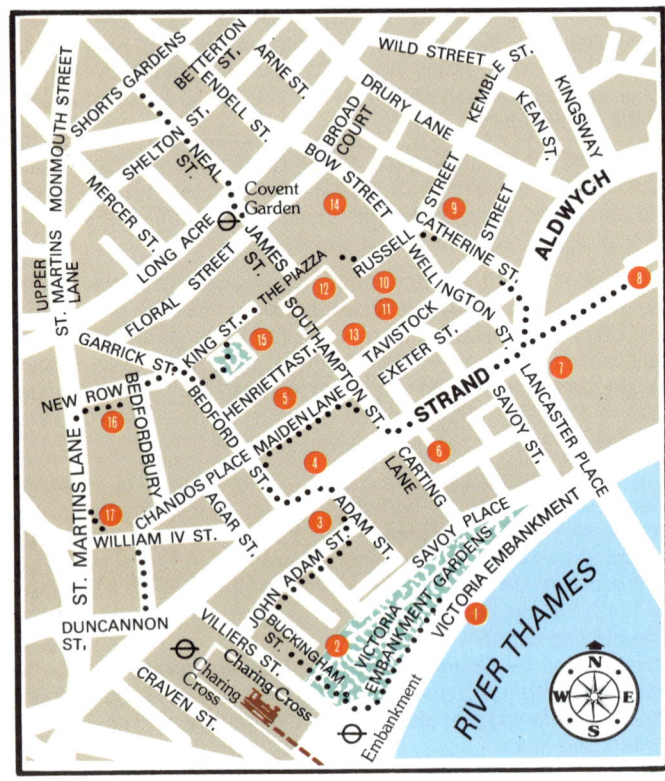

Index
1. Cleopatra's Needle
2. York Water Gate
3. Adelphi, Royal Society of Arts
4. Adelphi Theatre
5. Rule's Restaurant
6. Savoy Theatre, Savoy Chapel
7. Somerset House
8. St. Mary-le-Strand
9. Theatre Royal, Drury Lane
10. Theatre Museum
11. London Transport Museum
12. Covent Garden Plaza
13. Jubilee Market
14. Royal Opera House
15. St. Paul's Church
16. Goodwin's Court
17. Coliseum

*L*ONDON

Shops and cafés at Covent Garden Plaza

1870. Its devoted clientele enjoy personal recipes and mixtures formulated by the shop's founder a hundred years ago. Further down Russell Street, on the right-hand side, you will find *Brahms & Liszt Wine Bar*, named not after the two great composers, but after the Cockney slang for *drunk*.

On your left is the entrance to the **Theatre Museum**, which opened in 1987. (Open Tues.-Sun. 11am-7pm. Entrance fee. Tel. 831-1227.) The museum features an exhibit on the history of English theater from its birth to modern times. In addition to the exhibits, there is a small theater, a shop with appropriate souvenirs, and a café. Visitors can also purchase tickets for current London shows at the information desk.

Next to the Theatre Museum is the **London Transport Museum**. (Open daily 10am-6pm. Entrance fee. Tel. 379-6344.) The museum offers an interesting survey of the history of London's public transportation system, from carriages, carts, and horse-driven cabs to electric trolleys, double-decker buses, and the Tube. This museum is especially fun for children.

Opposite the museum is the large **Covent Garden Plaza**, which was the first square built in the city. Until 1974, Covent Garden housed the city's famous fruit and vegetable market. The area originally belonged to the monks of Westminster, who tilled a large plot of land here and sold their surplus produce. When the monasteries were closed in the sixteenth century by Henry VIII, the land became the property of the Crown. In 1552 it was given to John Russell, the

LONDON

first Earl of Bedford, who built his home here. He was followed by other nobility, who also built homes in this area, giving the streets their names: Drury Lane, Cecil Court, Exeter Street, etc.

The earls of Bedford continued to cultivate the land and to sell the produce. They were soon joined by other merchants; in time the place became solely a market and all farming ceased. Covent Garden's unique character was enhanced by the fourth Earl of Bedford, who was in need of a source of income for his family, and decided to develop the area for trade. Charles I charged him no less than £2,000 for the license. Architect Inigo Jones was selected for the project. Influenced by Italian piazzas, he designed a rectangular plaza bordered by colonnades. The square was originally called The Great Piazza, but later *Piazza* was used only in reference to the colonnades.

Trade in the square flourished. Gradually stands were added, some not absolutely legal, and the market expanded in size; it transformed the pleasant character of the area. The wealthy residents began to flee Covent Garden, and were replaced by market people, merchants, and even characters connected to the underworld. In the nineteenth century Parliament intervened to stop the deterioration. The stands were removed and architect Charles Fowler replaced them with a simple, charming building. Later an attractive structure was added in the eastern part of the square for the flower market; it now houses the Theatre Museum and the Transport Museum.

In 1974 the Covent Garden fruit and vegetable market was moved to a location more convenient for heavy vehicles, thus making the land in central London available for commercial and recreational purposes. The plan to give the area over to entrepreneurs with modern development proposals met with loud and strong opposition from various individuals and organizations concerned with preserving the district's special character. The planners were forced to retreat from their program and find an alternative that would maintain the traditional atmosphere as much as possible.

In the early 1980s Covent Garden reopened as a commerce and entertainment center that quickly became extremely popular. The streets were improved and paved, and the central market structure was renovated and turned into a place for specialty shops and boutiques. It also houses the **Light Fantastic Gallery of Holography**, which displays various holographic techniques, including artistic examples. (Open Mon.-Wed. 10am-6pm, Thur.-Fri. 10am-8pm, Sat. 10am-7pm, Sun. 11am-6pm. Entrance fee. Tel. 836-6423.) The adjacent **Jubilee Market**, a variety market open seven days a week, features arts and crafts.

After visiting the shops and observing the street performances that are almost a daily occurence, go around the market square from the right and turn onto James Street. On your right is the **Royal Opera House**. (Open daily 10am-8pm, when performances are not scheduled. Tel. 240-1066.) Built by E.M. Barry in 1858, this building symbolizes the constant bond between Covent Garden and the theater world. It houses the Royal Ballet, as well as the British Royal Opera, one of the best in the world, and a visit is highly recommended. The opera hall is extremely beautiful, decorated in red velvet, and is patronized by the rich in all their finery, who come to watch the opera or the ballet. Recently a plan was submitted to enlarge the building to include a commercial complex, at the expense of neighboring buildings worthy of preservation. The proposal met with fierce opposition from the public.

Continue north to Neal Street, which is packed full of charming stores selling everything from Oriental musical instruments at No. 64, to kites at No. 69, to copperware at No. 48.

Follow the same route back to the central market, and turn onto King Street, where you can still see one of the colonnades designed by Inigo Jones. The square is bordered on the north by **St. Paul's Church**, which owes its simple design to Jones. The Earl of Bedford's funds were low at this point; he acknowledged that the church could not be much more elaborate than a barn. Jones promised him the finest barn in the Kingdom. Unfortunately, most of Jones's work was destroyed by fire in 1795. Thomas Hardwick reconstructed the church according to Jones's original intentions. St. Paul's became known as the church of theater people. Under its eastern facade, which faces the square, George Bernard Shaw had Professor Higgins, on his way out of the opera, meet the flower vendor, Eliza Doolittle, in *Pygmalion*, the basis for the musical, *My Fair Lady*. The scene represented an encounter between high society and the masses who frequented the Covent Garden market.

Many important people have been christened, married, and buried in the church. The most picturesque personality of all belonged neither to the intellectual world nor to the theater. Frenchman Claude Duval, whom tradition tells us is buried on the church grounds, was the hero of the romantic fantasies of seventeenth-century women. Duval was a highwayman known for his chivalry, as well as for his success in seducing his victims of the opposite sex; it is said that only a few actually put up a fight when being robbed.

Further down King Street, before you turn into the churchyard hidden behind the building facades, take a look at No. 43, the last of the wealthy homes that once lined the streets of Covent Garden. At the intersection with Bedford Street there is a small lane to the right off Garrick Street, called Rose Street, site of the well-known pub, the *Lamb and Flag*. On the western corner of Bedford Street you will find *Moss Bros.*, a clothing store that has long been known for its formal-dress rental services.

LONDON

After visiting St. Paul's, cross the intersection to New Row. The old gas lighting continues to operate here; together with the paved streets, the area has a feeling of times gone by. At 12 New Row, on the corner of Bedfordbury, is *Arthur Middleton*, a wonderful store specializing in antique scientific instruments. Turn left and immediately right, onto the lane located between houses No. 23 and No. 24. This is **Goodwin's Court**, decorated with the bowed fronts of eighteenth-century houses. Once this little street was teeming with all sorts of needy, wretched, and drunk vagrants. It has since undergone extensive renovation, and boasts quite a respectable appearance.

Leave Goodwin's Court at the western end, and enter St. Martin's Lane. Turn south toward the **Coliseum**, home of the English National Opera, with an impressive globe perched on top. Unlike the Royal Opera, which performs operas in their original language, the English National Opera performs in English only. Before you come to the Coliseum, you will pass the *Café Pélican*, known for its pastries. Turn right onto William IV Street. On your right is London's General Post Office, which is open seven days a week. On the corner of Adelaide Street is a shop that specializes in postal goods.

Complete the tour at the **Charing Cross underground Station**.

LONDON

Whitehall and Westminster — Stronghold of the Regime

When Edward the Confessor moved his court from the City to Westminster in the eleventh century, the government, subject to the king, moved as well and settled in the same area.

Begin the tour of the stronghold of the British regime at **Charing Cross underground station**, where the village Charing was once located (*cierran* means "to turn" in Old English; the river turns eastward at this spot). The nineteenth-century monument in front of the station at **Charing Cross** commemorates the cross erected by King Edward I in memory of his beloved Queen Eleanor. When the queen died in 1290, she was buried in Westminster Abbey. King Edward erected thirteen crosses at thirteen stations along the path of her last journey. The original cross, which was destroyed in 1647, stood at the top of Whitehall, where there is now a **statue of King Charles I**. All distances to and from London are measured from this spot.

The memory of **Whitehall Palace**, which belonged to the Royal Family, is preserved by the street bearing the name Whitehall. Originally purchased by the Archbishop of York in 1240, the house became the official residence of his descendants for 300 years. When Cardinal Wolsey was appointed to the bishopric, he renovated the building in characteristic splendor, thereby arousing the envy of King Henry VIII, who lived in the medieval Westminster Palace. With the fall of Wolsey, Henry VIII quickly took over the palace and changed its name to Whitehall. He also purchased the property around the palace, and equipped it with recreational facilities such as tennis courts and an arena for cockfights.

In the days of Queen Elizabeth I, plays and performances were presented in Whitehall Palace, under the initiative of two great artists of the era: the author and playwright, Ben Jonson, and the architect Inigo Jones, who was a talented stage-designer as well. Inigo Jones also redesigned Whitehall Palace, planning an immense, awesome structure, but only a small part of this plan was executed, the Banqueting House. In 1698 the palace burned down, never to be restored. The royal court under William and Mary moved to St. James's Palace, and the king's attendants who had populated the grounds of the former palace were replaced by members of the government bureaucracy that developed in the area.

London

Walk south on Whitehall. On your right is the **Old Admiralty**, built around 1725. (Open by reservation, for groups only. Contact the Ministry of Defence, tel. 218-9000.) Admiral Nelson spent time in this building. When he died, the magnificent funeral procession of the highly praised admiral set out for St. Paul's Cathedral from here. Next to it is the **Admiralty House**, which is actually an addition made to the old building in 1788.

The next building on your right is the **Horse Guards**, built in 1760 on the site of the guardhouse of Whitehall Palace. It has an attractive stone exterior with a clock tower. The two mounted guards stationed here daily belong to the queen's Royal Horse Guards. There are also two additional guards patrolling by foot. Enter the yard and go into the **Horse Guards Parade**. On May and June evenings, a ceremony called *Beating the Retreat* is held here to the sound of marching music. (Tickets available at the Ticket Office on Bridge Street, near Westminster.) On the second or third Saturday in June, the *Trooping the Colour* ceremony is held here, the official celebration of the queen's birthday. (Tickets may be reserved by writing, before 1 March, to Household Division HQ, Horse Guards, SW1.)

Across the street is the **Old War Office**. To its right stands the **Banqueting House**, the primary remnant of Whitehall Palace and the only part of Jones's design that was completed before the fire. (Open Tues.-Sat. 10am-5pm, Sun. 2-5pm. Entrance fee. Tel. 930-4179.) Dating back to 1622, this was the first building in England to be designed in the Palladian classical style. The hall's high ceiling is decorated with fabulous paintings by Rubens. One morning in 1649, King Charles I stood on a scaffold leaning against the house, and delivered his final speech before his head was laid on the chopping block. The bust of the king, located in the attractive stairway, indicates the window from which he is thought to have exited for the scaffold.

To the right of the Banqueting House is the **Welsh Office**, and across the street is the **Scottish Office**. Both were built in the eighteenth century. In back of the Banqueting House is the huge Ministry of Defence building.

Next to the Scottish Office is the **Cabinet Office**, which used to house the Ministry of Finance. It borders on Downing Street. **10 Downing Street** has been the well-known residence of the prime minister of Britain since 1731.

Further down, Whitehall becomes Parliament Street. A massive building that looks like an Italian palace houses the **Home, Foreign, and Commonwealth Offices**. On the other side of the street, hidden by the old facades, construction of new, modern government offices is under way.

LONDON

In the center of the street is the **Cenotaph**, a monument erected in 1920 in honor of the victims of World War I. Later the victims of World War II were also memorialized here.

In between the two parts of the Italian palace is King Charles Street; turn right. At the end of this street you can visit the **Cabinet War Rooms**. (Open daily 10am-5:50pm. Entrance fee. Tel. 930-6961.) Nineteen rooms that were dug and fortified for Winston Churchill and other contemporary officials have been kept as they were. They include the Cabinet Room, Churchill's bedroom, the Map Room, and the transatlantic telephone switchboard which had a direct line to the White House. The American Bell Telephone Company, which installed the connection, had to keep the main installation in the basement of Selfridges on Oxford Street, because of its size.

Return to Parliament Street. Just before reaching Parliament Square, you will see on your left a pub called *St. Stephen's Tavern*, a favorite of members of Parliament.

Parliament Square was laid in the eighteenth century by Sir Charles Barry. In its center are a number of statues of governmental dignitaries, the most outstanding being the massive, slightly stooped figure of Churchill, erected in 1973. In the western part of the square is the Art-Nouveau building of the Middlesex Guildhall, now called the **Middlesex Crown Court**. In front of it stands a statue of Abraham Lincoln.

At the southern end of the square is **St. Margaret's Church**, the parish church of House of Commons. Edward the Confessor first built a church on this site in the eleventh century. The current church dates to the end of the fifteenth century, but has since undergone countless alterations and renovations. Its walls have witnessed many fashionable weddings and the funerals of numerous members of Parliament.

Next to this church is one of the most famous and most important churches in England, **Westminster Abbey**. (Nave, aisles, precinct open daily 8am-6pm, Wed. until 8pm. Free entrance. Ambulatory, transepts, chapels open Mon.-Fri. 9am-4:45pm, Sat. 9am-2:45pm and 3:45-5:45pm. Entrance fee. Guided Super Tours available Mon.-Sat., for a fee. Tel. 222-5152.) The Abbey is noted particularly for its beauty as a Gothic church, and because all the monarchs of England since 1066 (with the exception of two) were crowned here. Many monarchs and other members of the Royal Family are buried here.

Tradition dictates that a church was first built on this site in the seventh century. The first documented record, however, is of a Benedictine monastary established in the eighth century. Edward

WHITEHALL AND WESTMINSTER

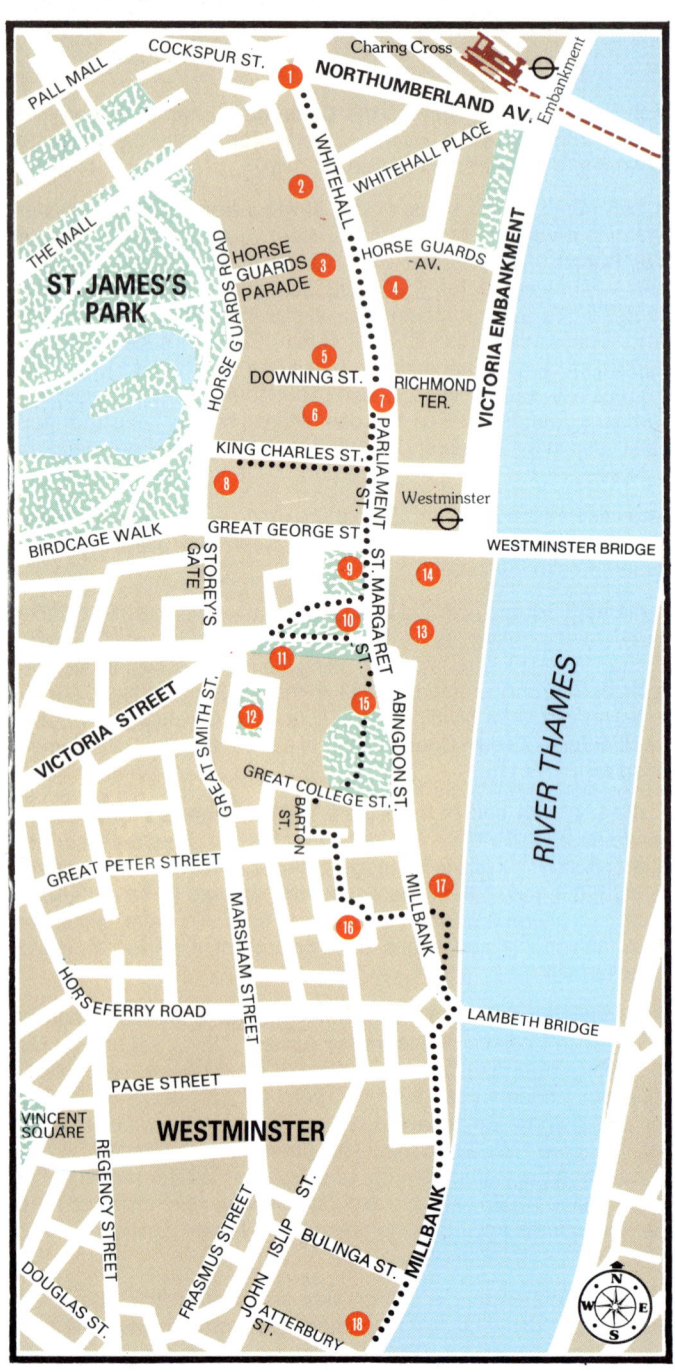

A sentinel of the Royal Horse Guard stands watch in Whitehall

Index
1. King Charles I statue
2. Old Admiralty
3. Horse Guards
4. Banqueting House
5. 10 Downing Street
6. Home, Foreign, and Commonwealth Offices
7. Cenotaph
8. Cabinet War Rooms
9. Parliament Square
10. St. Margaret's Church
11. Westminster Abbey
12. Dean's Yard
13. Houses of Parliament
14. Big Ben
15. Jewel Tower
16. St. John's, Smith Square
17. Victoria Tower Gardens
18. Tate Gallery

the Confessor then constructed a Norman church on this spot, close to his new palace at Westminster, which was dedicated shortly before his death; it was therefore natural that he should be buried there. William the Conqueror, his successor, was the first king to be crowned in the Abbey, establishing the tradition that has continued to this day. In 1245, in honor of the now cannonized Edward, King Henry III decided to rebuild the church in the lavish Gothic style. Construction progressed, with breaks, until its completion in the early sixteenth century.

The building was originally named West Minster, a reference to its location west of the City. Disputes within medieval Christianity caused the status of the site to change back and forth from monastery to church. Finally, under Elizabeth I in the sixteenth century, it became officially known as the Collegiate Church of St. Peter in Westminster. The original connection with a monastary makes it popularly known as Westminster Abbey.

The western exterior, with its twin towers, was altered in the eighteenth century by Nicholas Hawksmoor, and the northern front was redesigned in the nineteenth century by Sir George Gilbert Scott.

The church is built in the shape of a huge cross. Go in through the **west entrance**. As you enter, ribbed pillars rise before you, reaching to the arched ceiling; the effect is a fabulous expanse, lit with crystal chandeliers. Directly opposite the entrance is the **Grave of the Unknown Warrior**, decorated with blood-red poppy flowers. Behind you, above the door, is a huge 1735 stained-glass window, depicting Abraham, Isaac, and Jacob, with fourteen prophets.

In the eastern part of the **nave** is a partition decorated in Gothic Victorian style, which conceals the **choir**. Every day, 22 twelve-year-old boys, who study in the church school, sing in the choir. The **organ**, originally built in the eighteenth century, has since been extensively altered. Set into the partition, on the left, is a memorial to Sir Isaac Newton.

Ascend a few low steps to the **Sanctuary**. Approach the altar; behind it is a delicate mosaic depicting the Last Supper. The mosaic and the altar were designed in 1867 by Scott.

The transepts are almost overflowing with monuments and statues in memory of notable figures in British history. In the **north transept** you will find statues of Disraeli, Palmerston, and Gladstone, among others. The three chapels in the eastern part of the wing are usually closed.

Continue eastward, along the ambulatory to the north of the Sanctuary. On your left is the **Chapel of St. John the Baptist**, followed by the **Chapel of St. Paul**. The marked route leads you

*L*ONDON

up a flight of steps to the beautiful **Chapel of King Henry VII**, considered to be a masterpiece of late Gothic work. Its ceiling looks like delicately woven lace. Located in the center of the chapel are the lavish graves of *King Henry VII* and *Elizabeth of York*. A monument holding eight black pillars marks the graves of the sister queens, *Mary I* and *Elizabeth I*.

George Villiers, Duke of Buckingham, who was murdered in 1628, is buried in the chapel on the left. In the next chapel *Anne of Denmark*, queen of James I, is buried. The eastern chapel now belongs to the *Royal Air Force*. On the southern side is a vault containing the remains of *Charles II, William* and *Mary*, and *Queen Anne* and her husband, *Prince George of Denmark*. To the west of this vault are striking monuments to two women: *Margaret Beaufort*, mother of Henry VII, and *Mary, Queen of Scots*, mother of James I.

Cross the small bridge to the **Chapel of Edward the Confessor**. A monument to *Henry V* stands in the entrance. In the center is a small shrine, in honor of the saint king, Edward the Confessor, on which you can see the remains of original mosaics. Beyond the shrine stands the *Coronation Throne*, which has been used for crowning English monarchs since around 1300. On the right are monuments to *Edward I*, his wife *Eleanor of Castile*, and, most beautiful of all, the Gothic tomb of *Henry III*. The ambulatory is enclosed on the south by the **Chapel of St. Nicholas** and the **Chapel of St. Edmond**.

The south transept contains the **Poet's Corner**, so named because *Chaucer* and *Spencer* are buried here. The area is now occupied by the graves of many more poets, as well as plaques and monuments in honor of others not buried here.

From the south aisle of the nave go into the **cloisters**, which date to the mid-1400s. Here you will find a **Brass Rubbing Centre**. Brasses are memorial plaques engraved with various pictures — images of the people being memorialized, coats of arms, animals, and more. The center has replicas of some 100 brasses; the originals are embedded in church walls and floors, some in the Abbey and some in other churches. (Open Mon.-Sat. 9am-5pm. Rubbing fee.)

From the cloisters you can enter the **Chapter House**. (Open Mon.-Sat., April-Sept. 9:30am-5pm, Oct.-March 10:30am-4pm. Entrance fee.) Notice the original floor tiles and the huge windows with stained glass. Until 1547, the members of the House of Commons used to convene in this room, and to this day it belongs to the government and not the Abbey.

Enter the adjacent room, the **Chamber of the Pyx**, which is named for the monastery's coin treasures that were kept here in the past. (Open same hours as the Chapter House.) Later the monarchy kept

WESTMINSTER ABBEY

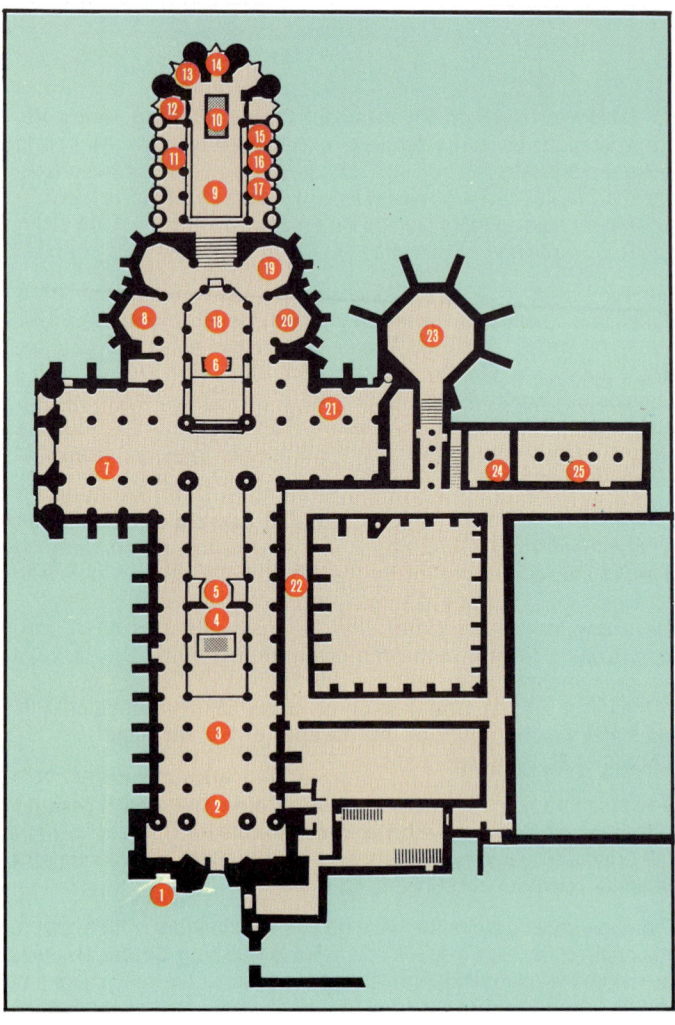

Index
1. West entrance
2. Grave of the Unknown Warrior
3. Nave
4. Choir screen
5. Organ
6. Sanctuary
7. North transept
8. Chapel of St. John the Baptist
9. Chapel of King Henry VII
10. Graves of Henry VII, Elizabeth of York
11. Graves of Mary I, Elizabeth I
12. Grave of the Duke of Buckingham
13. Grave of Anne of Denmark
14. RAF Chapel
15. Graves of Charles II, et al.
16. Grave of Margaret Beaufort
17. Mary, Queen of Scots monument
18. Chapel of Edward the Confessor
19. Chapel of St. Nicholas
20. Chapel of St. Edmond
21. Poet's Corner
22. Cloisters
23. Chapter House
24. Chamber of the Pyx
25. Abbey Treasure Museum

*L*ONDON

Statue of Richard the Lion-hearted against the House of Lords

the pyx, the box containing standard coin weights, in this chamber. It is part of the original structure built by Edward the Confessor, and it has the oldest altar in the monastery. The old Norman undercroft houses the **Abbey Treasure Museum**. (Open daily, 10:30am-4:30pm. Entrance fee.) Among the treasures displayed is the second crowning throne, which was prepared for Queen Mary in 1689 and has never been used since. The museum also has exhibits relating the history of the Abbey.

Continue toward the **Little Cloister**, which originally belonged to the monastery infirmary. (Open Thursdays, April-Sept. 10am-6pm October-March to 4pm. Free entrance.) Next to it is College Garden, which dates back at least 900 years. The adjacent buildings belong the Westminster School, which was first a monastic school founded by the monks in the twelfth century.

Outside the church grounds, on your left, go into the large **Dean's Yard**, which is surrounded on all sides by old residences, some of them from medieval times.

Go around Westminster Abbey from the northern side and cross the street to the **Houses of Parliament**. You may observe sessions from the Strangers' Gallery of each House. (In the *House of Commons* sessions are held Mon.-Thur. 2:30-10pm, Fri. 9:30am-3pm. Free entrance. Tickets are necessary if you wish to visit before 6pm. After 6pm and on Fri. you do not need tickets, and there is less of a line to get in. Tel. 219-4273. In the *House of*

LONDON

Lords sessions begin Mon.-Wed. at 2:30pm, Thur. at 3pm, and Fri. at 11am. Free entrance. Tel. 219-3107. Free guided tours are available of both Houses and include Westminster Hall. Advance tickets are necessary. In order to obtain free tickets for tours and parliamentary sessions, write to your embassy or to your member of Parliament.)

Edward the Confessor moved his court to Westminster Palace and renovated it for this purpose. The palace subsequently became the chief residence of the monarchs of England, until Henry VIII moved to Whitehall Palace in the sixteenth century. Parliament remained in the building until it was almost completely destroyed by fire in 1834. The Houses of Parliament were quickly rebuilt, in Gothic style according to a design by Sir Charles Barry and Augustus Pugin. They incorporated Westminster Hall and the cellars of St. Stephen's Chapel, which remained from the original building, into the huge new structure.

On your left as you face the building is the high clock tower that displays one of the most famous symbols of London, **Big Ben**. This huge bell, which strikes the hours, weighs over 13 tons and is likely named after Sir Benjamin Hall, the portly man who was responsible for its installation. When Parliament is in session at night, a light is lit at the top of this tower. The front part of the building, where there are usually long lines of people waiting to get in, is the old **Westminster Hall**. Beyond it is the **House of Commons**, and in front of it stands an 1899 statue of Oliver Cromwell. The right-hand section of the building contains the **House of Lords**, with a fine statue of Richard the Lion-Hearted in front of it. At the southern end is **Victoria Tower**, with its breathtaking view of the city. The tower contains hundreds of thousands of documents and decrees of Parliament. When Parliament is in session during the day, the Union Jack — the British flag — flies above the building. When the queen visits, her banner, the Royal Standard, is raised here.

Walk southward. To your right you will find a modest brick building, surrounded by the remains of an ancient moat. This is **Jewel Tower**. (Open Mon.-Sat. 9:30am-6:30pm, until 4pm in winter. Free entrance. Tel. 937-9561.) Dating back to the reign of Edward III, this is another remnant of Westminster Palace. It was erected to house the king's treasures, and was later used to store the documents of Parliament.

Cross the garden to the south, passing _Knife Edge_, a statue by Henry Moore. Turn off Great College Street onto Barton Street, one of the most charming streets built in the eighteenth century. Many notable people lived here, including T.E. Lawrence, known as Lawrence of Arabia. While living at No. 14 he wrote _The Seven Pillars of Wisdom_.

Continue south to Smith Square. In the center stands a strange-

LONDON

looking Baroque church from 1728, **St. John's**. Queen Anne, who evidently saw sketches of the design, likened it to a footstool turned upside down. The church was one of the first to be restored after World War II and it is now used as a concert hall.

Cross over to the west, toward **Victoria Tower Gardens**. Opposite you see a quaint monument, Buxton Memorial. In the northern part of the Gardens stands a bronze group statue by Rodin, the *Burghers of Calais*, in memory of the notables who surrendered their city to Edward III in the fourteenth century.

Exit the Gardens, passing Lambeth Bridge, to Millbank. In between Bulinga and Atterbury Streets, to the west, you will see the **Tate Gallery**, the last stop on the walk. (Open Mon.-Sat. 10am-5:50pm, Sun. 2pm-5:50pm. Free entrance. Tel. 821-1313.) The Tate, one of the most important galleries in London, presents a fantastic collection of Impressionist and modern art, and of English painting of all periods, including Hogarth, Reynolds, Blake, and Constable. In April 1987 the new *Clore Wing* opened, devoted to a splendid collection of work by the English artist J.M.W. Turner. The museum also has a good, inexpensive restaurant.

The lavish northern facade at Westminster Abbey

Rodin's "Burghers of Calais" in Victoria Tower Garden near the Houses of Parliament

LONDON

St. James's and Buckingham Palace — The Royal District

Ever since Edward the Confessor left the City and built Westminster Palace, the kings of England have made their home in this area, which covers no more than one square mile.

In order to attend the 11:30am changing of the guard ceremony at Buckingham Palace, begin this tour at an early hour.

The tour starts at **Trafalgar Square**, the most central and busy of London's squares. The square was designed by the architect John Nash, and construction began in the 1820s. The square is named for the famous battle of 1805, in which Admiral Nelson defeated the united Napoleonic fleet of France and Spain, and was fatally wounded at the moment of victory. The huge stone statue of the admiral, towering above a granite column in the center of the square, was erected in 1843 and is referred to as **Nelson's Column**. The bronze reliefs that decorate its base illustrate the battles in which Nelson fought against Napoleon.

The square is particularly popular among tourists, who come to feed the flocks of pigeons that gather here. Every year at Christmas time a huge fir tree is set up here, splendidly decorated with a myriad of colors and sparkles, and people gather around to sing Christmas carols.

The square is surrounded by a number of important buildings. To the west is *Canada House*, and opposite it, to the east, is *South Africa House*. To the northeast is one of the most famous and best liked of London's churches, **St. Martin-in-the-Fields**, which was constructed around 1725 by the Scottish architect James Gibbs and boasts an impressive spire. This church serves as the parish church for the monarch; the coat of arms of King George I is boldly engraved above the entrance. A great musical tradition developed at this church, from which the renowned academy of the same name emerged. In 1929 it had the honor of being the first church from which prayer was broadcast by radio. The musical tradition continues, with lunchtime concerts.

Immediately to the north of Trafalgar Square stands a large neoclassical building, the **National Gallery**. (Open Mon.-Sat. 10am-6pm, Sun. 2-6pm. Free entrance. Tel. 839-3321.) The museum contains one of the world's most important, largest, and richest collections of European art from the Renaissance to the present

LONDON

day The first step toward establishing this collection was made by Parliament in 1824, when a budget was allocated to purchase a collection from the estate of John Julius Angerstein. Initially the collection was displayed in Angerstein's home; in 1838 it was moved to the present building. The building has undergone several expansions, and recently a plan was approved to enlarge the museum to the west. The new wing will be modern, but the exterior will be designed to blend with the present one. It is expected to open in the 1990s.

The invaluable collection includes masterpieces from the Flemish school, such as Van Dyck and Rubens, the Dutch school of Rembrandt, the Italian Renaissance from Botticelli and Leonardo da Vinci to Michelangelo, as well as Spanish and German schools, French Impressionists and, of course, British artists. An absolute must.

The southwest exit from the square in the direction of the Mall is marked by an enormous arch, known as **Admiralty Arch**. It was erected as part of the architect Aston Webb's redesign of the Mall in honor of the late Queen Victoria. The Mall leads to Buckingham Palace and is currently used for royal parades; it was originally paved and fenced in for Charles II when he was young, so that he could play the ball game called pall-mall (from the Italian *palla*, "ball," and *maglio*, "mallet"). This street acts as the northwest border to St. James's Park.

Past the arch, on your left, stands an unassuming ivy-covered brown building. This is the **Citadel**, erected during World War II for government offices.

Continue walking along the Mall. On your right is the classical facade of the **Carlton House Terrace**, designed by John Nash in the nineteenth century. Several adjoining apartments, each with its own street entrance are typical of urban English construction of the eighteenth and nineteenth century. Various clubs and institutions now occupy the Carlton House Terrace. At No. 12 is the back entrance to the **Institute of Contemporary Art**; the public entrance is on the Mall next to the Duke of York steps. (Open daily noon-11pm. Entrance fee. Tel. 930-3647.) In addition to galleries exhibiting international contemporary art, the Institute also has a theater, cinematheque, and a nice cafe.

To your right is the **Duke of York's Column**. The statue standing on top of the tall granite pillar depicts Frederick, Duke of York, the second son of King George III. Frederick, the army's chief commander, and his mistress were infamous for their suspected willingness to sell army jobs to anyone who had the money. Frederick's indecision was also renowned, and this characteristic is satirized in a children's song:

*L*ONDON

> The grand old Duke of York
> He had ten thousand men.
> He marched them up to the top of the hill,
> And he marched them down again.
> And when they were up they were up!
> And when they were down they were down!
> And when they were only half-way up
> They were neither up nor down!

On the far end of the Mall, in a small square in the middle of the street, stands a second monument to Queen Victoria, also designed by Webb, the **Queen Victoria Memorial**. The marble statue of the queen is crowned above by a gilded bronze figure of Victory. On sunny days the reflection on the golden image is blinding.

On the other side of the Memorial is Buckingham Palace, where you can wait with the other peoples of the world for London's number one tourist attraction, the **Changing of the Guard**. (April-Aug., daily at 11:30, Sept.-March on alternate days, weather permitting. Tel. 930-4832 for details.) To the beat of the drums, a group of guards, wearing their famous hats, appears from the adjacent barracks and performs the ceremony in the open square opposite the palace, where the queen lives when in London. The Royal Standard flies on the pole at the top of the building when she is in residence.

Buckingham Palace was first built by John Sheffield, appointed Duke of Buckingham by Queen Anne. In 1762 George III bought the mansion for his wife, Queen Charlotte. Architect John Nash began enlarging it in 1825, and the building expanded to become the grand palace in which Queen Victoria lived after taking the throne.

The palace and the large garden behind it are not open to the public. You may, however, visit the **Queen's Gallery**, through Buckingham Gate. (Open Tues.-Sat. 11am-5pm, Sun. 2-5pm. Entrance fee. Tel. 930-4832.) Fine and decorative arts from the Royal Family's collection are displayed in rotating exhibitions.

Further down the street becomes Buckingham Palace Road. To your right is the **Royal Mews**, where you can view the royal carriages, still used for special occasions and royal visits. (Open Wed. and Thur. 2-4pm, closed during carriage processions and for a week in June during the Ascot horse races. Entrance fee. Tel. 930-4832.)

Turn left onto Bressenden Place, which is part of the business and trade district. Continue to Victoria Street. **Victoria Station**, to the west, is London's largest, most central, and most crowded train station. It has a Tourist Information Centre that also provides a service for reserving accommodations, and is worth dropping by to pick up some pamphlets on the current events in the city.

*L*ONDON

THE ROYAL DISTRICT

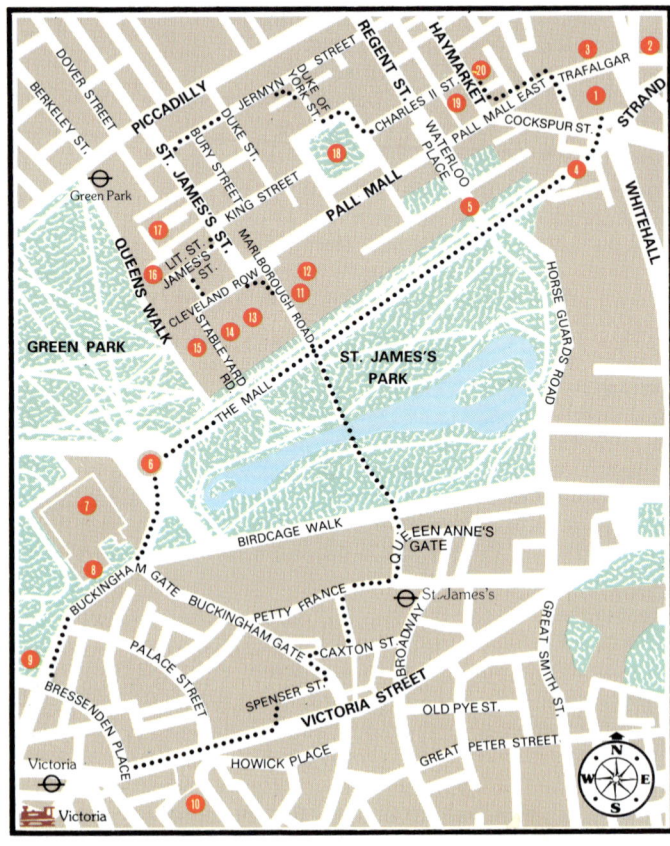

Index
1. Trafalgar Square
2. St. Martin-in-the-Fields
3. National Gallery
4. Admiralty Arch
5. Carlton House Terrace, Institute of Contemporary Art
6. Queen Victoria Memorial
7. Buckingham Palace
8. Queen's Gallery
9. Royal Mews
10. Westminster Cathedral
11. Queen's Chapel
12. Marlborough House
13. St. James's Palace
14. Clarence House
15. Lancaster House
16. Spencer House
17. Blue Ball Yard
18. St. James's Square
19. Her Majesty's Theatre
20. Theatre Royal, Haymarket

*L*ONDON

Taking a break at Trafalgar Square

Continue east on Victoria Street. A few meters down the street a plaza suddenly opens before you. The huge, Byzantine-style church bordering the plaza is **Westminster Cathedral**. (Open daily, 7am-8pm; bell tower open in the summer, daily 9:30am-5pm. Elevator fee. Tel. 834-7452.) Designed by John F. Bentley and built around 1900, the cathedral is the most important Catholic church in Britain, and the seat of the Archbishop of Westminster. The alternating gray stones and red bricks give the building a picturesque appearance. Part of its interior is decorated with golden mosaics. Most of the huge space is almost entirely empty, and its walls are being covered with marble at the rate that the contributions come in.

Further down Victoria street you will find a new branch of the *Army & Navy Stores* which began in the nineteenth century. On the other side of the street you can eat to your heart's content, or stop for a drink, at the Victorian *Albert Pub*.

Turn left at Spencer Street, then left on Buckingham Gate, to the corner of Caxton Street. An early eighteenth-century building houses the National Trust, the organization responsible for preserving buildings of historical importance and opening them to the public. Over the door stands a statue of a boy, a reminder of the building's former role as Blewcoat School, located here from 1709 to 1926.

Follow Palmer Street to Petty France Street, to the side of the

*L*_ONDON_

fortress-like building of the British Home Office. Beyond it you will find a small, quiet street, one of the most beautiful in London, which was built in the early eighteenth century. It is called **Queen Anne's Gate**, and serves as an excellent example of the elegance of the Queen-Anne style of English architecture. In front of No. 15 is a statue of Queen Anne.

You can take a light afternoon break in **St. James's Park**, London's oldest royal park. John Nash designed the park largely as it appears today. This is one of the most pleasant spots in London, with its small lake, birds, and abundant springtime flowers. On summer days, strollers can enjoy the music of an outdoor band.

Cross the Mall and continue north to Marlborough Road. On the right is the **Queen's Chapel**. (Open for prayer in the summer, Sun. from 10:45am.) Originally intended for the Catholic Princess Maria of Spain, the fiancée of King Charles I, the chapel was completed for the woman he actually married, who was also Catholic, Henrietta Maria. The design is the work of the architect Inigo Jones and the chapel was the first to be built in England in the Palladian style.

Slightly concealed by the chapel is **Marlborough House**. (Closed for extensive renovations until 1991.) The building was constructed by Sir Christopher Wren around 1710 for the Duchess of Marlborough, who was in charge of Queen Anne's bedchamber. In 1817 the house became property of the Crown; among those who lived here were Edward VII before he became king, George V as an infant, and later, his wife, Queen Mary.

On the other side of the street stands **St. James's Palace**, the oldest and most picturesque of the remaining palaces in London. Unfortunately, it is closed to the public, but the exterior is worth a look. The palace was constructed in 1532 by Henry VIII for his queen, Anne Boleyn, at a location which had formerly been the site of a leper hospital called St. James's. After the fire at Whitehall Palace in 1698, the royal court moved here. Although Buckingham Palace has been the London home to British monarchs of the past 150 years, St. James's is still the prescriptive royal residence.

Walk around the palace. On its northern side stands a sentry from the queen's Royal Guard, keeping watch over the original palace gate. From the Tudor period, its angular turrets add a traditional touch to the old building. Immediately to the right you see the long windows of the **Chapel Royal**. (Open for prayer only from October to Good Friday, Sun. from 10:45am.) The chapel, which was built for Henry VIII, was enlarged in the nineteenth century, but the Tudor ceiling, whose decoration is attributed to Holbein, remained. Several royal couples were married here, including William and Mary, Queen Anne and Prince George of Denmark, George IV

*L*ONDON

(who, to his new wife Caroline's great dismay, was already secretly married to someone else), and Victoria and Albert.

Turn left on Stable Yard Road. A path between the buildings leads to one of the palace courtyards, **Ambassadors' Court**. In the palace's capacity as official residence of the queen, it is here that she receives foreign ambassadors on state visits.

To the right of the entrance to the courtyard is **Clarence House**. It was built by John Nash for the Duke of Clarence, who became King William IV. The guard stationed in front testifies to its royal tenant: the queen mother, Elizabeth, widow of King George VI.

Across the street, facing Stable Yard, stands the impressive **Lancaster House**. (Open Easter-Nov., Sat. and Sun. 2-6pm. Entrance fee. Tel. 839-3488.) Frederick, Duke of York, began construction in 1825, but he did not live to see the building completed. He died only two years later, drowning in debts, and the house was sold by his creditors to the Duke of Sutherland. Queen Victoria, who would come to visit the duchess from nearby Buckingham Palace, praised its beauty in comparison to her own home by telling the duchess, "I have come from my house to your palace." Lancaster House is now used for official gatherings.

Follow Little St. James's Street into the prestigious St. James's district. On the left you can see **Spencer House**, one of the few aristocratic homes that is still privately owned. It belongs to the Earl of Spencer, the father of Lady Diana, Princess of Wales. In their glorious past, the nobility used to come to their city homes in "the season," that is, in the summer. In those days, in between attending the theater, opera and numerous parties, the nation's aristocracy used to present their sons and daughters in their best dress, in order to attain an appropriate match.

On the corner of St. James's Street, at No. 69, stands the **Carlton Club**, founded over 150 years ago. Members' clubs, a prominent status symbol of English society, are a unique phenomenon. They emerged out of the coffee houses that were once fashionable meeting places among the high society. The people who gathered there generally spent their free time drinking, debating, and gambling. In time the clubs started to provide overnight accommodation as well, and became increasingly exclusive, taking on political and social characteristics. At the same time, the lists of those requesting admission grew longer and longer. Naturally, the clubs were restricted to men, and to this day only a few have opened their doors to women.

At. No. 72-73 is the city's finest Japanese restaurant, *Suntory*. Along the street to your right are three shops which perhaps best represent the status of this area. The one farthest down, *Berry Bros. & Rudd*, is a wine merchant that has been situated here since 1730; its interior

*L*ONDON

Changing of the Guard at Buckingham Palace

decoration speaks of times past. At No. 6 is the hat store *Lock*, established in the eighteenth century and still faithfully serving the Royal Family. Next door is *Lobb*, the city's famous shoe makers. Its permanent customers also include members of the Royal Family, as indicated by the coat of arms displayed in front. The shoes are custom-made, and the store has a proud collection of plaster molds of the feet of famous figures past and present.

Continue north to the small court on your left, **Blue Ball Yard**. This surprisingly beautiful little spot was once the location of stables and wine cellars. No. 4 has a blue plaque noting that Chopin set out from here for his last concert in 1848. He died the following year.

Further along the street are two old clubs, one facing the other. On the left is *Brook's*, which was traditionally Whig; the handsome building on the right is *Boodle's*, founded in 1775. At the far end of the street, at No. 37-38 is *White's*, a Tory club and one of the oldest, dating to 1693.

Turn right onto Jermyn Street. Once occupied by all sorts of shady characters, the street now has a more respectable appearance, and numerous fine stores.

On your right, at No. 71, with the angels decorating the front, is the prestigious men's shirt store, *Turnbull & Asser*. At No. 87, a blue plaque hangs on a relatively new building, marking the place where the physicist Sir Isaac Newton lived. No. 89 is a small, long-standing perfumery, *Floris*; the coat of arms in front indicates that the store

*L*ONDON

The Irish Royal Guard in step in front of the house of the Queen Mother

serves the Royal Family. The smell emanating from the store at No. 93, *Paxton & Whitefield*, comes from dozens of different kinds of cheeses, which have been its specialty for some two hundred years.

Turn right onto Duke of York Street. On the right is one of the district's most interesting pubs, the *Red Lion*, which serves food that is reasonable both in taste and in price.

Walk south to **St. James's Square**. Of the lovely houses that surrounded it in the eighteenth century, only a few remain: No. 4, with a classical exterior, Nos. 5, 13, 15, and No. 20, which was designed by Robert Adam. At No. 14 is the **London Library**, founded in 1841 by Thomas Carlyle, and one of the largest private lending libraries in Britain. A statue of the mounted William III stands in the center of the square.

Leave the square to the west, in the direction of Regent Street. Down the street on the right lies **Waterloo Place**, where there is a monument to the Crimean War (1853-1856), the war based on the Eastern Question, the dispute between the Great Powers concerning authority over important sites in the Holy Land. Up the street at No. 12 is the *British Travel Center*, where information is available on tours throughout the country. Cross the street and continue to Haymarket, the site of the sixteenth century hay market.

On your right is the **Royal Opera Arcade**, a covered passage containing some charming shops, which was designed by Nash in

LONDON

the early nineteenth century. Next to it is **Her Majesty's Theatre**, founded in 1705 and since then rebuilt three times. Opposite stands the **Theatre Royal, Haymarket**, which opened in 1821. Up the street is the **British Design Centre**, where you can see exhibits of products created by British designers.

Turn right on Haymarket, and at the corner you will find the tall *New Zealand House*, which borders on Pall Mall, also named for the ball game that Charles II and other royalty enjoyed playing. The street is famous for its prestigious clubs, such as *Travellers*, which only accepts members who have traveled at least 1,000 miles outside of the British Isles, and *Athenaeum*, whose members are scientists, researchers, and the like.

Complete the tour at **Trafalgar Square**.

*L*ONDON

Mayfair — The Life of the Aristocracy

When they hear the name Mayfair, many Londoners think of elegantly dressed gentlemen and ladies emitting the delicate fragrance of expensive perfume as they step out of their chauffeur-driven Rolls Royce limousines.

Not so long ago, Mayfair was a highly fashionable and most desirable residential area. Its name comes from the general fair that was held at this location every May. The fair was known for its odd attractions, which became increasingly bizarre with the passing years. It was finally closed in the early 1700s after local residents complained that it was an undesirable nuisance.

Begin the tour at the **Piccadilly Circus underground station**. **Piccadilly Circus** was a part of architect John Nash's grandiose plan. The Prince Regent, who became King George IV, ordered the redesign of the entire area between Regent's Park (see "Regent's Park — The First Garden Suburb") and the Mall.

Nash designed a round area, which ultimately turned out to be triangular. Many plans for its renovation and redesign have been presented to the city leaders, but the large majority were rejected out of hand, as they would have changed its character beyond recognition. Plans were recently approved and the circus underwent extensive renovations. Traffic was reorganized, the underground station was improved, and an underground commercial center was constructed.

Not one of the original houses built around the circus exists today. To the north is a building covered with neon signs, which has become the trademark of Piccadilly Circus.

To the south stands a Victorian building that houses the **Criterion Theatre**, built half underground. The building was recently renovated and a restaurant with a bar, the *Criterion Brasserie*, opened on the premises. The golden ceiling and jeweled floor, remnants of the original building, are valued at more than £1 million.

The center of the circus is graced with a statue dedicated to Lord Shaftesbury, placed there in 1892, and known to all as **Eros**. Actually, the statue depicts the Christian Angel of Charity. The steps at the bottom of the statue have become a favorite meeting place for youth from the world over, and it is they who have helped make the area so famous.

Young people are also attracted to the well-known, multi-storied

*L*ONDON

MAYFAIR

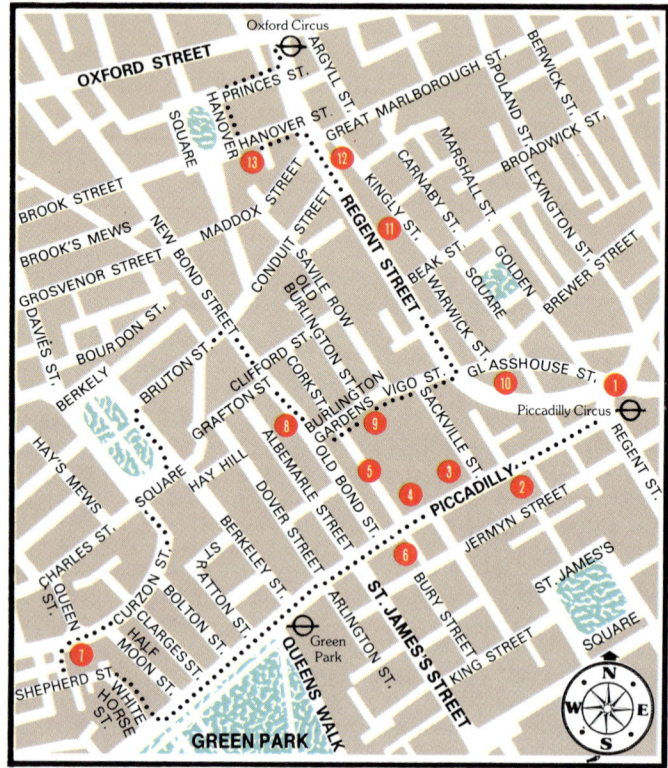

Index
1. Piccadilly Circus
2. London Brass Rubbing Centre, Church of St. James
3. Albany House
4. Burlington House, Royal Academy of Arts
5. Burlington Arcade
6. Piccadilly Arcade
7. Shepherd Market
8. Royal Arcade
9. Museum of Mankind
10. The Quadrant
11. Hamleys
12. Liberty
13. London Diamond Centre

music store, *Tower Records*. The store carries a huge selection of records, tapes, and CDs, a veritable feast for the ears of music-lovers.

Several streets run into Piccadilly Circus. To the northwest is Regent Street, with its neoclassical buildings that were an integral part of Nash's design. To the north is Shaftesbury Avenue, famous for its theaters. To the east is Coventry Street leading to Leicester Square, and to the west is Piccadilly.

The name of this street comes from a mansion, Pickadill Hall. Its owner, Robert Baker, manufactured the frilled lace collars (pickadills) that were so fashionable in Elizabethan England. Today this is one of the most prestigious streets in London. It is occupied by fine hotels, foreign airline offices, and exclusive stores.

On the right is a massive hotel, *Le Meridien, Piccadilly*, with the top floor built like a portico. Across the street stands *Simpson*, a high-class clothing store for men and women.

A few steps away, at the corner of the narrow Church Place, is the **London Brass Rubbing Centre**. (Open Mon.-Sat. 10am-6pm, Sun. noon-6pm. Free entrance; rubbing fee. Tel. 437-6023.) Even if you do not desire the image of a knight or a medieval lady, you should go in and have a look. The center, which plays medieval music in the background, has a collection of some 70 brass facsimiles from numerous churches. For a relatively small price you can get a piece of paper and wax pencils to produce your own brass rubbing, with surprisingly professional-looking results, even if you are all thumbs. Prices are based on the size of the rubbing.

Next door is the parochial **Church of St. James**, built in 1676 by the great architect Sir Christopher Wren. This is one of Wren's simplest churches, yet it was London's most fashionable and popular church during the eighteenth century. The church was seriously damaged by German bombs in 1940-1941, and was extensively renovated, including the addition of a new spire in 1968. The ceiling of the church is a barrel vault decorated with plaster applied around the fragments that remained after the bombing. The magnificent wood engravings are by Grinling Gibbons, as is the marble font depicting the Tree of Life with Adam and Eve on either side. The church is now used as an active cultural center, where lectures and concerts are held. A small, quiet yard on the side of the church offers refuge from the crowds and noise of Piccadilly.

Continue west on Piccadilly. Look up above the large glass window of an airline office at the busts of British artists set into the front of the building. The building once belonged to the Royal Institute of Painters in Water Colours.

Hatchard's, at No. 187, is one of London's oldest book stores,

LONDON

established here in 1797. Immediately next to it, at No. 185, stands another eighteenth-century store, *Swain, Adeney, Brigg*, which specializes in fancy umbrellas, leather bags and suitcases, as well as hunting clothes and equipment — a remnant of the sport that was popular among British nobility until the societies for prevention of cruelty to animals began to protest.

At No. 181 is *Fortnum & Mason*. A highly regarded department store particularly famous for its food section, it was established in the eighteenth century by a grocer named Mason and a courtier named Fortnum. In the food section you can buy a picnic hamper of the best there is to eat, with prices to match. In the back of the store is a café, a popular place to have English cream tea. Notice the clock on the front of the store painted in light green. Every hour on the hour the doors open and a figure of Mr. Fortnum and Mr. Mason, dressed in eighteenth-century garb, step out and bow to one another.

Cross the street. The small **Albany Court Yard** is one of the most prestigious lanes in London. **Albany House** was established in 1770 for Lord Melbourne, but it is named for Frederick, Duke of York and Albany, who later moved in. It was subsequently sold, enlarged, and divided into apartments, which became highly desirable residences mainly for bachelors.

The large buiding with the neoclassical facade that stands further west is **Burlington House**, currently occupied, by, among others, the **Royal Academy of Arts**. (Open daily 10am-6pm. Entrance fee for special exhibitions. Tel. 734-9052.) Construction of the building began around 1665, as a home of the Earl of Burlington. In the eighteenth century the structure was altered in the Palladian style by Colen Campbell; the following century it was renovated again in Victorian Renaissance style. In 1868 the Royal Academy of Arts moved here upon its centennial.

Go into the inner courtyard. A statue of Joshua Reynolds, the Academy's first president, sits in the center. Enter the building through the arches on the other side, and you will see an impressive staircase. Inside the rooms is a marvelous collection of English art. There is also an unfinished sculpture of the Madonna and Child by Michelangelo. Every summer an exhibit of British painting is held in the Academy gallery in recognition of the nation's young talent.

Immediately after Burlington House is a lovely covered passageway. **Burlington Arcade** was built in 1819 by Lord Cavendish. This is, by all accounts, the most exclusive and expensive shopping center in London. Two uniformed guards patrol it and signs warn visitors against running, whistling, or even singing. Across the street is another covered passageway filled with fancy stores, **Piccadilly Arcade**.

LONDON

Continue west down Piccadilly. On your left, after passing St. James's Street, is one of London's most renowned hotels, *The Ritz*, also a famous address for afternoon tea. Beyond it is the expansive **Green Park**, where you can have a pleasant rest in a natural setting.

On the northern side of the street, looking out on Green Park, are a number of offices, members' clubs, and fashionable hotels. At 94 Piccadilly is the *Naval and Military Club*. Turn right at White Horse Street, and you will come to Mayfair's most picturesque section. This is **Shepherd Market**, whose little lanes are lined with small stores, coffee houses, and traditional pubs. It is in this area that the fair in May was held.

Continue to Curzon Street and turn right. At No. 20 is a hairdressing salon, *Trumper's*, whose staff have styled the hair of the Royal Family since 1875. Walk along the street until you reach **Berkeley Square**, one of Mayfair's famous squares. It is named for Berkeley House, which stood at this spot from 1644 until 1733. Devonshire House, which replaced it, was destroyed in the present century. The charm of some of the eighteenth-century houses is preserved on the western side of the square, in particular at No. 14. In the center of the square is an early nineteenth-century pump house.

Leave the square via Bruton Street. **Le Fevre Gallery**, at No. 30 Bruton, specializes in impressionist and modern art. This prestigous gallery is one of many characteristic of Mayfair today. The *Time Life Building* stands on the corner of New Bond Street.

Bond Street is *the* street of London in general, and of Mayfair in particular. Development began here in the late seventeenth century, starting at its southern end — Old Bond Street — and spreading north to New Bond Street. It is named for Sir Thomas Bond, the treasurer of Henrietta Maria, wife of Charles I.

On this street you can purchase the prettiest, rarest, and most expensive of everything. At 26 New Bond Street you will find the jewelry store *Tessiers*, with its eighteenth-century exterior. At No. 34-35 is *Sotheby's*, the largest and most famous auctioneers in the world, established in 1744. Further north are the fashion houses of *Ralph Loren* (No. 143) and *Georgio Armani* (No. 123). Walk south toward Old Bond St., and you can window-shop for more designer fashions, jewelry, leather goods, furniture, antiques, and any other valuable items you can think of. To your right, at 28 Old Bond Street, is the **Royal Arcade**, location of the famous chocalatiers, *Charbonnet et Walker*. When you have had your fill of these riches, turn left on Burlington Gardens. The first street on the left is Cork Street, and it is lined with many of Mayfair's famous galleries.

On the right is the back of Burlington House, location of the **Museum of Mankind**. (Open Mon.-Sat. 10am-5pm, Sunday 2:30-6pm. Free entrance. Tel. 437-2224.) The museum holds the

The Royal Arcade

Liberty — a stately Tudor-style address

LONDON

ethnography section of the British Museum. Exhibits are rotated, in order to display all the museum's collections. It is worthwhile to check out what is being shown during your stay.

Past the museum is the back of Albany House. On the left is **Savile Row**, famous for its elite tailors. Any self-respecting English gentlemen has his suits made by one of these experts; to be discoverd in a suit purchased at a department store would be a dreadful embarrassment. At No. 3 are the offices of Apple, the record company of the Beatles. They held their last public concert on the roof of this building in January 1969. The performance was unfortunately cut short by the police, responding to complaints of uninspired neighbors.

Continue down Vigo Street to Regent Street. The descent to the right, going toward Piccadilly Circus, is called **The Quadrant**; Nash intended to confine the commercial section to this area. _Café Royal_, a favorite meeting place of writers, intellectuals, and royalty in the late 1800s, is located here. It is still a restaurant and a coffee house, and its widespread reputation competes with its high prices.

Regent Street is also famous for its fashionable stores, situated between the many airline offices. On the corner opposite you, at No. 100, is _Aquascutum_, a store for men's and women's clothing. At No. 112 is _Garrard_, the jewelers of the Royal Family, who are responsible for cleaning and maintaining the Crown Jewels.

Continue north along the street and peek into the clothing and china stores. The famous toy store, **Hamleys**, is one of the world's largest and takes up an entire block (No. 188-196). It was established in the eighteenth century, and the royal coat of arms hangs in front, testifying that little princes and princesses also enjoy its treats.

Further along, at No. 204, is _Jaeger_, which began by designing modern clothes and later added a department for household goods. It has now become a chain store.

Turn right at the next corner to Carnaby Street, which used to be popular with the youth of the lively 1960s. Only a pale shadow of the glory of those years remains today.

The next building is _Liberty_, a store that first opened in 1875, and became famous particularly for its printed cotton fabric (Liberty Prints), some designed by William Morris and his students. The back of the store, built in 1924 in the Tudor style, faces Great Marlborough Street.

From the other side of the street, to your left, is Hanover Street, which leads to Hanover Square. The **London Diamond Centre** is located here. (Open Mon.-Fri. 9:30am-5:30pm, Sat. 10am-1pm. Entrance fee. Tel. 629-5511.) In the center there is an exhibition of all that is relevant to diamond production, from the mine to the final product.

Complete the tour at the **Oxford Circus underground station**.

LONDON

Soho — Bohemian Chic

Soho once symbolized London's lively 1960s. The hippy fad emerged in its streets, mingling both the Bohemian and the salacious. Today's young trend-setters have moved to Kensington and the sex dens in Soho are being replaced by ethnic restaurants. Soho remains a nostalgic reminder of something dark and mysterious on the one hand, and young and vibrant on the other.

As early as the seventeenth century, Soho took on a special cosmopolitan character, with the arrival of the first Huguenot immigrants in the late 1600s following the 1685 revocation of the Edict of Nantes, the official recognition of rights given to the Protestants within the French Catholic kingdom. They were followed by Greeks, Germans, Italians, Spanish, and, most recently, immigrants from the Far East, particularly China and Singapore.

Begin the tour at **Piccadilly Circus**. Here you can still feel something of the '60s, when you see young wanderers gathering at the base of the Eros fountain. Turn east on Conventry Street. Immediately on your left you will see the **Trocadero complex**, which opened in 1984, and features a variety of stores and tourist attractions. (Open daily, 10am-10pm.) Among other things, you can watch *The London Experience*, a sound-and-light show of the city's history, accompanied by disturbing smoke effects (nothing of great interest). In contrast, a really special experience awaits the visitor at the **Guinness World of Records**, which presents a selection of the Guinness records with a combination of photography, demonstrations, music, and text that is fascinating for adults and children alike. (Open daily, 10am-10pm. Entrance fee. Tel. 439-7331.) Also located here is **Light Fantastic, the World Centre of Holography**, which displays this unique art form. (Tel. 734-4516.)

Outside Trocadero you will find open-roofed tourist buses, in which you can take an hour-and-a-half guided sightseeing tour of London's main tourist attractions. On the corner across the street is the **Swiss Centre**, with the best that the land of fondue and chocolate has to offer.

Cross over to **Leicester Square**, which is memorialized together with Piccadilly Circus in the famous World War I song:

> It's a long way to Tipperary
> It's a long way to go
> It's a long way to Tipperary
> To the sweetest girl I know

*L*ONDON

> Good-bye Piccadilly, farewell Leicester Square
> It's a long long way to Tipperary
> But my heart is right there!

The soldiers bid farewell to the square for a reason — it is the pulse of the London entertainment industry, an industry that influences the rest of the world. The fields of Leicester have always been common land. The square was delineated in 1670, named after the Earl of Leicester's house built here in 1631. Tenants here have included many artists, among them Hogarth and Reynolds, but both their homes and those of the nobility have now been replaced by London's busiest movie houses.

In the small kiosk at the western side of the square is the **Half-Price Ticket Booth** for same-day performances, operated by the Society of West End Theatres. (Open 12:30-2pm for matinées, 2:30-6:30pm for evening shows.) There is usually long line of people — mainly tourists — who have arrived early in order to get tickets for the most popular performances. On the northwestern corner of the square the distances between London and the capital cities of the British Commonwealth are marked on the sidewalk. On the southwest corner is a statue of Charlie Chaplin, the great entertainer, who was a native Londoner. A monument in the center of the square honors William Shakespeare.

Two small streets run north from the square. The eastern one, Leicester Place, is the location of a round church, **Notre Dame de France**, which is noted for its exquisite decoration by the Frenchman, Jean Cocteau.

Leave Leicester Square at the southeast corner, and walk to the **National Portrait Gallery**. (Open Mon.-Fri. 10am-5pm, Sat. 10am-6pm, Sun. 2-6pm. Free entrance. Tel. 930-1552). The gallery boasts a unique collection of portraits of British notables through history, many rendered by the greatest artists of the last few centuries. The portraits of the monarchs of England and of famous intellectuals are particularly interesting.

North of the gallery is the wide Charing Cross Road, best known and particularly loved by bookworms, who should not miss the opportunity to browse through its many new and used book stores. To the right, on the charming **Cecil Court**, you can find specialized book stores, with subjects such as theater, mysticism, travel, and history. The street was paved in the seventeenth century and is now a promenade lit with old gas lamps.

Continue north along Charing Cross Road and turn left on Little Newport Street. This area has recently taken on a sort of Asian atmosphere, its streets full of immigrants from the Far East who have made it their center. On Lisle Street you will find several good

SOHO

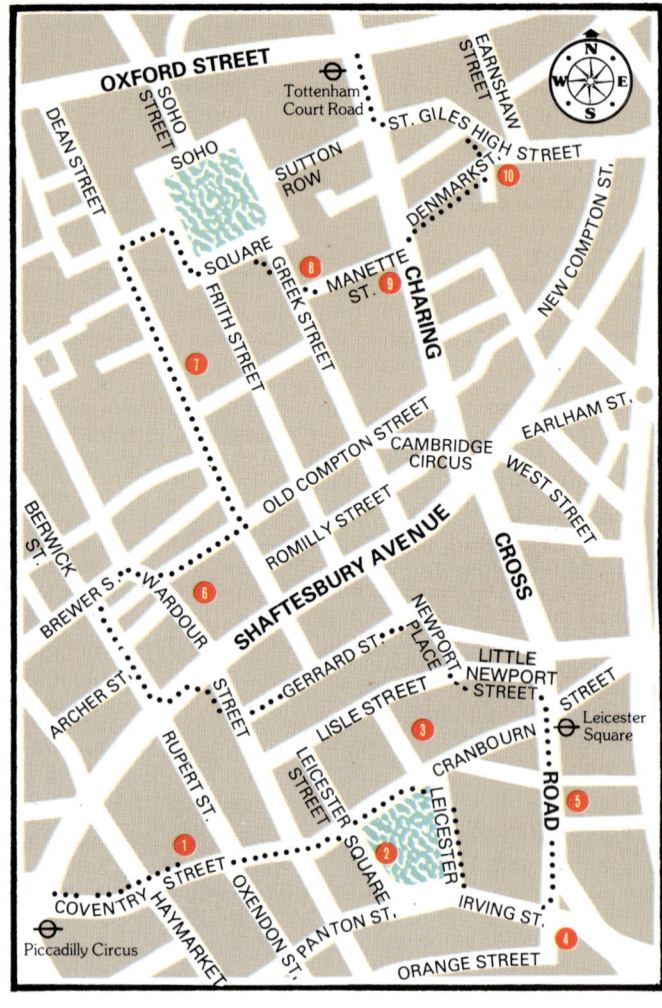

Index
1. The Trocadero
2. Half-Price Ticket Booth
3. Notre Dame de France
4. National Portrait Gallery
5. Cecil Court
6. St. Anne's
7. Leoni's Quo Vadis
8. House of St. Barnabas
9. Foyles
10. St. Giles-in-the-Fields

Distinctly British telephone booths — street-side museum pieces

Chinese restaurants, such as *Fung Shing* at No. 15, *Mr. Kong* at No. 21, and *Poons* at No. 27.

Gerrard Street has already become London's official Chinatown, with pagoda-type gates on both sides, Chinese book stores, a Chinese movie theater, and, of course, a wide selection of restaurants and supermarkets specializing in Chinese delicacies. On the weekend the street fills with families of Chinese immigrants, from grandparents to infants. The music of their language in the air makes you forget for a moment that you are on British soil.

Turn right on Wardour Street, then left on Shaftesbury Avenue. Like

*L*ONDON

Charing Cross Road, this wide boulevard was paved in the late nineteenth century in order to cut through the little streets of the giant slum that had emerged in Soho. Further east, at the intersection of the two streets is the uninviting **Cambridge Circus**, which is scheduled to be redesigned. On the western side of the circus is the **Palace Theatre**, built by Richard D'Oyly Carte in 1891. It was the home of England's national opera for only a year before becoming a variety theater, and is still in operation today while undergoing renovations. This is only one of many theaters concentrated along Shaftesbury Avenue. The names Apollo, Globe, Queen's, and Lyric are what make this district the very heart of London's West End.

Turn right onto Rupert Street. Its continuation is called Berwick Street, where you will find a lively fruit and vegetable market that was in operation as early as the eighteenth century. At its northern end there are wholesale stores that specialize in fabric, jewelry, and fashion accessories.

Turn right at Brewer Street — the name testifies to the distilleries that were once located here. To the west, the street leads to Golden Square, the center of the British film industry. The eastern end of the street is the center of the diminishing sex industry of Soho. Of the sex clubs and shops that once proliferated in this district, only a few remain — a result of strict regulations, and perhaps also due to the conservative reaction to the era of sexual permissiveness. Turn right again and go back to Wardour Street, where you will come to the ruins of the parish church of Soho, **St. Anne's**. It was almost completely destroyed in World War II, leaving only its tower, which has been restored.

Head east on **Old Compton Street**, named for Henry Compton, dean of the Chapel Royal. This used to be Soho's major commerce street, and today it still boasts a number of delicatessens and bakeries, such as *Patisserie Valerie* at No. 44. These have been joined by several ethnic restaurants, such as the Italian *Amalfi* at No. 29-31.

Turn north on Dean Street, also named for Henry Compton. On the southern end of the street, at No. 49, is a well-known popular pub. Until recently, it was officially called the York Minster, but became known as the "French pub," because of the nationality of its father and son owners; eventually the name was formally changed to **French House**.

The northern end of the street is graced by attractive eighteenth-century buildings. At No. 26-29 is another Italian restaurant, **Leoni's Quo Vadis**. In a tiny apartment above it, Karl Marx, his family, and his children's nurse lived in terrible poverty from 1851 to 1856. At No. 88 is a magazine store called *Rippon* with a charming Rococo front

*L*ONDON

from the late 1700s. There are also two good Indian restaurants on this street, *Trusha* at No. 11-12, and *The Red Fort*, at No. 77.

Turn right toward **Soho Square**, which was laid out in 1681. The name Soho is said to originate from the cry local hunters used to send their dogs out on the hunt. The Duke of Monmouth, one of the illegitimate children of Charles II, built himself a huge house near the square. He chose "Soho" as his slogan in the fateful Battle of Sedgemoor (1685) in which he rebelled against the Crown. Other members of the nobility also built mansions around the square, and it quickly became a fashionable residential area that attracted wealthy Huguenot immigrants and, later, foreign ambassadors.

A statue of Charles II built by Caius Gabriel Cibber (1681) stands in the square. In 1876 is was taken by W.S. Gilbert to the garden of his home, but it was returned in 1938. None of the original buildings of the square have survived. On its eastern side stands **St. Patrick's Church**, rebuilt in Italian style in the late nineteenth century. On the northwest corner you will find the **French Protestant Church** of London, established in 1550. The present building was constructed in 1893.

The southeastern corner is occupied by a building whose unassuming facade does not hint at its luxurious interior. This is the **House of St. Barnabas**. (Open Wed. 2:30pm-4:15pm, Thur. 11am-12:30pm. Free entrance.) Built in 1746, its treasures include plaster Rococo decoration, wood engravings, and fine metal work. The building became a home for the poor and the needy, and now houses homeless women.

The house faces Greek Street, so called because of the Greek immigrants who settled here after fleeing the Ottoman Empire. There are two good restaurants on this street from the Land of the Magyar (Hungary), *The Gay Hussar* at No. 2, and *Old Budapest* at No. 6. You can get an inexpensive and delicious Greek meal around the block at *Mykonos*, 17 Frith Street.

Turn left at the first little street, Manette Street, and you will come back to Charing Cross Road. On the right-hand corner, at No. 113-119, sits London's largest book store, **Foyles**, maybe the world's largest as well. The store was founded by two brothers, William and Gilbert Foyle. Upon failing their civil service exams in 1904, the two decided to sell their textbooks. In light of the enthusiastic returns, they became book merchants. Their empire includes an antique books section. An entire five-floor building overflows with books on every subject in the world, and managers claim that Foyles stock numbers some six million books. A visit to Foyles is a must for book-lovers the world over.

Cross the street and turn onto Denmark Street. A few meters down

LONDON

the street you will approach a striking church with a handsome Baroque steeple towering 50 meters above. This is **St. Giles-in-the-Fields**, built originally as a chapel in 1101 in connection with a leper's hospital founded by Matilda, wife of King Henry I. It was named for Saint Giles, patron saint of the ostracized and wretched. In the course of time the chapel became a parish church and its yard became filled with the graves of plague victims and executed prisoners. In 1733 it was rebuilt by Flitcroft, who incorporated many elements of the former building, such as the engraving in oak above the western entrance, depicting Judgement Day. Inside the church is a beautiful organ dating to 1671.

On your way to the end of the tour at the **Tottenham Court Road underground station**, you will pass another Greek restaurant, *Rodos*, situated nearby at 59 St. Giles High Street — bon appetit!

Giving directions

The HMS Belfast on the stretch of the Thames

LONDON

Bloomsbury — The Home of Writers and Poets

As early as the seventeenth century the **Bloomsbury** district was the residence of the well-to-do. In the eighteenth and nineteenth centuries the district developed extensively and numerous houses rapidly appeared around its famous squares.

In the past century the area became particularly popular among writers and artists. The most famous residents of these squares were the members of the Bloomsbury Group — Virginia Woolf, Vanessa Bell, and others who greatly influenced the literature and art of the first half of the twentieth century.

Begin the tour at the **Tottenham Court Road underground station**. The street of the same name runs north; it is famous both for its electronics stores and its furniture stores. Turn north and immediately right to Great Russell Street. Because of its proximity to London's greatest cultural institution, the British Museum, this street abounds in stores for antique books and maps.

Turn left toward the attractive **Bedford Square**, which has changed very little since it was demarcated. Late eighteenth-century and nineteenth-century terrace houses surround it on all sides.

Go back to Great Russel Street via Bloomsbury Street. On your left is the huge classical building that houses the **British Museum**. (Open Mon.-Sat. 10am-5pm., Sun. 2:30-6pm. Free entrance. Tel. 636-1555.) The museum contains one of the largest, most comprehensive, and most interesting collections of antiques and antiquities in the world, of inestimable value.

Its items were attained by serious researchers, enthusiastic collectors, antique dealers, and simple adventurers. The foundations for the museum were laid by Sir Hans Sloane, who left his library and antiquities collection to the nation in 1753, thereby influencing Parliament to establish a national British Museum. The museum was initially set up at Montagu House, and valuable collections of medieval manuscripts were added to it. The exhibits, which were opened to the public on a limited basis in 1759, soon drew 10,000 visitors a year. The area of the museum was too small for the increasing accumulation of items, and in 1823 construction of the present building began.

Enter the museum and go to the Information Desk to get a floor plan.

LONDON

The museum contains marvelous collections of ancient Assyrian and Egyptian objects, including the Rosetta Stone, an Egyptian obelisk, and Egyptian mummies and their decorated sarcophagi. The Greek-Roman collection includes sculptures, temple ruins, painted ceramic implements, mosaics, monuments, and coffins, as well as a fine sampling of Etruscan art. The museum also has a collection of Oriental art, from lands such as India, China, Japan, and their neighbors, and exhibits art and archeological finds from the British Isles.

The building also houses the immense **British Library**, repository of over 16.5 million volumes (approximately half of which are kept in other buildings throughout London). In the Round Reading Room, where Karl Marx wrote *Das Kapital*, you will be surrounded by some 100,000 books. (Reading rooms open Mon., Fri., and Sat. 9am-5pm, Tues.-Thur. 9am-9pm. Tel. 636-1544.) The library includes an invaluable collection of ancient manuscripts, some of which are displayed, such as the Magna Carta.

A visit to the museum will probably take a few hours. Afterward, continue east toward **Bloomsbury Square**. The square was laid in the seventeenth century by the fourth Duke of Southhampton, for whom it was first named. The original buildings did not survive, but it is still an attractive place. Continue along Bedford Place, with its lovely eighteenth-century houses on either side, most of which are used as offices or small hotels.

The next square is **Russell Square**, the largest of the Bloomsbury squares. On its southern side lie the buildings of **London University**, founded in 1836. London was the last of Europe's major capitals to establish its own university. In 1878 this was the first university in Britain to admit women to academic studies with full rights.

The little street that runs from the northwest corner of the square leads to Woburn Square. The **Courtauld Institute Galleries** is located at its western end. (Open Mon.-Sat. 10am-5pm, Sun. 2-5pm. Entrance fee. Tel. 580-1015.) It contains a wonderful collection of impressionist and modern art. The collection is scheduled to be moved to Somerset House in August 1989.

At the edge of the square on the right stands the **Percival David Foundation of Chinese Art**, which displays a unique and comprehensive collection of Chinese ceramics from the tenth through the eighteenth centuries. (Open Mon. 2-5pm, Tues.-Fri. 10:30am-5pm, Sat. 10:30am-1pm. Free entrance. Tel. 387-3909.)

Gorden Square is also surrounded by attracitve homes reminiscent of the past. Cross to the right in the direction of **Tavistock Square**. The spirit behind the Bloomsbury group, Virgina and Leonard Woolf, lived here. Turn left onto Upper Woburn Place. On the corner is the **Jewish Museum**, which houses a collection of Jewish ritual

*L*ONDON

BLOOMSBURY

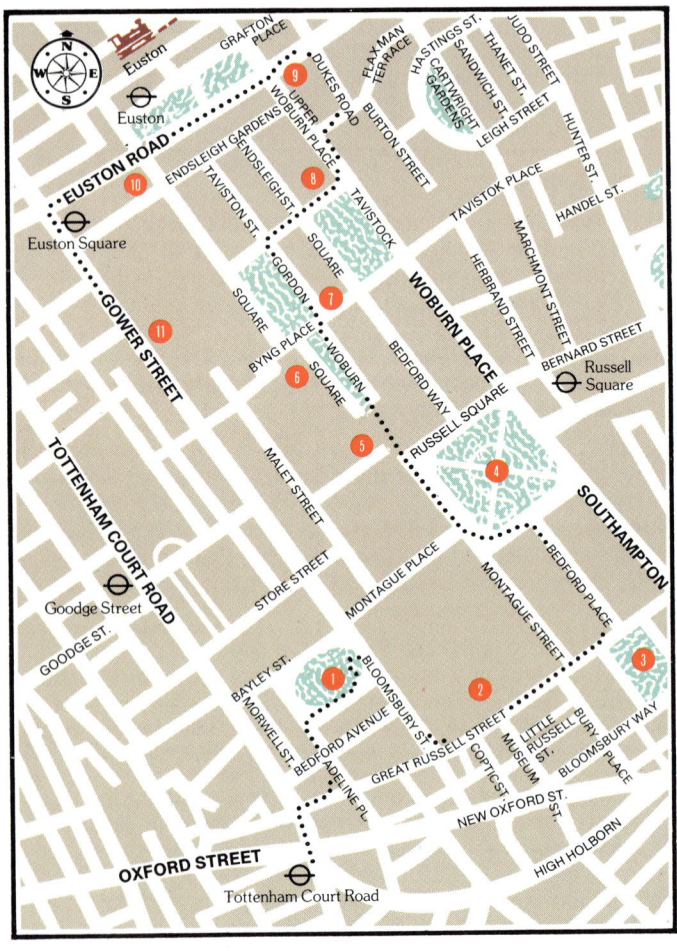

Index
1. Bedford Square
2. British Museum
3. Bloomsbury Square
4. Russell Square
5. London University
6. Courtauld Institute Galleries
7. Percival David Foundation of Chinese Art
8. Jewish Museum
9. St. Pancras Church
10. Wellcome Institute for the History of Medicine
11. University College

*L*ONDON

Four caryatids of the St. Pancras Church

and religious articles. (Open Tues.-Fri. 10am-4pm, Fri. in winter and Sun. 10am-12:45pm. Free entrance. Tel. 388-4525.)

Turn right onto Woburn Walk, where there are some charming shops with eighteenth-century exteriors. Continue on Dukes Road, until you reach the back of **St. Pancras Church**, which was built in 1822 in Greek Revival style. On the northern exterior of the church is a veranda, an imitation of the Erechtheum at the Acropolis in Athens. The four figures of women are not particularly good copies of the caryatids on its exterior.

Busy Euston Road runs from east to west. Towering in the distance to the east you see the turrets of **St. Pancras Chambers** (originally the Midland Grand Hotel), a Victorian Gothic fantasy built by Sir George Gilbert Scott in 1869. It is now used as an office building. Below it is **King's Cross train station**, built in the same era, which, in striking contrast, represents the glory of Victorian modernity in a huge building of iron and glass.

Turn left on Euston Road. At No. 183 is the **Wellcome Institute for the History of Medicine**. It houses a medical history library and sponsors changing exhibitions related to health and medicine. (Open Mon.-Wed. and Fri. 9:15am-5:15pm, Thur. 9:15am-7:30pm. Free entrance. Tel. 387-4477.)

LONDON

Turn left on Gower Street. The western side of this street, lined with Georgian buildings, has been occupied by many of England's artists and intellectuals, among them the John Millais, P.M. Roget (who wrote the thesaurus), D.H. Lawrence, Charles Darwin, and others.

On the eastern side of the street is **University College** of London University, a classical building with a Corinthian exterior. Inside are a number of interesting exhibits worth visiting. In the **Flaxman Gallery** you will find a collection of paintings, drawings, and plaster models by John Flaxman. (Open Mon.-Fri. 10am-5pm. Free entrance. Tel. 387-7050.)

The **Petrie Museum**, somewhat small for the number of exhibits, houses an extraordinary collection of Egyptian archeological items, from the prehistoric to the Coptic periods, including rare fragments from the letters of El Amarna. (Open Mon.-Fri. 10am-noon and 1:15-5pm. Free entrance. Tel. 387-7050, ext. 2884.)

The exhibits of the college are completed with the "self-portrait" of Jeremy Bentham, who died in 1832 and asked that his body be preserved and displayed, which it is, clothed in his finest, in a glass coffin.

Other Sights in the Area

Dickens House Museum is where the talented author lived from 1837-1839. (48 Doughty St. Open Mon.-Sat. 10am-5pm. Entrance fee. Tel. 405-2127.) While here he wrote *Oliver Twist*, and finished *The Pickwick Papers* and *Nicholas Nickleby*. The items exhibited include the author's personal belongings.

The **Thomas Coram Foundation for Children** exhibits the art treasures of the Foundling Hospital that was established by Captain Thomas Coram in 1739. (40 Brunswick Square. Open Mon.-Fri. 10am-4pm. Sometimes closed for conventions. Entrance fee. Tel. 278-2424.) Hogarth, Gainsborough, Reynolds, and others donated their works to the hospital, so that they would be exhibited and would draw public attention and donations.

*L*ONDON

Oxford Street and St. Marylebone — A Shopping Paradise

Every year millions of tourists come to London. Many are attracted to the wide variety of consumer goods, and they leave millions of pounds sterling in the cash registers of shops and department stores, a considerable contribution to the British economy.

A large portion of this commercial activity occurs in a place whose name has become renowned among those who like to shop: **Oxford Street**. This street, which runs from Marble Arch in the west to Tottenham Court Road in the east, was apparently paved as early as the days of the Romans. It was named relatively late — in the eighteenth century — for the De Vere family, sixteenth-century Earls of Oxford.

Begin the tour at the **Marble Arch underground station**, and head east. It would be impossible to mention all the stores along the street, so we will just note the most important.

On the first block on the right at 527-531 Oxford Street is the huge record store *Smithers and Leigh*, which is said to offer everything worth hearing. At No. 506, on the corner of Portman Street, is *Littlewoods*, which specializes in fairly inexpensive clothing. Further down, on the left at No. 485, is a branch of London's most popular and famous clothing chain, **Marks & Spencer**, which has stores throughout the city and the country, and even overseas. Marks & Spencer is best known for its reasonable prices and quality goods — from clothing to smoked salmon.

Before turning left on Orchard Street, visit the reputable department store that gave a street its fame and prestige — **Selfridges**. Established in 1908 by an American, Gordon Selfridge, its formidable neoclassical exterior dominates the street; notice the lady on the front. Selfridges is particularly famous for its cosmetic, food, and clothing sections, and its prices are generally sky-high. It is a fantastic experience visiting the shop during the Christmas season.

It was in the basement of this building that Bell Telephone housed the "mixer" system that it installed for establishing a direct line beteween the U.S. President and the British Prime Minister, Winston Churchill.

Walk along Orchard Street to the heart of the **St. Marylebone** district, which developed mainly during the eighteenth century. At

OXFORD STREET AND ST. MARYLEBONE

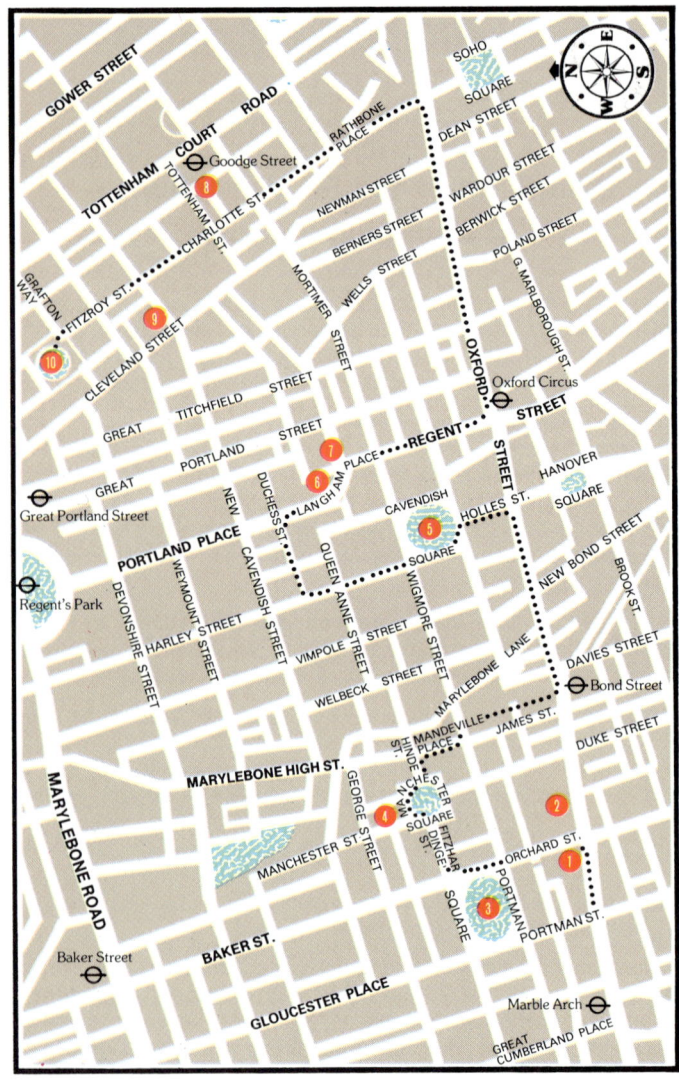

Index
1. Marks & Spencer
2. Selfridges
3. Portman Square
4. Wallace Collection
5. Cavendish Square
6. BBC building
7. All Souls Church
8. Pollock's Toy Museum
9. British Telecom Tower
10. Fitzroy Square

*L*ONDON

London transport on Oxford Street

Portman Square two of the old houses, Nos. 21 and 20, have remained; the latter was constructed in 1776 by Robert Adam and now houses the **Courtauld Institute of Art**.

Turn right at Fitzhardinge Street and you will come to **Manchester Square**, designed in 1776, at the same time as the home of the fourth Duke of Manchester. In 1872 the house was sold to Richard Wallace, the Marquis of Hertford, and it now houses his immense art collection, the **Wallace Collection**. (Open Mon.-Sat. 10am-5pm; Sun. 2-5pm. Free entrance. Tel. 935-0687.) One of the richest and most important collections in Britain, it opened to the public in 1900 and includes a large number and wide range of beautiful works, from the paintings of major artists to furniture and household items. Among the treasures are paintings by Rembrandt, Velázquez, and Rubens. Do not miss this exceptional museum.

When you leave the building, turn east. In this region there are several winding streets that follow the ancient channel of the Tyburn River. Turn right at Mandeville Place and continue back to Oxford Street via St. Christopher's Place. This promenade, lined on both sides with Victorian buildings, is full of boutiques and fashionable restaurants.

Continue east on Oxford Street. Close to the Bond Street underground station, you will find a small, pleasant commercial center worth checking out. Next to it is the large *HMV* record store.

LONDON

The next department store is *Debenhams* at No. 334-338, which has also become a nationwide chain. It offers a selection of high-quality clothing at attractive prices. It is worth a visit, especially to see its tasteful interior design.

At the popular *John Lewis* you will find a wide selection of moderately priced fabrics and household items. Turn left onto Holles Street, which will take you to **Cavendish Square**. At lunch time Londoners flock to the square for a break from work in the shade of the trees here, enjoying a sandwich and drink.

Cavendish Square was laid out in 1717 for Robert Harley, whose name was given to the street that runs from its northwest corner. Walk along this street. Attractive eighteenth-century houses line both sides. Harley Street has become particularly popular among medical specialists, and the prestige of the location is reflected in their fees.

Turn right onto Duchess Street, and follow it to Portland Place. This street, which runs from Regent's Park, was part of Nash's grandiose plan of the early nineteenth century (see "Regent's Park — The First Garden Suburb").

Walk south. On your left standing at the eastern end of Portland Place is the huge building which has housed the **BBC** since 1931. The building replaced one that was constructed by Nash as part of his design of the street; Nash built that one to replace Foley House of the eighteenth-century.

Next door is **All Souls Church** on the curve of the street, now called Langham Place. It was also part of Nash's plan (1824). The church was damaged in World War II, and the present interior is relatively modern.

Regent Street starts at this point. Go to Oxford Circus and turn left to continue on Oxford Street. This part of the street also offers a wealth of stores, for clothing, shoes, jewelry, records, and more.

You can end your tour at this point or walk further along the street until you reach Rathbone Place. If you look up to your left you can see the **British Telecom Tower**, which was constructed in 1965. It is popularly referred to as the Post Office Tower (its original name), and, at some 189 meters (620 feet), is one of the tallest buildings in London.

Turn left. The upper part of the street, which is called Charlotte Street, is lined with restaurants. On Scala Street you will find **Pollock's Toy Museum**, where a varied collection of toys from the nineteenth and twentieth centuries is exhibited. (Open Mon.-Sat. 10am-5pm. Entrance fee. Tel. 636-3452.) The museum is particularly interesting to those nostalgic about childhood.

LONDON

Pass the British Telecom Tower and complete the tour at the lovely **Fitzroy Square**. It is surrounded by late eighteenth-century buildings designed mainly by Robert Adam. At the beginning of the century many members of the Bloomsbury Group lived here, including George Bernard Shaw at No. 29, later followed by Virginia Woolf. The square has now become a popular spot, and many restaurants have popped up around it — a nice place to end an exhausting day of shopping.

*L*ONDON

Regent's Park — The First Garden Suburb

Regent's Park, a pleasant, cheerful spot in the center of the British metropolis, represents one of London's most successful design and development projects — a combination of residential buildings with wide areas left to nature.

This district, which was called Marylebone Fields, was first enclosed by King Henry VIII, who loved hunting, and it remained the property of the Crown until the Civil War in the seventeenth century, when Oliver Cromwell divided the land and leased it as farms. When the leases expired in 1811, the land was returned in its entirety to the Crown, and the Prince Regent, later to become King George IV, decided to redesign the area.

The task was assigned to the renowned nineteenth-century architect, John Nash. He designed a neighborhood of parks with a lake, trees, large grassy lawns, huge villas, and an inner and outer ring of splendid terrace houses. A wide boulevard was planned to lead from the park to the center of town, with its southern end devoted to commerce.

The grandiose plan was only partially realized. Of the twenty-six villas planned, only eight were built, and none of the terrace houses on the inner circle were constructed. Nevertheless, the part of Nash's design that was actualized continues to this day to be a refreshing oasis in the midst of the London metropolis. Its beauty attracts many visitors throughout the year.

Begin the tour at the **Regent's Park underground station**. When you exit the station you will see a half-circle of houses along the southern edge of a square. This is **Park Crescent**; from its center the avenue runs south to the center of London. Look north across the large **Park Square**. Terrace houses with Ionic-style exteriors surround the square on both sides. The houses on the right were used in the nineteenth century for the diorama, an entertainment show that was in fashion prior to the introduction of moving pictures. On the northeast corner opposite the square is the **Royal College of Physicians**, built in 1964.

Enter the park on Broad Walk. This avenue runs through the park from south to north. Beyond the lawns to your right, along the outer ring of the park, you can see some of Nash's handsome terrace houses, in the following order: Cambridge Terrace, Chester Terrace, and Cumberland Terrace (the most impressive). Next to these stands the **Danish Church**, which was built in neo-Gothic style

REGENT'S PARK

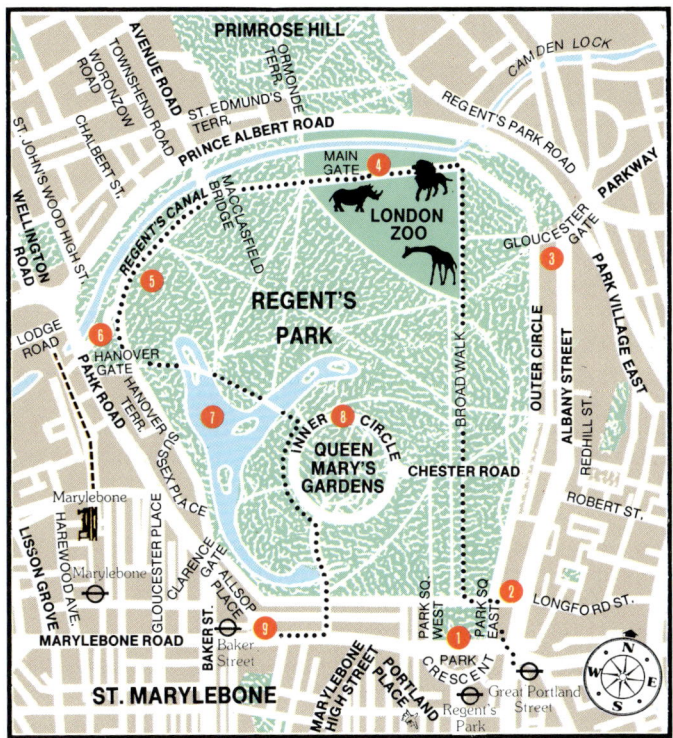

Index
1. Park Square
2. Royal College of Physicians
3. Danish Church
4. London Zoo
5. Winfield House
6. London Mosque
7. Regent's Park Lake
8. Open Air Theatre
9. Madame Tussaud's Wax Museum, London Planetarium

---

in the nineteenth century and initially named for Saint Katherine. The Danish community made this its center in the 1950s. The building north of the church, **Gloucester Lodge**, is the border of Nash's project on this side.

Continue to the end of the avenue to **Regent's Canal**. Dug in 1820, it borders the park on the north. In the summer, the Waterbus leaves from the pier on the canal bank for **Little Venice**, a tranquil spot to the west of the Park surrounded by attractive Victorian buildings, and full of small coffee houses, just right for spending a pleasant afternoon.

On the northern side of the canal lies the grassy **Primrose Hill**. On the left you see the fence of the famous **London Zoo**. (Open

*L*ONDON

April-Oct., Mon.-Sat. 9am-6pm, Sun. 9am-7pm; Nov.-March, daily 10am to dusk. Entrance fee. Tel. 722-3333.) The London Zoo is the oldest zoo in the world. It was designed in 1825 for the members of the Zoological Society and in 1847 opened twice a week to the public. From the first 5 acres on which it began, the zoo has expanded to some 35, and its inhabitants include a wide range of mammals, birds, reptiles, and other creatures, from all corners of the world. There are many attractions here for the whole family, including the Children's Zoo, where the young ones can touch, pet, and even ride some of the animals.

Continue west along the Outer Circle. After a few hundred meters, as the road curves south, you will come to the **Winfield House** on the left. This is one of the few villas located within the park. It was built in 1936 in place of one of the original houses, for the wealthy heiress Barbara Hutton, and is now the home of the U.S. Ambassador to Britain.

Go a few steps further, and on your right you will see the minaret and golden dome of the impressive **London Mosque**, built in 1977. The buildings adjacent to it serve as a cultural center for London's Moslem population.

Turn left and follow the path to a bridge across **Regent's Park Lake**. The lake was part of Nash's original plan; its water comes from the underground Tyburn stream. Continue to the next bridge to the Inner Circle of the park. Opposite you is the **Open Air Theatre**. Performances have been staged here since 1932 and are still held during the summer, weather permitting.

Instead of the terrace houses that were planned for the Inner Circle, a garden was planted under the auspices of the Royal Botanic Society. When the society was disbanded, Queen Mary, wife of King George V, wanted to preserve the garden, hence the name **Queen Mary's Gardens**. There is an exquisite rose garden here, and a bandstand with musicians to entertain passersby during the summer months. In 1982 a bomb planted under the stage by a terrorist organization exploded, injuring many orchestra musicians. A cafeteria is also located here.

Leave the park to the south, passing between two terrace houses at its edge, and go out onto busy Marylebone Road. Turn right and complete your tour at one of the best-known and best-loved tourist attractions in London — **Madame Tussaud's Wax Museum**. (Open daily 10am-5:30pm. Entrance fee. Tel. 935-6861.) Madame Tussaud, a Frenchwoman, began her career designing wax figures of the French royal family, and went on to make the death masks of those taken to the guillotine during the French Revolution. After living in England for many years she founded her museum in London in 1835. The current directors of the museum try to keep

*L*ONDON

up with the times, and the exhibits change along with the rise of new stars. Only lasting all-time favorites are kept on the permanent display. Among others, you can see the hottest pop stars, politicians, the Royal Family, important historical scenes, a re-enactment of the Battle of Trafalgar, and the obligatory hall of terrors, with its chilling reconstruciton of an execution.

Adjacent to the museum is the **London Planetarium**. (Open daily 11am-4:30pm. Entrance fee. Combined tickets with Madame Tussaud's available. Tel. 486-1121.) Here the universe is spread before you hourly. Have a great time.

*L*ONDON

Hyde Park and Kensington Gardens — Oasis in the City

Hyde Park encompasses wide expanses of lawns, trees, flowers, pools of water, reserves for birds, riding paths, and facilities for sports and recreation, concentrated in the very heart of the crowded metropolis. All these elements make it the city's most famous park and a favorite of Londoners. It is pleasant to stroll here any day of the week, and in particular on Sunday, when there are special activities.

Begin the tour at the **Marble Arch underground station**, located at the northeastern edge of the park. When you come out of the station, you face the huge **Marble Arch**, designed by John Nash for the entrance to Buckingham Palace. Nash was inspired by the Arch of Constantine in Rome. In 1851 the arch was moved from the palace to its present location, and when the roads in the area were widened, it was left standing in the middle of a traffic island.

Running south from the arch is Park Lane, lined with London's most prestigious hotels. Undoubtedly the most famous of these is the *Dorchester*. Of the original houses built along the street in the early nineteenth century, only few remain, from Nos. 93 to 99.

At the end of Park Lane is **Wellington Arch**, originally erected in 1828 at the southeast entrance to the park. The arch now stands opposite **Apsley House**, which was designed by Robert Adam in the 1770s. In 1817 the house was purchased by the first Duke of Wellington, who was chief commander of the army in the early nineteenth century. In 1952 the **Wellington Museum** opened here; it contains mementos, personal items, and a large art collection that belonged to the "Iron Duke." (Open Tues.-Thur. and Sat. 10am-6pm, Sun. 2:30-6pm. Entrance fee. Tel. 499-5676.) The museum and the arch are situated in the middle of a traffic island and the whole area is called **Hyde Park Corner**.

A little to the west of the Marble Arch station is another traffic island. In the center is **Tyburn Memorial**, a reminder of one of the most chilling aspects of London's history. From the twelfth to the eighteenth century, this spot on the bank of the Tyburn was the site of the executions of those sentenced to death by order of the royal courts. Initially a simple tree that stood here was used for hanging the condemned. When their numbers grew, permanent gallows were

HYDE PARK AND KENSINGTON GARDENS

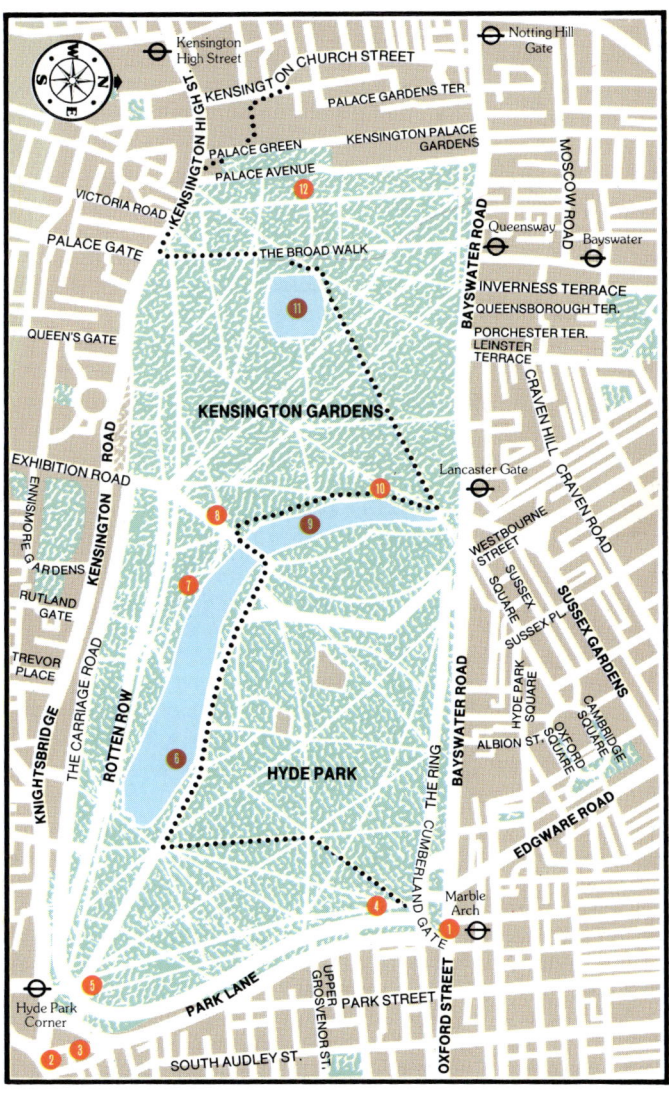

Index
1. Marble Arch
2. Wellington Arch
3. Apsley House, Wellington Museum
4. Speakers' Corner
5. Achilles statue
6. Serpentine
7. Lido
8. Serpentine Gallery
9. Long Water
10. Peter Pan statue
11. Round Pond
12. Kensington Palace

erected to make a sort of triangle, so that 15 executions could be handled at once. The executions attracted large audiences, from paupers to the nobility, who sometimes were treated to "special" attractions, such as beatings, torture, and quartering.

Across the street in the park you will come to **Speakers' Corner**. In 1872 Parliament issued a bill permitting mass gatherings here. Today, any person is allowed to speak his mind, as long as he does not harm the public welfare and sensitivities. On Sundays the corner is crowded with Londoners, and even more so with tourists. The speakers compete for the audience, vocal debates resound through the air, and on more than one occasion the spirited arguments have come close to the point of physical blows.

Walk along the paths of the park. **Hyde Park** was originally part of the Eia Estate. King Henry VIII, true to character, wanted this area for himself — it was abundant in deer and wolves. In order to turn it into a royal hunting area, he persuaded the owners, the monks of Westminster Abbey, to exchange it for an area that was less useful to him, and he fenced in the land that he received.

In 1637 King Charles I designated Hyde Park as the first royal park to be opened to the public. At that time the **Ring**, a road along the borders of the park, was already paved, and it quickly became a fashionable place for carriage riding. In the eighteenth century the park was a somewhat dubious place, and perhaps for this very reason it became popular among the sons of the aristocracy, who made use of its hidden areas to hold illegal duels. In the early nineteenth century the park's status improved and it became increasingly popular.

Walk south on the path to the bank of the **Serpentine**, the long artificial lake that winds around like a snake, enjoyed both by water fowl and by bathers, the latter on **Lido** beach on the southern shore. Along the southern part of the park Rotten Row was paved. In 1851 the area between it and Knightsbridge was turned into the grounds for the Great Exhibition. In honor of the fair, Joseph Paxton built the famous Crystal Palace, which was later disassembled and moved to another location. Recently a monument was erected in this area in memory of the Jewish victims of the Holocaust. Further east, close to the Hyde Park Corner entrance, is the **Achilles statue** erected in memory of the Duke of Wellington and his soldiers.

Walk along the northern bank of the Serpentine, pass the boat dock, and cross the lake on the last of John Rennie's bridges that is still in use in London. On the southwestern side of the lake is the *Serpentine Restaurant*, and next to it is the **Serpentine Gallery**, famous for its modern art exhibits (check the newspapers for current shows). The northern section of the lake is located within the territory of Kensington Gardens, and is called the **Long Water**.

LONDON

Continue north along the western bank of the lake. Pass the **statue of Peter Pan**. To the north of it are fountain gardens. Begin your tour of **Kensington Gardens** here. These gardens, which seem to be a continuation of Hyde Park, are more formally designed, and prettier. Cross through to the southwest until you come to **Round Pond**, decorated with colorful flower beds. The pool lies opposite **Kensington Palace**, the London residence of Charles and Diana, the Prince and Princess of Wales.

William III purchased the building in 1689 and instructed Wren to renovate and enlarge it. William and Mary were the first king and queen to live here; they were followed by Queen Anne, George I, and George II.

Queen Victoria was born in Kensington Palace and lived here until she was eighteen, when she was crowned. In 1899, in honor of her eightieth birthday, she opened the **State Apartments** to the public. (Open Mon.-Sat. 9am-5pm, Sun. 1-5pm. Entrance fee. Tel. 937-9561.) The entrance is on the eastern side, through the garden.

There are many treasures to be found in the palace rooms. The **Queen's Staircase** was designed by Wren to provide public access to the State Apartments. The **Queen's Apartments** have changed only slightly since they were built by Wren. In the **Queen's Gallery** are some exquisite engravings. The **Privy Chamber** has a painted ceiling, depicting the god Mars wearing the Order of the Garter, and tapestries illustrating the four seasons of the year. The ceiling of the **Presence Chamber** shows Apollo. The **King's Staircase** was also designed by Wren; the wrought-iron balustrade, the work of Jean Tijou, was added later.

The ceiling of the **King's Gallery** depicts scenes from the Odyssey. Part of the gallery was used as a sitting room for the Duchess of Kent, Queen Victoria's mother. Here, on 20 June 1837, in the middle of the night, Queen Victoria was informed of her aunt's death and was declared queen.

In the **Duchess of Kent's Dressing Room** the decor is reproduced to match that of its nineteenth-century occupant. In the room next to it, Queen Victoria's toys are displayed. Go through **Queen Victoria's Bedroom**, which she shared with her mother, and continue until you come to the **Cupola Room**, where Queen Victoria was baptized in 1819. The window in this room looks out at Round Pond.

On the ground floor, which opened in 1984, is the fabulous **Court Dress Collection**. The collection includes the clothing of men and women who appeared in the royal court over the past two centuries. In the nineteenth century the nobility customarily presented their sons and daughters who had come of age to the court. Special clothes were worn for the occasion. Notice the headgear that was

*L*ONDON

Speaker and his crowd at Speaker's Corner, Hyde Park

fashionable with Queen Victoria and her ladies-in-waiting: a long, white net scarf affixed to the hair.

Outside the house is the **Orangery** building, which is generally closed to the public. Go to Broad Walk and turn south. Pass the **Queen Victoria statue**, sculpted by her daughter Princess Louise in 1887, and you will approach Kensington Road. This busy thoroughfare connects the eastern part of London to the west.

Turn west and walk toward the commercial center of Kensington, where today's fashion trends are set for the punk generation.

At Palace Green turn right. Along this green boulevard, enveloped in almost stoic calm, stand some nineteenth-century London mansions. Most of them now house foreign consulates.

Turn left and cross over to Kensington Church Street, a long and winding road with something of a rural feeling, a reminder of the days when Kensington was a picturesque village. The street is lined with stores selling books and antiques, making it a charming place to walk. Treasure-hunters with money to spend will have no trouble finding interesting channels for investment here.

Complete your tour at the **Notting Hill Gate underground station**. In this area, every August, the Notting Hill Carnival is celebrated. This colorful, lively, noisy affair is held by the West Indies immigrant population. A must for reggae and calypso lovers. If it is Saturday, we recommended that you continue a short distance north toward the colorful **Portobello Road Market**.

Enjoying Hyde Park on horseback
Royal Albert Hall

*L*ONDON

Knightsbridge and Kensington — Shops and Museums

Knightsbridge, Brompton, Belgravia, and Kensington have always been names associated with money, status, culture, and all that characterizes the upper class. Today these areas have continued to maintain a special blend of glamour, prestige, and cultivation.

Begin the tour at the **Knightsbridge underground station**. This area is filled with the prestigious shops of elite fashion designers. Go to Brompton Road and enter **Harrods**, the world-famous department store. Dating back to 1849 and originally a small grocery store, Harrods steadily grew and developed. In the 1890s the first escalator in any London store was installed here. In 1905 the store moved to its present location. Harrods claims to sell every item on the face of the earth. Legend has it that its marketing manager was once asked whether the animal section could supply an elephant; his answer was, "Of course, but what kind of elephant would you prefer, Indian or African?" It is an exhilarating experience to wander through the store, walking between the halls of food, cosmetics, and clothing. Each section has its own character. Harrods is partiuclarly popular during the Christmas season when locals and tourists come to search for presents. A Tourist Information Centre can be found here, on the fourth floor.

Across the street at 70 Brompton Road is the **IBA Broadcasting Gallery**. (Open Mon.-Fri., book in advance for guided tours. Free entrance. Tel. 584-7011.) A permanent audio-visual exhibition recreates the history of radio and television broadcasting.

Continue along the street. The luxurious stores of *Lanvin*, *Gianni Versace*, and others line both sides. Turn right onto Montpelier Street. Built in the first half of the nineteenth century, it still has its own special charm. The grey building on the left side is *Bonham's Montpelier Galleries*, an auctioneer house in operation since 1793.

Return to the main street. On the left is a small lane called Beaufort Gardens, which is surrounded by handsome terrace houses. At the next street, Beauchamp Place, turn left. Walk among the fashionable boutiques and the china shops, called the *Reject China Shops* (their merchandise is discounted, and some is seconds). Most of the important English manufacturers exhibit their goods here. It is worth a look around; you may find some bargains.

LONDON

Walk down the street to Walton Street. Here you see a striking contrast created by the white eighteenth-century terrace houses situated next to the red-brick Victorian houses.

Turn right and return along Ovington Square, also surrounded by terrace houses. The basements common to all these houses used to serve as servants' quarters; today they are highly desirable and very expensive apartments.

Go back to Brompton Road. Further down the street on the right stands a building in Italian Baroque style. This is **Brompton Oratory**, one of the most important Catholic churches in London today. Covered by a large dome, the building opened in 1884. Behind it, on Cottage Place, is the neo-Gothic **Holy Trinity**. Built in 1829, this church was one of the first examples of the Gothic revival.

Where Brompton Road runs into Cromwell Road, you reach the stronghold of London culture. It is difficult to absorb this entire group of museums and colleges, situated one next to the other, in a single tour. The large building on the right is the **Victoria and Albert Museum**. (Open Mon.-Thur. and Sat. 10am-5:50pm, Sun. 2:30-5:50pm. Free entrance. Tel. 589-6371.) Prince Albert, husband of Queen Victoria, took great interest in the arts and design. To encourage their development, he established the Museum of Manufacturers, which included some exhibits that were originally shown at the 1851 Great Exhibition. In 1857 the museum moved to its present location, and in 1899 its name was changed to Victoria and Albert.

The many exhibits displayed in the spacious rooms cover a wide range of the arts and include, to mention only few, the following: plaster copies of the best classic creations; Japanese, Chinese, and Indian art; furniture, china, silver, and gold produced in recent centuries; a marvelous collection of jewelry; and an exhibit of fashion design from the Middle Ages to the present day. It takes several visits to really get the most out of this museum. The pleasant restaurant on the ground floor offers good inexpensive food, and sometimes afternoon visitors are treated to harp music.

Further down Cromwell Road is the picturesque neo-Gothic building that houses the **Natural History Museum**. (Open Mon.-Sat. 10am-6pm, Sun. 2:30-6pm. Entrance fee includes combined ticket with Geological Museum. Tel. 589-6323.) One of the most interesting exhibits includes life-size skeletons of dinosaurs and a whale. Other exhibits cover plants and animals, human biology, an introduction to ecology, and various other natural subjects.

Turn right on Exhibition Road. Next to the Natural History Museum is the **Geological Museum**. (Open Mon.-Sat. 10am-6pm, Sun. 2:30-6pm. Entrance included with Natural History Museum ticket. Tel. 589-3444.) The museum contains a fascinating collection of gems

KNIGHTSBRIDGE AND KENSINGTON

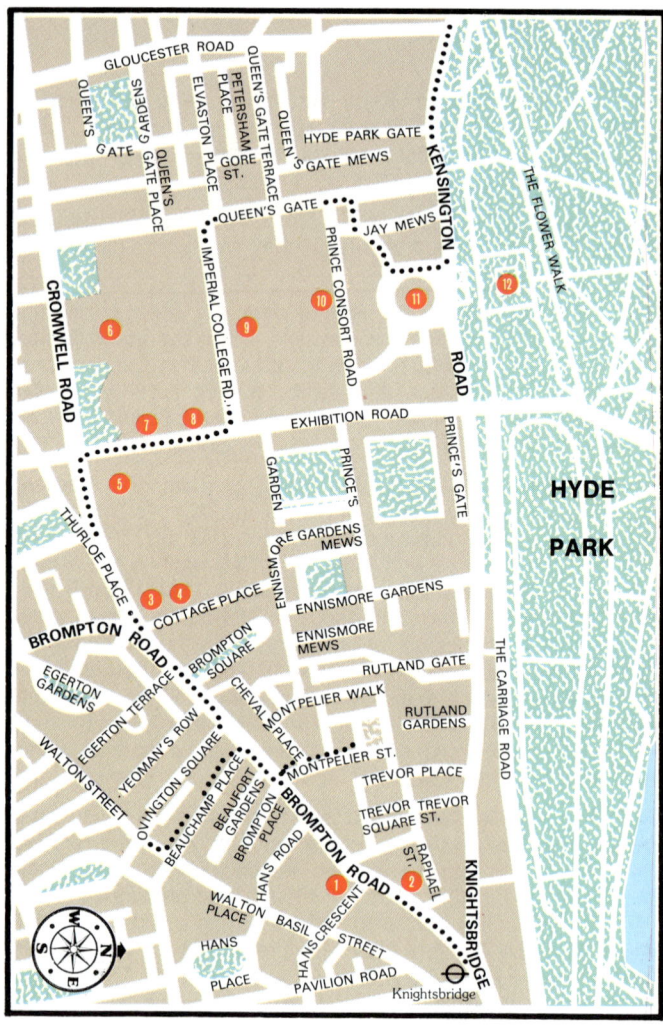

Index
1. Harrods
2. IBA Broadcasting Gallery
3. Brompton Oratory
4. Holy Trinity
5. Victoria and Albert Museum
6. Natural History Museum
7. Geological Museum
8. Science Museum
9. Queen's Tower
10. Royal College of Music
11. Royal Albert Hall
12. Albert Memorial

LONDON

Harrods dominates a city block

and minerals. Other exhibits let you experience the sensation of an earthquake, get acquainted with fossils millions of years old, understand the solar system, and learn about our use of natural resources.

The last museum on the tour is the **Science Museum**. (Open Mon.-Sat. 10am-6pm, Sun. 2:30-6pm. Free entrance. Tel. 589-3456.) This popular museum warrants a special trip. It contains a wealth of technology exhibits, from old steam-driven train engines to automobiles, to space-age equipment. The latter, for instance, takes up a large area and includes a part of the Apollo 10, which circled the moon in 1969. Other exhibits include the development of flight, computers, and hands-on displays. The **Wellcome Museum of the History of Medicine** occupies two floors of the building.

When you leave the museum make an immediate left from Exhibition Road onto Imperial College Road. On both sides you can see buildings of the **Imperial College for Science and Technology**. On the right, way above you, is the **Queen's Tower**, with two lions guarding its base, a remnant of the Imperial Institute of the nineteenth century. Turn right on Queen's Gate. Walk along the wide boulevard and notice the handsome terrace houses across the street. On Prince Consort Street is the **Royal College of Music**, which contains the **Museum of Instruments**. (Open during academic year by special request only. Entrance fee. Tel. 589-3643.)

On the next small street, Bremner Road, turn right. You will be facing the round **Royal Albert Hall**, built in memory of Prince Albert,

*L*ONDON

the beloved husband of Queen Victoria. Various performances are held here, including the summer Promenade Concerts, which draw long lines outside.

Directly across the street from the hall, to the north, stands a large, Gothic-style monument. This is **Albert Memorial**, designed by Sir George Gilbert Scott and erected in memory of Prince Albert with donations provided by his subjects. The money left over was used for the construction of the hall.

Finish the tour in the commercial district of Kensington Road, to the west.

Other Sights in the Area

The **Commonwealth Institute** has exhibitions covering different aspects of the cultures in the British Commonwealth countries. There is also an art center, a library, and a cinema. The building itself is an unusual example of modern architecture. (230 Kensington High St. Open Mon.-Sat. 10am-5:30pm, Sun. 2-5pm. Free entrance. Tel. 603-4535.)

Linley Sambourne House was the home of the chief political cartoonist of the humorist journal *Punch* at the end of the nineteenth century. The interior has changed little since Sambourne lived there, and the original furnishing is displayed. (18 Stafford Terrace. Open March-Oct., Wed. 10am-4pm and Sun. 2-5pm. Entrance fee. Tel. 994-1019.)

LONDON

Chelsea — A Fashionable Address

As early as the sixteenth century **Chelsea village** was considered a highly fashionable residential area. A part of its picturesque charm has remained to this day and it is still an extremly sought-after residential district.

Begin the tour at the **Sloane Square underground station**. Two theaters are located in the square. The better-known is the **Royal Court Theatre**, which presented original productions by playwrights such as George Bernard Shaw, John Osborne, and David Storey. On the other side of the square is a large department store, *Peter Jones*, which specializes in textile products. The facade of the building itself is of architectural interest.

Running from the square is **King's Road**, one of the longest roads in central London. It is named for King Charles II, who used it as a route connecting his palaces at Whitehall and Hampton Court. In the 1960s the street became famous as the center of avant-garde dress. The well-known Mary Quant set up her fashion house here, followed by many others, and thus Chelsea began to set the tone in youth fashion. After a slow period in the early 1970s, the area is now recovering, but it is no longer the trend-setter it once was. Walk along King's Road. After a few dozen meters, on the left, are some neoclassical buildings. These military offices, called the **Duke of York's Headquarters**, were originally built in 1801 as an orphanage for the children of soldiers.

Turn left on Cheltenham Terrace and you can see the Headquarters more clearly. Here you can take a walk through the quiet, pleasant streets of Chelsea, which still have the atmosphere of the days in which they were built. Turn right onto St. Leonard's Terrace; the houses lining it are particularly attractive. The Irish writer Bram Stoker, creator of *Dracula*, once lived here, at No. 18. Sir Laurence Olivier, the highly praised British actor, resided at No. 7 for several years. The large shaded lawn to your left is **Burton's Court**. Once it was part of the Royal Hospital.

At the end of the street make the first left and you will come to one of the most famous works of the architect Sir Christopher Wren: the **Royal Hospital, Chelsea**. (Grounds open Mon.-Sat. 10am-dusk, Sun. 2pm-dusk. Great Hall, Museum, and Chapel open Mon.-Sat. 10am-noon and 2-4pm, Sun. 2-4pm. Free entrance. Tel. 730-0160.) The hospital was built as a home for veterans, under King Charles II, who was inspired by the Hôtel des Invalides established by Louis XIV in Paris. Wren began construction in 1682

CHELSEA

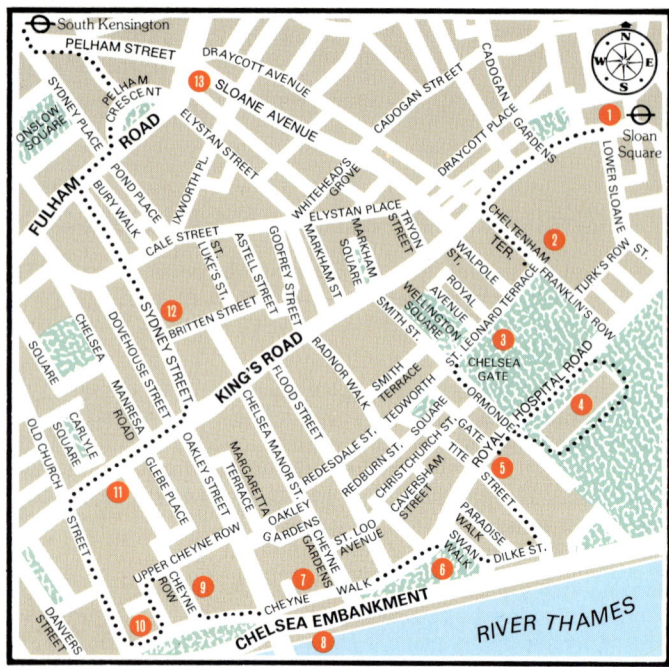

Index
1. Sloane Square
2. Duke of York's Headquarters
3. Burton's Court
4. Royal Hospital, Chelsea
5. National Army Museum
6. Chelsea Physic Garden
7. Cheyne Mews
8. Cadogan Pier
9. Carlyle's House
10. Chelsea Old Church
11. Argyll House
12. St. Luke's Church
13. Michelin House

---

and the hospital was completed ten years later. The major features of the square-shaped structure are the **Great Hall** and **Chapel**, connected by an impressive domed room. The exterior dome can be seen from a distance and has become the trademark of the hospital.

Currently over 400 military pensioners live at the hospital. Notice their blue or red uniforms, the style of which has not changed since the eighteenth century. Every year around May 29 they customarily hold the *Oak Apple Parade*, commemorating Charles II's safe return home to London on that date in 1660.

A small **Museum** with an exhibit on the history of the hospital is located to the east of the building.

To the southeast lie the beautiful **Ranelagh Gardens**. Since 1913, the Chelsea Flower Show has been held here every May.

The colorful tones of Chelsea

Leave the hospital grounds. Near Royal Hospital Road is the **National Army Museum**. (Open Mon.-Sat. 10am-5:30pm, Sun. 2-5:30pm. Free entrance. Tel. 730-0717.) Here you will find two floors of exhibits describing the 500-year history of the British Army, from 1485 to 1914. Particularly interesting are the soldiers' uniforms from past centuries, and the skeleton that the museum claims belonged to Napoleon's horse.

Past the museum, turn left on Tite Street. No. 34 was the home of Oscar Wilde, the nineteenth-century playwright and author. Wilde lived here with his wife and sons for several years, but his involvement in a scandalous trial related to his homosexual

*L*ONDON

inclinations (highly illegal in Victorian England) led to his arrest and loss of the house.

Further down the street on the left, at No. 25, stands a modern white building where the owners of Mustique Island (a popular Carribean resort) lived in the 1970s. In the nineteenth century another white house stood in the same spot, occupied in the 1870s by the American Impressionist painter James Whistler.

Turn right on Dilke Street. The second turn on your right leads to a small courtyard, Clover Mews. The little alleyways in London called *mews* were once used for stables with rooms built above. Most of the old stables have been converted into garages for the owners' automobiles, while the small rooms above have been made into fashionable apartments. These have become increasingly popular recently and their price has risen accordingly.

Take the next right onto Swan Walk, a quiet street with several particularly lovely buildings. The fence on the other side of the street bars the view of the **Chelsea Physic Garden**. (Open Apr.-Oct., Wed. and Sun. 2-5pm. Entrance fee. Tel. 352-5646.) England's second botanical garden, it was established in 1673 for research purposes by the Society of Apothecaries. The cotton seeds developed here were sent across the ocean to the colony of Georgia, where they played a significant role in the development of the southern United States, and the development of slavery.

At the end of Swan Walk turn left. This street meets up with the continuation of Cheyne (pronounced *chainy*) Walk, one of the most famous and most exclusive streets in London. Over the last two hundred years the handsome eighteenth-century Georgian homes overlooking the river and the pier along it have housed many famous English artists and intellectuals. In the 1970s, 3 Cheyne Walk was occupied by Keith Richards, the Rolling Stones guitarist. A century earlier, the controversial author George Eliot spent the last weeks of her life at No. 4. Also in the nineteenth century, the Pre-Raphaelite painter Dante Gabriel Rossetti lived at No. 16, after his beloved wife's death. In the garden he raised exotic animals, such as a kangaroo, armadillos, and others.

Behind 19-26 Cheyne Walk, on **Cheyne Mews**, stood Henry VIII's Chelsea Palace until 1753. Two of his queens, Anne of Cleves, whom he divorced, and his last wife, Catherine Parr, lived here. Elizabeth I also lived here when she was young, as did Lady Jane Grey, who is known for her very short period on the throne — just nine days — before she was imprisoned by Mary I and executed at the age of sixteen.

Go back to Cheyne Walk. Facing you is **Albert Bridge**, built over the Thames in 1873. To its left is **Cadogan Pier**. Every year in July a rowing competition is held from London Bridge to Cadogan Pier.

LONDON

Dating back to the 1715 celebration of the crowning of George I, it is perhaps the oldest competition in London. It is popularly called *Doggett's Coat and Badge Race*, after the prize offered by the race's original sponsor, eighteenth-century actor Thomas Dogget. Today some of the participants dress up in clothing of that period. The race is currently organized by the Fishmongers Company.

Continue west along the street. In the 1970s, Mick Jagger of the Rolling Stones lived at No. 48, before moving across the Atlantic.

Turn right at Cheyne Row. No. 16 dates to 1708, according to a plaque on the exterior wall. No. 24 is **Carlyle's House**. (Open Apr.-Oct., Wed.-Sat. 11am-5pm, Sun. 2pm-5pm. Entrance fee. Tel. 352-7087.) Thomas Carlyle, a nineteenth-century historian and theorist, lived here from 1834 until his death in 1881. The house was left as it was, and many of his personal belongings are exhibited.

Continue along the street. This is one of Chelsea's quietest areas. Turn left at Upper Cheyne Row, and left again onto Lawrence Street. Close to the corner of Cheyne Walk is a pub, *The Cross Keys*, where you can rest and refresh yourself with food and drink.

A few steps further down Cheyne Walk you will come to **Chelsea Old Church**. Although it was severely damaged in the World War II bombings, some thirteenth- and fourteenth-century sections of the church have survived.

In front of the church, overlooking the river, is a statue of Thomas More, author of *Utopia*, who lost his head for refusing to concede to King Henry VIII's Act of Supremacy. After his execution in London Tower, his body was buried within the citadel, and his head was taken to Canterbury Cathedral for burial. The Catholic Church declared him a saint, while Henry VIII acquired More's house in Chelsea, where he built the adjacent manor house.

Turn right onto Old Church Street. When you reach King's Road, turn right. Chelsea is famous for its antiques market, and a few steps down you can see the charming antique shops, many of which are quite exclusive.

A few steps further on King's Road, at Nos. 229 and 231, are two stores said to date back to 1620, although it is difficult tell from their appearance. Past them is a Palladian-style building, **Argyll House**, built in 1723 for the Duke of Argyll.

Turn left on Sydney Street. A few steps up the street on your left, is *Chelsea Farmers' Market*, where you can buy plants, fish, and dairy products, and you can also sit down and enjoy a meal, direct from the English farm.

Further up the street, on the right, stands **St. Luke's Church**, built in 1820. This was one of the first Gothic revival churches in London. It

LONDON

was built as a parish church to take the place of Chelsea Old Church, which was too small for the expanding community. In 1836 Charles Dickens was married here. Opposite the church, on the left, is a line of attractive nineteenth-century houses.

Continue along the street and turn right on Fulham Road. Walk through this well-developed, flourishing commercial center, looking at the large store windows. Further down the street on the right is **Michelin House**, built in 1910, which is one of London's prime examples of Art-Nouveau architecture. Turn left on Pelham Crescent and continue along Pelham Place, a boulevard with blossoming trees and lovely houses.

Complete the tour at the **South Kensington underground station**.

*L*ONDON

Southwark — The City South of the Thames

Begin your tour on the northern bank of the Thames River, at the **Tower Hill underground station**. Walk around the Tower of London on the eastern side and cross the river via the Victorian **Tower Bridge**. (The suspended passageway is open daily 10am-6:30pm, in winter until 4:45pm. Entrance fee. Tel. 407-0922.) The bridge offers a breathtaking view of the city. It opened in 1894 and was built in pseudo-medieval style, to blend in with the adjacent citadel. The bridge was an impressive technological achievement; it is composed of two hanging panels, each weighing some 1,000 tons, which can be raised within two minutes in order to allow tall ships to pass underneath.

The mechanism for opening the bridge was originally operated by steam power, but it now runs on electricity. The machine room at the base of the southern tower can be visited for a fee. Originally the bridge was raised several times a day, but as the river traffic declined, so did the use of the bridge, and it now opens just two or three times a week. Nevertheless, you may be lucky enough to see the massive panels rise.

When the bridge is raised, all traffic stops. In 1952 a double-decker bus driver who failed to stop in time managed to leap over the space that began to open under his wheels.

Exit on the southern bank. At the same time that the City of London emerged on the two rubble hills on the northern bank of the Thames River, another settlement began to develop on the southern bank. It continued to grow along with London since its establishment in the first century A.D.

Southwark, or as the Saxons called it, Sud Werk ("the southern work"), was originally settled by fishermen and seamen. The town attracted all types of craftsmen, builders, glassmakers, tanners, and others, who had access to the northern city over the ancient London Bridge.

At the same time many inns were set up in the area for passersby and sailors. Southwark was considered London's entertainment area for the masses. As Shakespearean theater flourished in the sixteenth century, so did the semi-institutionalized brothels. The South Bank became associated with the shady, the sensual, and the progressive.

In the nineteenth century, when the British Empire was at its peak of expansion, Southwark swarmed with longshoremen and

*L*ONDON

sailors from the many merchant ships that anchored here. In the twentieth century Southwark suffered from decline and deterioration. The Empire dwindled and with it the marine activity. The German Blitz left the area in ruins, and its reconstruction is still in progress.

Many renewal plans have been drawn up for the area, and the conversion of the huge docks and wharves along the river into a residential, commercial, and business area is progressing steadily. Every day something changes in this part of London, but there is still a long way to go.

Turn west and take the path to the riverbank, toward the warship anchored in the water. If the path is barred, make a right on Tooley Street.

The **HMS Belfast** today serves as a floating sea museum. (Open daily 11am-5:50pm, until 4:30pm in winter. Entrance fee. Tel. 407-6434.) Set to sea in 1938, the cruiser was hit in the beginning of the war, was repaired, and managed to return to battle before the war ended. The ship continued to serve until 1963, when it seemed destined for the junkyard. The Imperial War Museum helped prevent this fate. In 1971 the HMS Belfast finally anchored in its present location, and was converted into a museum of the sea battles of the two world wars. Those who board are invited to wander through a warship that has changed very little since its active duty. The deck, the command bridge, the battle equipment, the cabins, and the narrow corridors can all be observed up close. Be careful — the steep steps and narrow passages may be hard to maneuver for small children or people who have difficulty walking.

From the ship you see the opposite shore, where the Tower of London stands in all its glory. There is a ferry between the boat pier at the Tower and the ship.

Leave the ship and take Vine Lane to Tooley Street. Walk along the street to the west. At No. 88 is the *Shipwrights Arms*, a remnant of the nineteenth-century public houses that were frequented mainly by sailors and longshoremen. The maiden decorating the exterior tells of activities that occured in the inner rooms.

A sign on the right guides you to **Crown Court, Southwark**, Southwark's modern courthouse, which opened in 1982. Next to it is **Hay's Wharf**, an area that has recently undergone extensive development. It is quickly being converted into an attractive district for commerce and offices.

On the left is a huge, long brick building, the **London Bridge Station**. Everyday thousands of Londoners come here from throughout the city, cross London Bridge by foot and go to their places of work in the City on the north bank.

A dark opening under the bridge at 34 Tooley Street leads you

*L*ONDON

to the **London Dungeon**. (Open daily 10am-6pm, until 4:30pm in winter. Entrance fee. Tel. 403-0606.) Here anyone seeking a chilling experience is promised the satisfaction of the horror stories of London, presented with wax models. Recommended for terror-lovers and those with strong nerves.

Continue down the street to the intersection and turn left onto Borough High Street, a busy road that leads to London Bridge. A short way along it to your left is St. Thomas Street, where you will find the **St. Thomas's Old Operating Theatre**, the only remaining nineteenth-century operating room in Britain. (Open Mon., Wed., and Fri. 12:30-4pm. Entrance fee. Tel. 407-7600.)

A bit further down Borough High Street you will come to a Victorian yard on your left called **King's Head**; above the house there, which was built in 1881, is a bust of Henry VIII. Two meters down is the site of **George Inn**, the last of the inns typical of Southwark in past centuries. The original medieval structure was frequented by pilgrims on their way to Canterbury. The present building was constructed in 1676, and only its southern wing remains, now the location of a pleasant pub where you can refresh yourself.

Go back the way you came and turn to one of the most impressive and most important monuments in London in general and on the South Bank in particular, **Southwark Cathedral**. The largest Gothic church remaining in London, it began as a seventh-century convent. In 1106 the Augustinian Priory of St. Mary Overie was established here. In 1540 the priory was converted to the parish Church of St. Saviour. Finally, in 1905, the structure became a cathedral; the official name is Cathedral and Collegiate Church of St. Saviour and St. Mary Overie. After 800 years of construction and restorations, the building is absolutely beautiful.

In the southern garden of the cathedral there is a modern sculpture depicting the Holy Family, by Kenneth Hughes. Go in through the southern entrance. The interior of the church was rebuilt in the nineteenth century after it had greatly deteriorated. As you tour inside, pay special attention to the attractive monuments, which were placed together in one location after the renovations. The Gothic stained-glass window, covering the entire eastern wall, is a rare beauty. Near the north transept is the Harvard Chapel, dedicated to the British John Harvard. Baptized in the church in 1607, he later moved to America and founded the well-know college which bears his name.

As you leave the cathedral, notice the market next to it on the southern side. Go around from the west and turn right. This area has undergone extensive changes in the last few years. Next to the river is a new residential building, *Minerva House*. There is a spectacular view of the City from the riverbank plaza.

London

SOUTHWARK

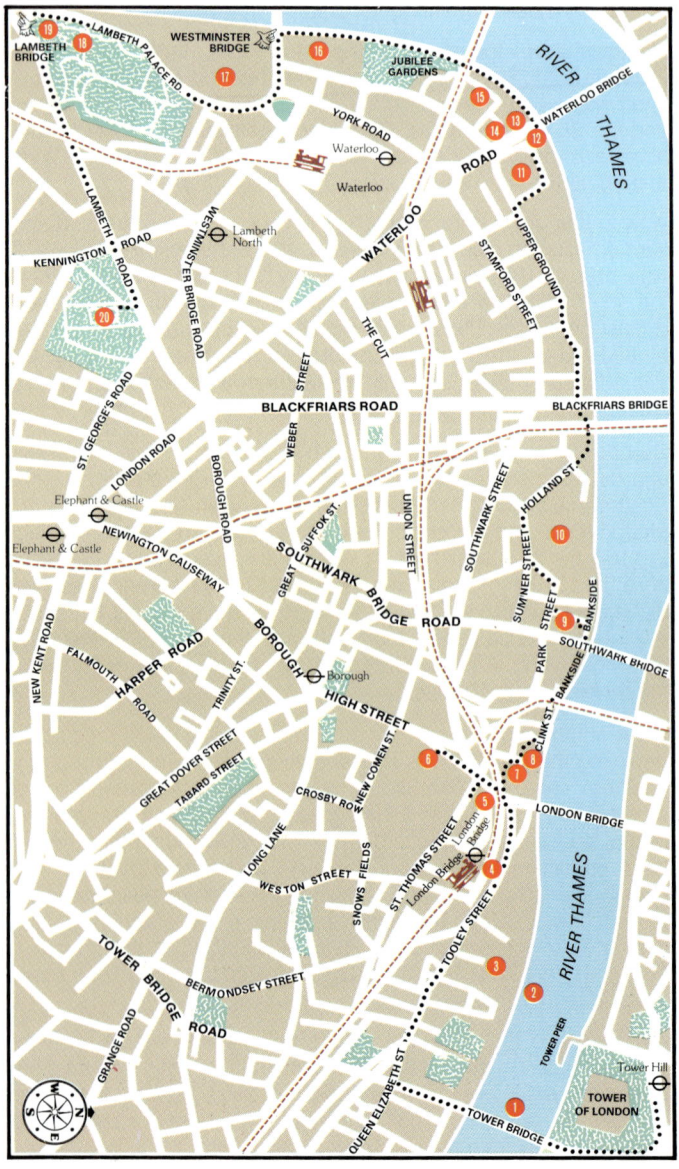

*L*ONDON

A stroll toward County Hall

Index
1. Tower Bridge
2. HMS Belfast
3. Crown Court, Southwark
4. London Dungeon
5. St. Thomas's Old Operating Theatre
6. George Inn
7. Southwark Cathedral
8. Kathleen & May
9. Bear Gardens Museum
10. Bankside Power Station
11. National Theatre
12. National Film Theatre
13. Queen Elizabeth Hall, Purcell Room
14. Hayward Gallery
15. Royal Festival Hall
16. County Hall
17. St. Thomas's Hospital
18. Lambeth Palace
19. Tradescant Trust Museum of Garden History
20. Imperial War Museum

*L*ONDON

Go back the way you came and turn west toward the narrow **St. Mary Overy Dock**, built in the sixteenth century. This was a free dock — those who came to the Church of St. Saviour could unload their merchandise without paying any fee. **Kathleen & May**, a river schooner built around 1900, is anchored here and can be explored. (Open daily 10am-5pm. Entrance fee. Tel. 403-3965). Next to the dock are some coffee shops and pubs where you can sit and watch the river.

Continue to Clink Street. Pass the *Old Thameside Inn*, which has been skillfully renovated. Next to it is Pickford Wharf, adjacent to some very old buildings, a few of which date back as far as the Middle Ages. This was the street of the **Clink Prison**, of which nothing remains except the name, now common slang for jail.

Cross under the railroad bridge to Bankside, an old embankment. On the corner, at No. 1, is an old pub founded in 1775, *The Anchor* (see the emblem). On a nice day you can sit on the terrace overlooking the river, and enjoy a refreshing drink.

The **Bankside** district was London's entertainment area in the sixteenth century, much as the West End is today. Many theaters operated here, including the *Swan*, the *Rose*, the *Hope*, and the *Globe*, where Shakespeare presented his work. These exotic names were all derived from the brothels that also prospered in that period, and which attracted the crowds no less. Shakespeare's famous **Globe Theatre**, a theater-in-the-round, went up in flames in 1613. It was rebuilt but later closed again in 1642 under Puritan pressure. Currently nothing is left of the original theater, but a plan was recently approved for its reconstruction next to the Bankside Power Station further west. The plans also include a Shakespeare museum and an educational and entertainment center. Funds are now being raised for the project. The area itself appears to be abandoned, and many of the construction and renewal programs have yet to move beyond paper.

Follow Bankside past **Southwark Bridge** and make your first left, which will lead you to the **Bear Gardens Museum**. (Open Thurs.-Sat. 10:30am-5:30pm, Sun. 2-4pm. Entrance fee. Tel. 928-6342.) The museum is located in a warehouse from the Georgian period, built on the last bear-baiting arena that operated in this district between 1662 and 1682, next to the Elizabethan Hope Playhouse. The museum preserves the memory of the glorious history of this former entertainment district, and includes a replica of a seventeenth-century theater, used for current performances.

When you leave the museum, continue northwest along Park Street to Summer Street. Next to the empty lot, which may one day hold the new Globe Theatre, on your right, reigns a massive brown monster,

LONDON

unmistakably the **Bankside Power Station**. Go around the station on Holland street to Blackfriars Bridge.

On the southwest corner of the bridge is a pub called *Doggett's Coat and Badge*, named after a boating race held annually on the Thames (see "Chelsea — A Fashionable Address"). Continue west on Upper Ground. Along the river is an embankment which has not been completed; in fact, the entire area around this street is undergoing extensive alterations. The wharves that served the Port of London are being converted for modern use, and the old and the new are blending.

A few hundred meters down you will come to a block of buildings that has made this area, called **South Bank**, a cultural center of London. Pass the London Weekend Television building and turn right to the embankment. On left are a number of modern buildings, constituting the **South Bank Arts Centre**. The complex originated with the Festival of Britain in 1951, although most of the buildings were added in the mid-1960s. The first building on your left is the **National Theatre**, with three auditoriums: the Lyttleton, the Olivier, and the Cottesloe. These, together with the restaurants and exhibits held here, form the most important cultural center in London.

Pass under Waterloo Bridge and you will come to the **National Film Theatre**. Quality films and industry classics, often focusing on specific themes, are generally presented here. The screenings are for members only, but anyone can join at weekly or monthly rates. There is also a good inexpensive restaurant on the premises, where you can sit outside and enjoy the view of the river. On the embankment in front of the building you will usually find people selling old books, pictures, and newspapers — a good spot for treasure-hunters.

The next building of the complex houses two concert halls: **Queen Elizabeth Hall** and **Purcell Room**. In back of this building, somewhat hidden by it, is the **Hayward Gallery**, famous for its exhibits, which generally focus on twentieth-century works. (Open Mon.-Wed. 10am-8pm, Thur.-Sat. 10am-6pm, Sun. noon-6pm. Entrance fee. Tel. 928-5708.)

The final building of the South Bank Arts Centre is the first one built. The **Royal Festival Hall** was erected for the Festival of Britain. It contains a 3,000-seat concert hall known for its acoustics. There

An aerial view of Westminster

LONDON

are also restaurants here, as well as a book store where you can purchase copies of the finest musical and theatrical stage works.

At this point you can complete the tour with a walk along the river. On the way you will pass Jubilee Gardens, which opened in 1977 in honor of Queen Elizabeth's 25 years on the throne. To the south is the huge **County Hall**, erected in 1922, where the Greater London Council was housed until it was dissolved in 1986. Cross Westminster Bridge to the underground station of the same name.

If you are not too tired you can continue walking to a few more sights. Turn east and then south on Lambeth Road. Walk around **St. Thomas's Hospital**, most of which was built in the nineteenth century. Follow the road to the medieval **Lambeth Palace**, which has served as the seat of the Archbishop of Canterbury since the thirteenth century. (Open by arrangement only. Free entrance. Tel. 928-8282.) Its special charm lies in the late Gothic style, and much of the building is medieval in appearance.

Next to the palace is the **Tradescant Trust Museum of Garden History**, located in the church of St. Mary-at-Lambeth. (Open March-mid-Dec., Mon.-Fri. 11am-3pm, Sun. 10:30am-5pm. Free entrance. Tel. 373-4030.)

Turn left on Lambeth road and complete the tour at the **Imperial War Museum**. Here there is an exhibit of the twentieth-century military history of the United Kingdom and the British Commonwealth. (Open Mon.-Sat. 10am-5:50pm, Sun. noon-5:50pm. Free entrance. Tel. 735-8922.)

*L*ONDON

The East End — An Immigrant's Haven, a Seaman's History

From the sixteenth century on, the East End district of London has been one of the city's sources of commercial strength and the home of much of its immigrant population — two characteristics of the area that are tightly intertwined.

The district, located outside the walls of the City, is known to have been populated as early as the twelfth century. In the sixteenth century, with the development of trade, Dutch merchants began to settle here alongside the French Huguenots, English craftsmen who found they could make a good living here, and Irish immigrants who worked at the docks.

The French, who were seasoned merchants, brought with them the art of weaving and opened dozens of workshops in the area. They were followed by Jewish immigrants, who in the late nineteenth century dominated the area around Whitechapel.

In the later years of the nineteenth century the residents of the area were horrified by the cruel murders of a few prostitutes. The murderer, who was never captured, was nicknamed Jack the Ripper and became a legendary figure.

After World War I the Jews began to leave, and were replaced by immigrants from the West Indies and the Far East. Today the area's population is predominantly Pakistani, Indian, and Bangladeshi.

This tour can be divided into two parts.

Part A

Begin the tour of the East End at the **Aldgate underground station**. Turn west; at the corner you will see a church, **St. Botolph Aldgate**. It is dedicated to the patron saint of travelers and was built in the eighteenth century on the foundations of a Saxon church.

Notice the road that winds south, Jewry Street. It is named for the Jewish community that first came to this area in the early seventeenth century.

Turn right and cross the underpass to Dukes Place. Its continuation, Bevis Marks, is the site of the **Spanish and Portuguese Synagogue,** also referred to as the **Bevis Marks**. Built in 1701, it strongly resembles the Portuguese Synagogue in Amsterdam. If the synagogue keeper is there, it is very much worth a look; the interior

*L*ONDON

THE EAST END

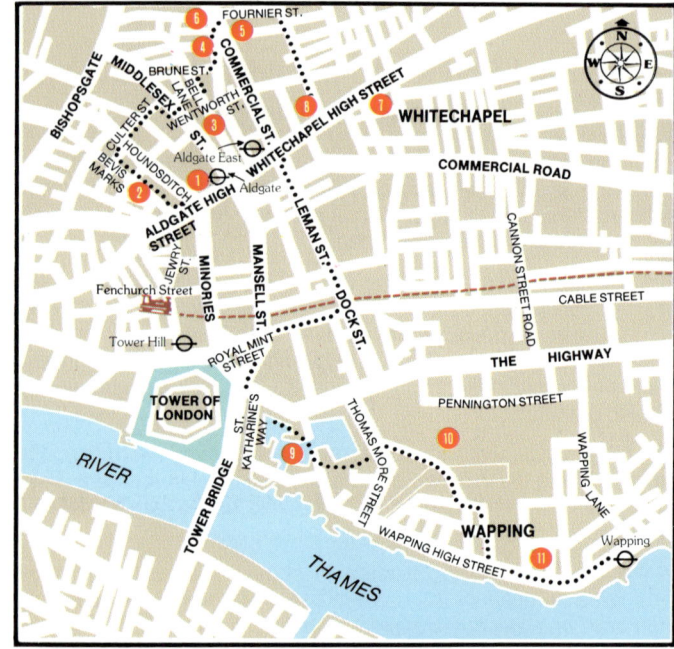

Index
1. St. Botolph Aldgate
2. Spanish and Portuguese Synagogue
3. Petticoat Lane market
4. Soup Kitchen
5. Christ Church, Spitalfields
6. Spitalfields Market
7. Whitechapel Bell Foundry
8. Whitechapel Art Gallery
9. St. Katherine's Dock
10. Sir Thomas More Court
11. St. John church tower

---

has not changed since the building was erected. The architect who designed the building, Joseph Avis, refused payment and eventually converted to Judaism.

The little street to the left after the synagogue is Bury Street. On the corner where it bends is a blue plaque commemorating the original synagogue that stood here from 1657 to 1701.

Turn right, cross Houndsditch to Cutler Street, and walk east to Middlesex Street. Every Sunday this street and those running from it turn into one of London's most famous and most popular open-air markets. **Petticoat Lane market**. As early as the fifteenth century, trade in clothing and fabric prospered here, which is how the market

*L*ONDON

Victorian facade of Soup Kitchen

got its name. The influx of Jewish immigrants to the East End in the eighteenth century added to local commerce, and the Sunday market grew and developed; it is still going strong. Most of the trade occurs between 9am and 2pm, and the streets are so crowded you can hardly move.

Walk on Cobb Street and turn left on Bell Lane. The blocks of buildings on your right are the result of public initiative. Built at the end of the last century, they were intended to solve the housing problem of the immigrants who flooded this area beyond its borders. The buildings are used as housing for the poor today as well, and have been designated for renewal projects.

Continue along the street and turn right at Brune Street. Just a few steps down you will see a late Victorian building. This is the **Soup Kitchen** that the Jewish community in London opened for their elderly and poor. The kitchen still supplies hot meals to more than a hundred Jewish elderly residing in the East End.

Continue to the left on Commercial Street. At the corner on the right is the attractive **Christ Church**, **Spitalfields**. Built in the early eighteenth century, it served the Huguenot population who settled in the area.

LONDON

Across the street is a huge covered structure. This is the **Spitalfields Market** for fruits and vegetables, which operates very early in the morning. It was set up at the beginning of the century on the site of a market that functioned here as early as the seventeenth century. The market spreads over a wide area of priceless land, and construction is currently underway for a commercial center to house stores and restaurants.

Turn right onto Fournier Street. The houses here were built in the eighteenth century by the Huguenot immigrants, who used the upper floors for spinning and sewing workshops. People recognizing the architectual value have recently begun purchasing and renovating these buildings in order to restore their former charm.

Walk along the street. At the eastern end, on the left, is a mosque of the Bengalese population of the East End. The history of this building reflects the history of the East End. Originally built as a church for the Huguenots and later converted by the Jews into a synagogue, today it is a Moslem house of prayer.

Turn right onto Brick Lane. This street has also seen many changes. It is now lined with stores and restaurants owned by immigrants from eastern Asia. *Truman Brewery* is as old as the street itself. Originally called the Black Eagle Brewery, it was founded in the seventeenth century. On Sunday the market spreads to this street too, where an interesting selection of clothing, household items, fruits and vegetables, and various other goods are offered.

Down the street you will come to Whitechapel High Street, which is perhaps best known as the Jewish center of the East End. Look east and you can see the minaret of the East End Mosque. Closer, at No. 34, is the **Whitechapel Bell Foundry**, established in 1570 and located at its present site since 1738. This foundry is responsible for the sound of many of the bells that ring in London and elsewhere, including the famous Big Ben.

Turn right and walk a short way down the street to **Whitechapel Art Gallery**, built in Art-Nouveau style in 1901. (Open Tues.-Sun. 11am-5pm, Wed. 11am-8pm. Free entrance. Tel. 377-0107.) The gallery exhibits contemporary art, with a special emphasis on local artists.

Next to the gallery is the small Angel Alley, location of the *Freedom Press Bookshop*, which specializes in anarchistic literature. Next to it is a print shop by the same name, which used to publish two newspapers in Yiddish, initiated by Jewish anarchists.

Past the alley, at No. 90, you will find *Bloom's*, a kosher Jewish restaurant and deli, popular among lovers of Eastern European Jewish cuisine. Its prices are reasonable and it is recommended to anyone hungry for a kosher meat meal.

London

Just to the right, on Commercial Street, is **Toynbee Hall**. Named for the respected historian, Arnold Toynbee, it was erected in 1884 for the purpose of educating the East End community.

Not far from this intersection, tens of thousand of East End residents assembled in October 1936 to prevent a parade of the fascist "Black Shirts." In the end, the parade was diverted to another route, but the events of that day contributed greatly to the decline in power of the fascists in England.

This completes the first part of the tour.

Other Sights in the Area

The **Geffrye Museum** is housed in an eighteenth century building that served as an almshouse supported by the Ironmongers. The museum has a magnificent collection of furniture and woodwork of different styles and periods. (Kingsland Road. Open Tues.-Sat. 10am-5pm, Sun. 2-5pm. Free entrance. Tel. 739-8368.),

The **Bethnal Green Museum of Childhood** contains a varied and interesting collection of toys, doll houses, model theaters, and games. (Cambridge Heath Road. Open Mon.-Thurs. and Sat. 10am-6pm, Sun. 2:30-6pm. Free entrance. Tel. 980-2415.)

Part B

The second part of the tour takes you to a completely different section of London's East End: the docks and wharves along the Thames. Turn left on Leman Street and right at Royal Mint Street, named for the royal coin mint that was located here until a few years ago.

Continue left to Mansell Street and you will come to a busy intersection. Across the street to the west is the Tower of London; you will be going in the other direction, east.

Turn onto St. Katharine's Way and cross over into the complex, called **St. Katharine's Dock**. Its name comes from St. Katharine's Hospital, which was founded here by Queen Matilda in 1148. For hundreds of years the hospital and the surrounding area provided refuge for London's immigrant population, until the land was sold in the early nineteenth century for redevelopment and the residents were relocated.

In 1828, Thomas Telford began constructing the dock and building warehouses and wharves along it. The success of the dock was based on its proximity to the City, and for some one hundred years it faithfully served the ships that unloaded their goods along its piers.

The Port of London's decrease in activity in the twentieth century led

*L*ONDON

to the decline of St. Katharine's Dock. The death blow was struck by the air raids in World War II, which transformed the entire Thames dock area into a burning torch. The dock's redevelopment did not begin until 1968. It was converted into a marina accommodating private yachts, and the warehouses along the front were turned into apartment buildings, restaurants, and stores.

The dock is closed in on the west by the *Tower Hotel*, one of the largest hotels in London. Next to it is the **World Trade Centre**, built on the site of one of the warehouses destroyed in the bombings, and designed to look like an old warehouse. The only building remaining from the original period is **Ivory House**, which has become an expensive apartment building, with shops occupying the ground floor. Next to it is a relatively new pub, *Dickens Inn*, built inside a former shed. On the eastern side of the wharf is the **Historic Ships Collection**. (Open daily 10am-5pm. Entrance fee.) The collection portrays the transition from sailing ships to steamships. Particularly interesting is *Discovery*, the ship in which Captain Robert Scott made his journey to the South Pole.

Cross the bridge over the marina. Walk through the area of apartment houses built to the south and east of the dock. This next wide expanse is currently in the process of intensive development, and the daily changes make it difficult to keep up with what is going on there. Many of the docks that were located here have been filled in, and the large warehouses are rapidly being converted into housing, both private and government-subsidized.

The history of the dock area in the last few centuries is closely related to that of the British Empire. The colonies established across the sea in the sixteenth and seventeenth centuries encouraged trade throughout the Empire, and the growth of the British fleet demanded parallel development of places for anchoring, loading, unloading, and storage. Most of the docks were built east of the Tower of London.

In the nineteenth century the Port of London reached a pinnacle of greatness. The docks, however, were little used after the fall of the empire, and the devasting effects of the World War II bombings left them virtually abondoned.

In recent years the London authorities began tearing down the walls enclosing the docks, which were built to prevent the removal of merchandise without paying customs. The large majority of anchorages were filled in, and implementation of many development plans for the area has begun.

Cross Thomas More Street and continue toward the former **London Dock**, which is now being developed as a residential area. It is said that when the old warehouses surrounding the wharf were demolished, hidden cellars packed with dozens of cases of wine

*L*ONDON

Yachts in St. Katherine's Dock

were discovered. Apparently these had been hidden from the customs agents in the nineteenth century, but the merchants never managed to take them out of hiding and sell them. Aged wine is an important finding — and not only for historians — but the customs authorities stood their own. The tax on the wine had never been paid, and therefore it had to be destroyed.

The new residential area at the London Dock, **Sir Thomas More Court**, is populated mainly by young couples. The buildings are designed in suburban, semi-rural style, right in the heart of the city. North of the docks, along Pennington Street, are the new homes of *The Sun* and *The Times*, newspapers who broke the famous Fleet Street tradition by moving to this district.

Turn right, walk around the block of buildings toward the river, and you will come to Wapping High Street. In recent centuries, **Wapping** used to be the district of seamen and others who made their living off the sea, directly or indirectly. When you cross the street to the east, notice the warehouses located on both sides. The cranes and the ramps that were used for lifting and moving merchandise are now idle. In many of the warehouses-cum-residences, the cranes are being left and the ramps are being made into porches to preserve the original character of the buildings.

Pass the *Town of Ramsgate* pub, a remnant of the 36 public houses that once were located on this street and served sailors. Next to it is the **Oliver Wharf** building, whose warehouse exterior has been well preserved while the building has been converted for another use.

LONDON

The lovely tower on the left belonged to the eighteenth-century **St. John**; the rest of the church was bombed in World War II. A few steps further you see a completely modern building, which belongs to the police. At No. 94 is another nicely preserved warehouse.

Complete the tour at the **Wapping underground station**. From here the train crosses the river in a tunnel built by Marc Brunel in 1843. The first public passage built under the river, the tunnel initially served pedestrians, and was later converted for use by the underground train.

Other Sights in the Area

The **National Museum of Labour History** portrays the history of the English labor movement. (Limehouse Town Hall, Commercial Road. Open Tues.-Sat. 9:30am-5pm, Sun. 2:30-5:30pm. Free entrance. Tel. 515-3229.)

LONDON

Hampstead — An Artist's Retreat

Almost since its inception, **Hampstead** has been a center of attraction for intellectuals, artists, and musicians. Its picturesque, somewhat rural character is still a favorite for Londoners. Lately the area's growing appeal has led to skyrocketing real-estate prices, which have made it one of London's more prestigious districts.

The village began with several manor houses situated adjacent to the large common ground called **Hampstead Heath**. In the eighteenth century a number of springs were discovered in the vicinitiy. Word of their therapeutic powers spread rapidly, and soon the area became a popular health center. In the nineteenth century the quality of the water was examined, and was found to be extremely poor, irreparably polluted in fact; this, however, did not detract from Hampstead's allure.

The village developed and became a highly regarded residential area for writers and artists. It became all the more attractive after 1907, when the underground reached the district, making the five-mile stretch from the center of London only a ten-minute trip.

Begin the tour of Hampstead at the **Hampstead underground station** at the corner of Heath Street and Hampstead High Street. Fashionable boutiques have recently been opened along these streets and the area has gradually become an extremely successful commercial center.

Walk down Heath Street. Tucked in between the boutiques you will find delicatessens, coffee houses, and the local residents' favorite pubs. Wander through the little streets that run off Heath Street, where you will discover hidden treasures and interesting shops.

A few dozen meters down turn right on Church Row. The street is lined on both sides with handsome early eighteenth-century terrace houses. Notice that the windows over the entrances each have their own special design. Before street lighting was installed, the distinct pattern of light shed through these windows helped the residents find their homes at night.

At the end of the street is Hampstead's parish church, **St. John's**, which was also built in the eighteenth century. The **cemetery**, located in the courtyard, behind the fence on the right-hand side of the street, is particularly interesting — the names of eminent figures in literature and the arts are on many of the gravestones. Walk around the cemetery fence and along Holly Walk, with its lovely early nineteenth-century houses.

London

HAMPSTEAD

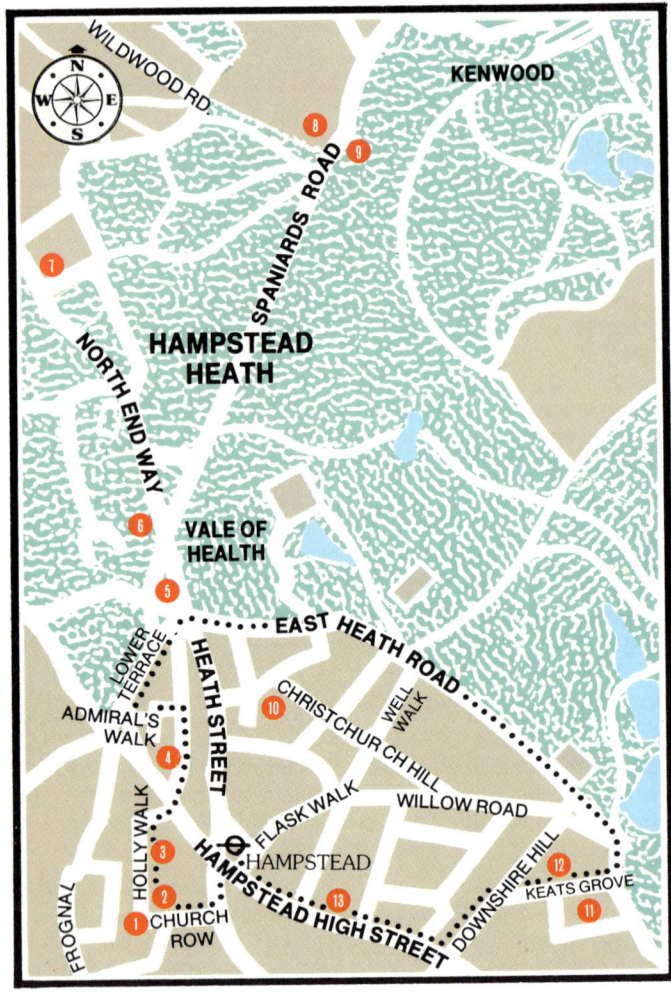

Index
1. St. John's
2. St. John's cemetery
3. St. Mary's Catholic Church
4. Fenton House
5. Whitestone Pond
6. Jack Straw's Castle
7. Old Bull and Bush pub
8. Spaniards Inn
9. Tollhouse
10. Christchurch
11. Keats House
12. St. John's Church
13. Old Brewery Mews

*L*ONDON

Suburban charm of Flask Walk in Hampstead

A short way down you will approach **St. Mary's Catholic Church**. Built in 1816, it was one of the first Catholic churches established in London after the Reformation in the sixteenth century.

At the end of the street turn right and walk down to Mt. Vernon Junction. At the corner is an attractive house built in the 1790s. An engraved plaque indicates that it was the home of the painter George Romney. On the left you see the striking facade of the **Institute of Medical Research**.

Turn right. On your left is a fence with an impressive gate belonging to **Fenton House**. (Open March, Sat. and Sun. 11am-5pm; April-Oct., Sat. and Mon.-Wed. 11am-6pm, Sun. 11am-2pm. Entrance fee. Tel. 435-3471.) Built around 1693, the house is named after the Fenton family, who lived in the nineteenth century. The house contains a magnificent collection of ceramics from the West and the East, as well as a collection of musical instruments. The beautiful entrance gate is the work of Jean Tijou.

A left turn leads you to the small, charming Admiral's Walk, dominated by a house resembling a ship. This is **Admiral's House**, built in the eighteenth century for a colorful, if not always lucky, admiral. In the nineteenth century the house was occupied by Sir George Gilbert Scott, the famous architect.

LONDON

Adjacent to the Admiral's House is **Grove Lodge**, in the past the home of the Nobel-prize-winning author John Galsworthy, best known for *The Forsyte Saga*. It was in this house that most of the book was written.

Continue to Lower Terrace, and turn right to **Whitestone Pond**, a triangular pool at the top of the hill. The pond may once have been used for bathing the legs of horses; today children delight in paddling their legs there. On the opposite side of the pond is a light-colored building, **Jack Straw's Castle**. An old pub known to have existed as early as the beginning of the eighteenth century, the present building is a reconstruction of the original.

To the north is a fork in the road. To the left, leading northwest, is North End Way, which takes you to Golders Green neighborhood and **Golders Hill Park**, a charming, gracefully designed park. Along the road you will also find the **Old Bull and Bush** pub, once home of the painter William Hogarth. Further on, to the left, is the house where the famous dancer Anna Pavlova lived. The building, **Ivy House**, holds a small museum displaying Pavlova memorabilia. (Open Sat. 2-6pm. Free entrance. Tel. 237-6472.)

The right-hand fork, running northeast, is Spaniards Road, named for the famous hostel that was there. Now a pub, **Spaniards Inn** is thought to have been the home of the Spanish ambassador in the seventeenth century. In the eighteenth century it became a hostel. Next to it, the road is partially blocked by the accompanying **Tollhouse** of the same period. Although the house slows the flow of traffic considerably, the building has not been removed because of its historical importance. Further down the road is Kenwood House (see "In the Lap of Nature — Parks and Gardens"), and past it another picturesque area of London, **Highgate**. *Highgate Cemetery* is worth a visit for those who wish to see Karl Marx's tomb as well as the final resting place of other important figures.

Turn right onto East Heath Road to Queen Mary's Maternity Hospital. The narrow street below leads to the neo-Gothic **Christchurch**, with its high spire. Continue along the street eastward. On your left is the expansive Hampstead Heath (see "In the Lap of Nature — Parks and Gardens"), where you can rest and enjoy the natural beauty.

When you reach Keats Grove, turn right. On this street you will find **Keats House**, home of the English poet John Keats. (Open Mon.-Sat. 10am-1pm and 2pm-6pm, Sun. 2pm-5pm. Free entrance. Tel. 435-2062.) The house was built in the early nineteenth century and contains personal items from the poet's estate.

Next to the house is a handsome church with a neoclassical exterior, **St. John's Church**. It was built in 1818, about the time that Keats came to live next door.

LONDON

Turn left on Downshire Hill, then right on Hampstead High Street. A few dozen meters down, you will pass a lane that runs to the right. Called **Old Brewery Mews**, it was once a stable yard and today houses offices.

Further along is a pedestrian path called **Flask Walk**, the name an unwarranted reminder of the reputation of Hampstead's spring water. Take the path and walk around the pretty houses.

Complete the tour at the **Hampstead underground station**. (For further information about Hamstead Heath see `In the Lap of Nature — Parks and Gardens.')

Other Sights in the Area

The **RAF Museum** in Hendon houses some 40 airplanes depicting the history and development of military aviation in Britain. (Colindale underground station. Open Mon.-Sat. 10am-6pm, Sun. 2-6pm. Free entrance. Tel. 205-2266.)

Next door are two more museums. (Both open same hours as RAF museum. Entrance fees.) The **Battle of Britain Museum** is a monument for the participants in the great air battle of 1940, which virtually saved Britain from the German conquest in World War II. Also on display are some of the enemy's aircrafts. The **Bomber Command Museum** is situated on Hendon's former airstrip. It displays a fabulous collection of bombers, including the most up-to-date models.

Towers floating in the City

LONDON

Greenwich — A Different Time

Greenwich is the point of reference both for determining time and for world-wide cartography. On your tour of Greenwich you will unsuspectingly pass between the western and eastern hemispheres of the earth, crossing the 0° meridian time and time again.

You can reach the Greenwich or Maze Hill train station from the center of London by taking British Rail from the Charing Cross station. Trains leave often at all hours of the day. You can also get there on the riverboat that leaves from Charing Cross Pier and Tower Pier. This mode of transportation is highly recommended on a nice day when it is not too cold.

Begin the tour at **Greenwich Pier**. Opposite you, on a dry dock, proudly stand the masts of the **Cutty Sark**, world renown as the fastest sailing ship of its time. (Open Mon.-Sat. 11am-6pm, Sun. 2:30-6pm, in winter until 5pm. Entrance fee. Tel. 858-3445.) Set to sea in 1869, the clipper was initially used for the tea trade with China, but the opening of the Suez Canal, and the development of the steam ships at approximately the same time, led to a decline in the use of sailing ships. In 1922 the Cutty Sark was turned into a training school for young sailors, and in the 1950s it was dry-docked. The interior was partially restored and made into a museum in which various exhibits are presented as a tribute to this type of ship.

In the wide plaza, somewhat dwarfed by the larger boat, is **Gipsy Moth IV**, the 11-ton yacht in which Sir Francis Chichester sailed solo around the world in 1966-1967. (Open same hours as the Cutty Sark. Entrance fee.)

Between the boats stands a small structure that serves as the entrance to **Greenwich Foot Tunnel**, an underwater pedestrian walk. It comes out on the northern bank on the **Isle of Dogs**, apparently so named because the king's hunting dogs were let free here when they were not being used. In the nineteenth century wide docks were built along the coast of the peninsula; these are rapidly being converted for housing and commerce.

Leave the plaza to the southeast at King William Walk and tour royal Greenwich. Greenwich was a royal estate as early as the days of King Alfred the Great. In the fifteenth century King Henry V's brother Humphrey, Duke of Gloucester, decided to turn the estate into a fortified palace. He fenced in the park and erected an observation tower at the top of the hill, in order to spot enemies

LONDON

attempting to invade London via the river. The duke called the palace *Bella Court*, but when he died it was handed to Margaret of Anjou, wife of Henry VI, who changed the name to *Placentia*. Placentia Palace was particularly popular with the members of the Tudor dynasty, and King Henry VIII and his daughters, Queen Mary and Queen Elizabeth, were all born in Greenwich. Henry also began several of his famous romances with his queens here. In the area near Greenwich, Henry VIII built wide docks for the ships of his increasingly powerful fleet, thereby laying the foundation for the maritime tradition of Greenwich.

In 1615, King James I invited Inigo Jones to design a home for his queen, Anne of Denmark, on the site where the entrance gate to Placentia Palace stood. Jones built England's first Palladian-style villa. The queen died before the villa had been completed, and Charles I later gave it to his wife, Henrietta Maria, and the structure became known as the *Queen's House*.

In the period of Cromwell's Commonwealth, Placentia Palace was irreparably damaged. Wanting more room than the Queen's House provided, Charles II hired Jones's student, John Webb, to build a new wing in keeping with Jones's design. For lack of resources, Charles had to stop construction before his beautiful palace was completed. The work was only resumed at the initiative of William and Mary in 1694. They preferred to live at Hampton Court Palace, but approved the establishment of a Royal Hospital for seamen in Greenwich, similar to the Royal Hospital in Chelsea. The task was assigned to Sir Christopher Wren, who characteristically presented several plans; the finished product can be seen today.

The Queen's House remained as it was, and when the old Placentia was destroyed, it gained a marvelous view of the river. The wing that was originally built for King Charles II was integrated symmetrically with three additional wings, named for King William, Queen Mary, and Queen Anne. Two parallel domes indicate the location of the Hall and the Chapel.

The project was completed more than half a century after it began, and many people were involved in it at various stages. In 1873, the hospital became the **Royal Naval College**. (Open daily, except Thur., 2:30-5pm. Free entrance. Tel. 858-2154.) The nineteenth-century curriculum included sail-stretching, compass-reading, and cannon-firing. The college now trains NATO forces in submarine navigation and nuclear warfare.

Go into the courtyard and enter the **Painted Hall**. The walls and ceiling were elaborately decorated by Sir James Thornhill in the early eighteenth century. Among the fabulous paintings are portraits of William and Mary. Opposite the Hall you will find the **Chapel**. It

London

GREENWICH

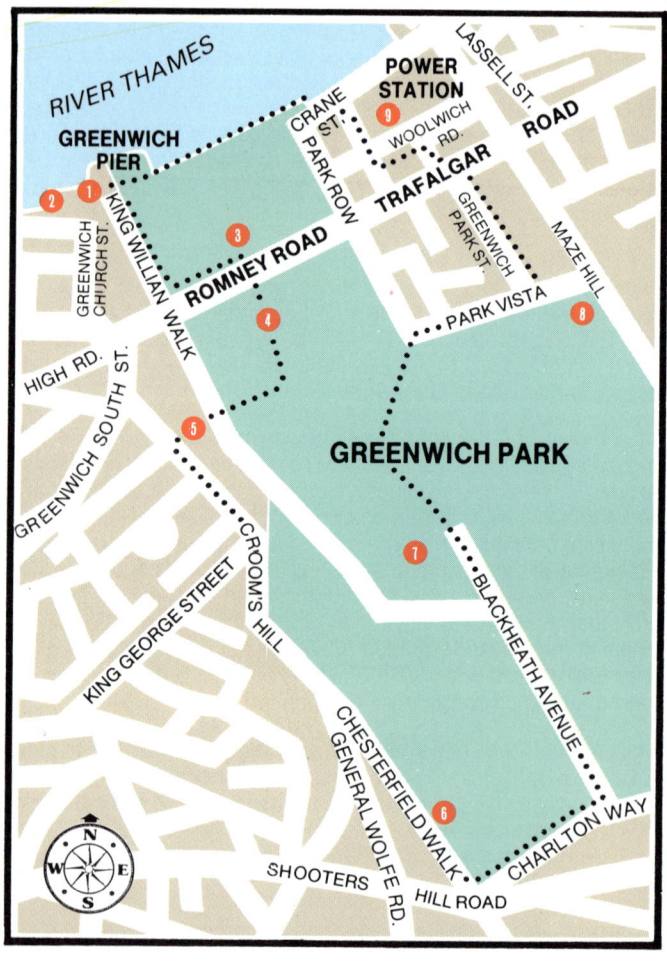

Index
1. Cutty Sark
2. Gipsy Moth IV
3. Royal Naval College
4. National Maritime Museum
5. Greenwich Theatre
6. Ranger's House
7. Old Royal Observatory
8. Vanbrugh Castle
9. Trinity Hospital

*L*ONDON

The Cutty Sark

was damaged by a fire in 1779, and was redesigned by James "Athenian" Stuart in delicate Wedgwood colors.

Exit the courtyard through the south gate and cross Romney Road to the **National Maritime Museum**. (Open summer, Mon.-Sat. 10am-6pm, Sun. 2-6pm, in winter until 5pm. Entrance fee; combined ticket with Old Royal Observatory available. Tel. 858-4422.) In the center of the complex stands the **Queen's House** that was designed by Jones and enlarged by Webb. After the Battle of Trafalgar, Daniel Alexander designed two additional wings, which were used as a school for seamen's children. The school was located here until 1933; in 1937 the National Maritime Museum opened.

LONDON

During the past few years the museum has undergone extensive alterations, and the Queen's House has been closed for this purpose. It is expected to reopen in the summer of 1989. The most impressive part of the Queen's House is undoubtedly the square entrance hall, which displays collections of exquisite paintings and of navigating instruments. The museum's two other wings contain a wealth of maritime information: pictures related to the sea and ships; models of ships; exhibits on sea trade, wars at sea, the exploration of the Poles, noteworthy seamen; and displays explaining marine archeology, sea and river life, and more. You can spend an entire day wandering through the rooms.

Walk through **Greenwich Park**. The park was fenced in 1433, thereby becoming the first royal estate to be designated for private use. It covers more than 175 acres of hilly land and boasts a small flock of deer (the descendants of those once hunted by the kings). The landscape is breathtaking.

Turn right and continue on the path until the park exit. Just to the north is the **Greenwich Theatre**. It has a Victorian exterior, although it was rebuilt in the late 1960s. Turn south on Croom's Hill, which serves as the park's western boundary. The houses built along it date mainly to the seventeenth and eighteenth centuries. Down the street are four seventeenth-century buildings: the Grange, Gazebo, Heath Gate House, and Manor House. At the top of the hill stand Macartney House and next to it **Ranger's House**. (Open daily, 10am-5pm, in winter until 4pm. Free entrance. Tel. 853-0035.) Built in the late seventeenth century, this became the park ranger's house in 1814. In 1974 the building and its art collections, including the Suffolk Collection of portraits, opened to the public.

Walk down Croom's Hill, which becomes Chesterfield Walk, and turn left into the park along Charlton Way. Turn north on the wide Blackheath Avenue, until you reach the **Old Royal Observatory**. (Open Mon.-Sat. 10am-6pm, Sun. 2-6pm, in winter until 5pm. Entrance fee; combined ticket with the National Maritime Museum available. Tel. 858-1167.) Built in 1675 by Wren for King Charles II, the Observatory originally served British seaman only. In 1767 it began printing the *Nautical Almanack*, a yearly publication that contained information about the location of the stars and enabled all seamen to measure their location relative to the Greenwich longitude. Soon this became the universally accepted point of reference, and many maps were drawn accordingly. In the late nineteenth century, 75% of all maps in the world were based on the Greenwich meridian, and an international convention held in 1884 in Washington accepted Greenwich Mean Time as a universal standard.

The Observatory is composed of several buildings. **Flamsteed House** was designed by Wren for the first Royal Astronomer, John

*L*ONDON

Flamsteed. Inside are his navigation instruments, considered the best available during his time.

Next door is the **Meridian Building**, erected in the eighteenth century. Some of the telescopes exhibited inside are still adjusted for astronomic observation, although the London air pollution makes viewing difficult. The 0° longitude meridian runs right through this building, hence its name.

Walk northeast from the Observatory and turn right onto Park Vista. On both sides of the street are graceful eighteenth-century buildings. On your right, hidden behind the gate, is the picturesque **Vanbrugh Castle**, a sort of medieval mini-fortress, with numerous turrets and towers, built around 1717 by the architect and playwright, Sir John Vanbrugh.

Turn left onto Greenwich Park Street and follow it until you come to Woolwich Road, where you will see the fence of **Trinity Hospital**, built in the seventeenth century. Past the power station to the right and to the north is **Ballast Quay**. The eighteenth-century buildings that line it include the *Cutty Sark Tavern*, with some more recent additions.

Turn left, walk along Woolwich Road, and make your first right. This is a somewhat neglected district, which bears no resemblance to those visited earlier. On Crane Street turn left again. Here you will find two interesting, well-known pubs, *The Yacht Tavern*, from the eighteenth century, whose windows look out over the Thames, and next to it the nineteenth-century *Trafalgar Tavern*, where diners are sometimes treated to a play or other performance.

Complete your tour at the quay along the river; the view on the left captures the perfect symmetry of the Royal Naval College.

Other Sights in the Area

The **Thames Barrier** is a huge dam that was built in order to prevent a hazardous flooding of London by an unexpected rising of the North Sea. The width of the Barrier is 520 meters (a third of a mile), and it is a unique achievement of British engineering. Its construction costs reached approximately £480 million. Next to it there is the **Thames Barrier Visitors Centre**. (Open Mon.-Fri. 10:30am-5pm, Sat. and Sun. 10:30am-5:30pm. Free entrance. Tel. 854-1373).

The barrier can be reached by boat from central London and from Greenwich Pier, or by British Rail from Charing Cross station. The train stops at Greenwich on the way to the Barrier.

Greenwich

Greenhouse at Kew Gardens

*L*ONDON

Kew Gardens and Richmond — From the Finest of Parks to the Finest of Viilages

Kew Gardens, the most famous botanical gardens in the world, are an absolute must for plant-lovers. In fact, Kew Gardens should be included in any tour of London, particularly if you come at the peak of the spring flower season.

You can reach Kew Gardens throughout the year by taking the underground to the Kew Gardens station. In the summer you can also get there on a riverboat that sails from Westminster Pier in central London, an enjoyable journey.

The **Kew Royal Botanic Gardens** began as part of the royal park and estate of Richmond. (Open daily 9:30am to dusk. Entrance fee. Tel. 940-1171.) In the 1720s King George II and his wife Queen Caroline lived in Ormonde Lodge, which was part of the Richmond Estate. Their son Frederick, Prince of Wales, leased the adjacent area called Kew and lived there until his death in 1751. His widow, Princess Augusta, began planting the botanical gardens in 1759, thereby laying the foundations for what you now see.

Her son George III inherited her part of the land with the buildings she had constructed, along with the Richmond estate, which he inherited from his grandfather. He began developing the gardens with the assistance of Sir Joseph Banks, who is responsible for their appearance today.

In 1841, a royal decree transferred the gardens to the custody of the state. Since then Kew Gardens have served as an international center for the preservation and study of the foliage of all areas of the globe. A research center offers young people from the world over a three-year course culminating with a recognized degree in horticulture.

The gardens now encompass collections of dried plants containing almost six million specimens (closed to the public), and of plants and seeds that are becoming extinct, a museum for economic uses of botany, planting areas, and several buildings and hothouses, with plants from all the climates of the earth.

Palm House contains a collection of palms and huge tropical plants.

Water Lily House contains a collection of tropical water lilies.

*L*ONDON

Aroid House contains plants that need high moisture and heat, as found in tropical rain forests.

Tropical Conservatory is the location of a variety of large tropical flora. The adjacent buildings house succulents, ferns, and the like.

Alpine House contains plants that need particularly cold temperatures in order to grow.

Temperate House contains plants from moderate and Mediterranean climates.

Australia House holds plants from that continent.

In addition to the hothouses, the gardens are divided into areas in which groups of plants and trees are concentrated, from Lebanon cedars and eucalyptus trees to azaleas, rhododendrons, magnolias, and more. The blooming season reaches its peak in May, and the gardens look their best at this time.

The garden grounds also include other buildings, devoted to various functions. **Museum No. 1**, next to The Pond, contains a collection of economically beneficial plants. The **Wood Museum**, on the northern edge of the gardens displays a variety of wood and wooden objects. (Both museums open Mon.-Sat. 9:30am-4:30pm, Sun. 9:30am-5pm.) The **Orangery**, designed by Sir William Chambers in 1761, features temporary exhibits and also houses a souvenir and book shop.

Kew Palace, or Dutch House, was built in 1631 by a London-based Dutch merchant. (Open April-Sept., daily 11am-5:30pm. Entrance fee. Tel. 977-8441.) George III leased it and commissioned an expansion to the south, which was destroyed. The house remained, and Queen Charlotte continued to live in it until her death in 1818. In 1899 Queen Victoria gave Kew Palace to the state and opened it to the public.

Queen's Cottage, a picturesque building, was built in the 1770s for Queen Charlotte as a country house, mainly for day outings. (Open April-Sept., Sat. and Sun. 11am-5:30pm. Entrance fee.) It was not really intended for long-term visits and the grounds were left semi-wild, in contrast to the other, carefully designed parts of the garden.

The **Pagoda**, built for Princess Augusta, was also designed by Chambers in 1761. The ten-story structure reflects a Far Eastern influence.

Throughout the park one also finds several small sanctuaries, artificial "ruins," and gates, which were meant to add a special touch and perhaps to give the area something of a Mediterranean atmosphere.

The park has the usual amenities — drinking fountains, public rest rooms, and refreshments stands. Plan to spend an entire day here, absorbing the luscious surroundings.

East of the gardens lies **Kew Village**, with many handsome houses, mostly from the eighteenth and nineteenth centuries. Across Kew Bridge, on the northern bank of the Thames, to the left, is the **Kew Bridge Engines and Water Supply Museum**. (Open Sat.-Sun. 11am-5pm. Entrance fee. Tel. 568-4757.) The museum features several nineteenth-century steam engines, which operate on a rotating schedule.

South of the gardens is another verdant area, **Old Deer Park**, which is just above the village of Richmond.

Richmond, the prettiest, greenest, most picturesque of London's villages, was a royal estate occupied by the monarchs of England for hundreds of years. During the Tudor period it was particularly popular, and Queen Elizabeth I died here. Charles I of the Stuart dynasty also liked Richmond, and he opened two parts of the estate for two parks, now known as Richmond Park and Old Deer Park.

In the eighteenth century Richmond was occupied successively by King George II, Prince Frederick, and his son George III; they were the moving force behind the development of the area. Many aristocrats who aspired to live near the royal court built homes along the river, and to this day the area is a treasure of interesting historical buildings, such as Ham House and Marble Hill House.

Richmond is now an urban village, both picturesque and lively, with interesting alleyways and wide expanses along the river — an ideal place for a weekend outing. One of the most enjoyable places to visit is **Richmond Green**, a green area overlooking old Richmond Palace and surrounded by handsome seventeenth- and eighteenth-century homes. In the charming little streets that run from the park there are a variety of stores and pubs. To the east is **Richmond Theatre**, an interesting building constructed at the turn of the century. It stands out because of its two unique turrets.

The embankment along the river is quiet and tranquil. The old bridge leads to **Twickenham**, another charming village on the opposite bank of the river. The river itself is very narrow at this spot, and you can rent a rowboat here.

South of the village lies the large **Richmond Park** (see "In the Lap of Nature — Parks and Gardens"). If you walk along the river to the south you will come to one of the most striking historical houses in London, accessible from Richmond by buses 65 and 71. **Ham House** represents the best of Jacobean architecture in London, and is worth a visit. (Open Tues.-Sun. 11am-5pm. Entrance fee. Tel. 940-1950.) It was built in 1610 and enlarged in the 1670s by the Duke and Duchess of Lauderdale, who filled its rooms

*L*ONDON

KEW GARDENS

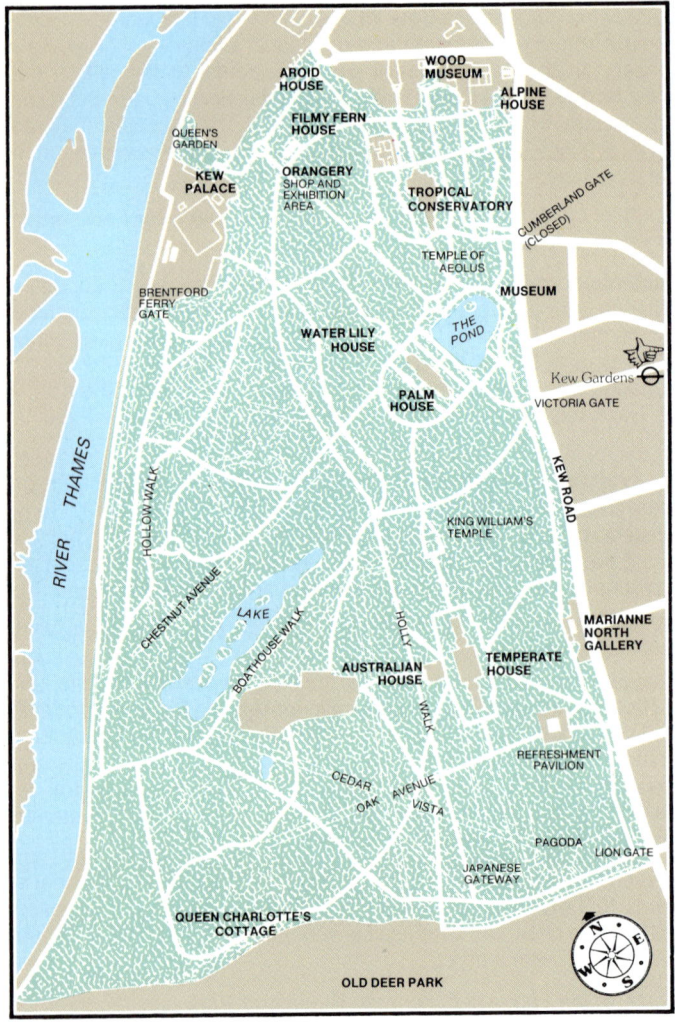

London

RICHMOND

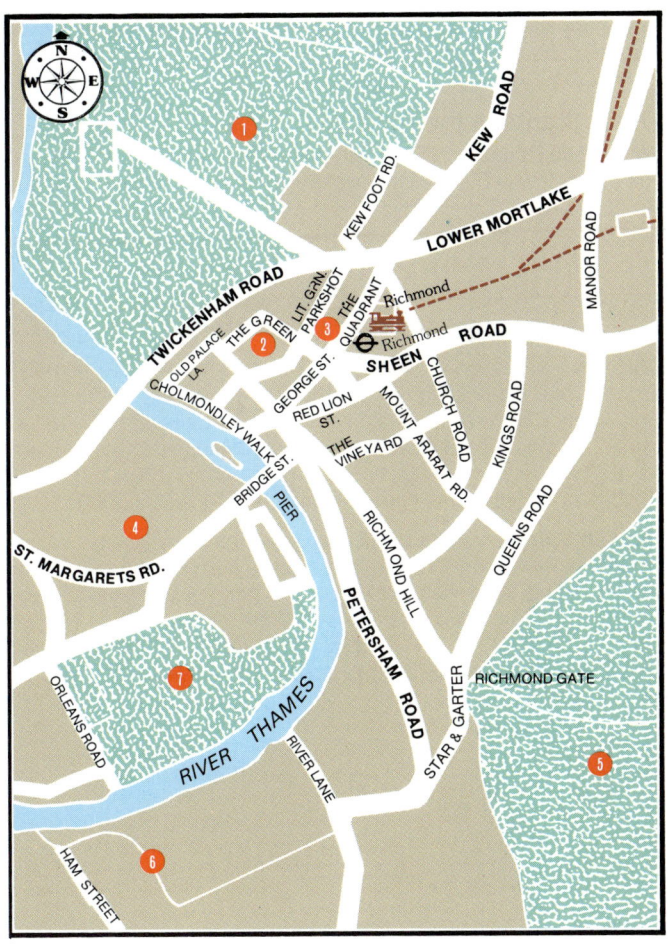

Index
1. Old Deer Park
2. Richmond Green
3. Richmond Theatre
4. Twickenham
5. Richmond Park
6. Ham House
7. Marble Hill House

LONDON

with beautiful items. The paintings of England's greatest artists, decorative furniture, and other *objects d'art* are tastefully presented.

You can return to London from the **Richmond underground station** in the center of the village.

Other Sights in the Area

Marble Hill House is a Palladian-style house built in the 1720s for Henrietta Howard. The mistress of King George II, she later became the Countess of Suffolk. The house contains a collection of furniture and pictures. (Richmond Road, Twickenham. Open daily, except Fri., 10am-5pm, in winter until 4pm. Free entrance. Tel. 892-5115.)

The following sights are west of Kew, across the Thames in Chiswick, and can be reached from the Turnham Green underground station.

Chiswick House, a wonderful example of Palladian-style architecture, was designed by Richard Boyle, the third Earl of Burlington. The interior design and the gardens are by William Kent. This was the home of the Prince of Wales who later became King Edward VII. (Burlington Lane. Open daily 9:30am-1pm and 2-6:30pm, in winter until 4pm. Entrance fee. Tel. 995-0508.)

Hogarth's House is where the eighteenth-century painter William Hogarth lived during the later years of his life. He documented the society of his time with drawings and engravings. The museum contains personal items and a collection of his works. (Hogarth Lane, Great West Road. Open Mon. and Wed.-Sat. 11am-6pm, Sun. 2-6pm, in winter until 4pm. Free entrance. Tel. 994-6757.)

LONDON

Hampton Court — Majestic Estate of the Kings

The kings of England built many palaces over the generations. The memory of some has been lost in oblivion and the memory of others has been preserved in name only, while others have remained standing to this day. **Hampton Court** was one of the later palaces to be built and it is undoubtedly the most lavish and luxurious of those that have survived. The enormous, majestic structure, filled with priceless treasures, gives testimony to the legendary wealth accumulated by the British monarchs over the centuries.

You can reach Hampton Court from central London by taking British Rail to the station of that name. In the summer you can also get there by boat from Westminster Pier. The palace is open April-Sept., Mon.-Sat. 9:30am-6pm, Sun. 11am-6pm; Oct.-March, Mon.-Sat. 9:30am-5pm, Sun. 2-5pm. Entrance fee. Tel. 977-8441. The gardens are open daily 7am-dusk. Free entrance.

Construction of Hampton Court Palace was started in 1514 by Cardinal Wolsey, on land by the Thames obtained from a religious order, the Knights Hospitallers of St. John of Jerusalem. Tradition has is that Wolsey chose this site for his vacation home after he conferred with various physicians and learned men, who strongly recommended the excellent quality of the air and water here. It is said that the palace built by Wolsey contained some 1000 rooms, and that his staff numbered close to 500. Wolsey spared no luxury, pleasure, or comfort. The floors were covered with lush carpeting, the furniture was upholstered in silk and velvet, and veritable treasures were hung on the walls. An excellent drainage system was also installed in the palace to maintain sanitary conditions, and a network of pipes brought clean water for drinking from a spring located some three miles from the palace.

Henry VIII visited Hampton Court, and, true to character, wished to have what he saw. Wolsey, who was a prominent cardinal and a brilliant politician, felt that his power was waning, and presented the palace to the king as a gift. Nonetheless, Wolsey still fell from grace, and Henry moved in in 1529. Before Wolsey died in 1530 — on the way to being tried for treason — Henry began enlarging the palace, adding living quarters for himself and his queen.

For the next two hundred years Hampton Court was the favorite home of the sovereigns of England. William III recruited the renowned

*L*ONDON

HAMPTON COURT — MAJESTIC ESTATE OF THE KINGS

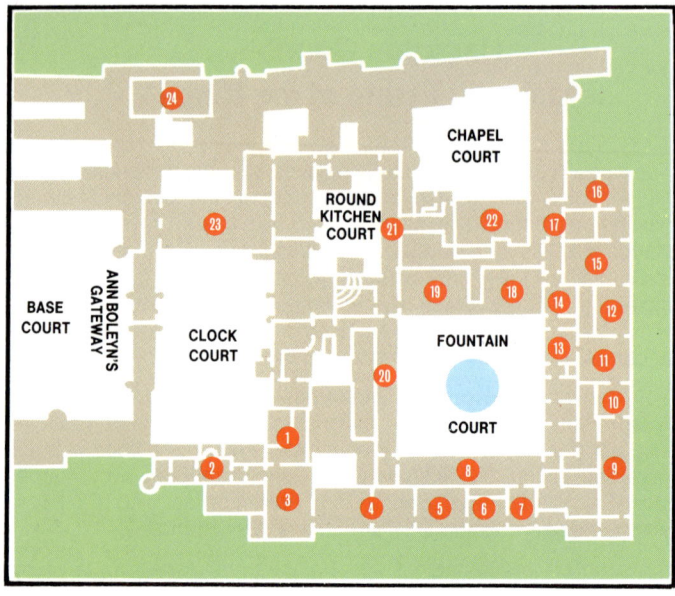

Index
1. King's Staircase
2. Guard Chamber
3. Wolsey's Rooms
4. First and Second Presence Chambers
5. King's Audience Chamber
6. King's Drawing Room
7. William III's Bedroom
8. Cartoon Gallery
9. Queen's Gallery
10. Queen's Bedroom
11. Queen's Drawing Room
12. Queen's Audience Chamber
13. Private Chapel
14. Private Dining Room
15. Public Dining Room
16. Prince of Wales Suite
17. Prince of Wales Staircase
18. Queen's Guard Chamber
19. Queen's Presence Chamber
20. Communication Gallery
21. Haunted Gallery
22. Chapel Royal
23. Great Hall
24. Kitchens

architect Wren to redesign the palace. Wren left the Tudor facade with its angular turrets, but demolished most of the building that had been added to Wolsey's palace by Henry VIII, and rebuilt it in heavy Baroque elegance, complementing red bricks with white stone.

After the death of George II the palace ceased to be a home for royalty. In 1838 Queen Victoria opened the State Apartments to the

*L*ONDON

Gardens in bloom

public. Today sections of the palace house pensioners of the Crown. In 1986 a serious fire broke out in the southern wing of the palace, evidently from a candle left burning by one of the residents, and many treasures were lost for good. The wing is now being renovated, and when the work is completed it will again be opened to the public.

The front of the palace faces west. It is guarded by statues of mythological animals, called the "King's Beasts;" they protect the original Tudor entrance, the Gatehouse. The yard on the other side of the gate, **Base Court**, is surrounded by the original structure built by Wolsey. Cross it and go through **Ann Boleyn's Gateway**, named for King Henry VIII's wife who was executed for adultery. The next yard is called **Clock Court** because of the astronomical clock built for Henry VIII in 1540, which shows the hour, date, month, year, zodiac signs, and cycle of the moon.

Enter the **State Apartments**. Pass the *King's Staircase*, with its fabulous wall murals painted by the Italian artist Antonio Verrio. From there go to the *Guard Chamber*, its walls adorned with hundreds of weapons, and next to it peek into *Wolsey's Rooms*. The next row of rooms was part of the State Apartments but was badly damaged in the fire: the *First and Second Presence Chambers*, the *King's Audience Chamber*, the *King's Drawing Room*, and *William III's Bedroom*. The walls of the adjacent *Cartoon Gallery* were once hung with Raphael cartoons describing the life of the Apostles Paul and Peter. These sketches are now kept in the Victoria and Albert

LONDON

Museum in London; replacing them in this gallery are tapestries based on their designs.

The king's quarters lead to the queen's quarters. The walls of the *Queen's Gallery* are hung with tapestries depicting the life of Alexander the Great. In the *Queen's Bedroom* there is a luxurious scarlet bed. The *Queen's Drawing Room* is decorated with wall paintings by Verrio. Adjacent to the *Queen's Audience Chamber* are her *Private Chapel* and *Private Dining Room*.

The rooms located in the northern wing of the palace include the *Public Dining Room*, the *Prince of Wales Suite*, including rooms once inhabited by Prince Frederick. The bedroom is decorated with paintings of the "Hampton Court Beauties" by Sir Godfrey Kneller, and the fancy *Prince of Wales Staircase* next to it has a a banister by Jean Tijou.

The *Windsor Beauties*, painted by Sir Peter Lely during the reign of Charles II, are hung in the *Communication Gallery*, which is connected to the *Queen's Guard Chamber* and the *Queen's Presence Chamber*. Past them is the *Haunted Gallery*. When Catherine Howard, the fifth wife of Henry VII, was sentenced to death, she tried to appeal to the king when he was in the Chapel Royal. The guards discovered her and dragged her away against bloodcurdling screams; her ghost is said to reside in the gallery to this day.

The *Chapel Royal*, built by Wolsey, has a beautiful wood ceiling. Even more impressive is the engraved wood ceiling of the *Great Hall*, built by Henry VIII.

Other interesting sights in the palace are the Tudor-period *Kitchens*, with huge ovens and antique utensils, as well as Henry VIII's wine and beer cellar.

The gardens surrounding the palace are beautiful and worth visiting. Each resident left his special mark on them. Wolsey began to design the garden south of the palace toward the river, and Henry VIII continued to develop this area. Here you find the *Pond Garden* and adjacent *Banqueting House* next to the Elizabethan *Knot Garden* and *Privy Garden*, which is set apart from the river by an exquisite iron gate by Tijou.

Tennis courts from the Tudor period are located north of the palace; they are still sometimes used for games and competitions. Beyond the courts lies the **Wilderness**, where you can find a cafeteria, and in its northern part is the **Maze**. (Open March-Oct., daily 10am-6pm. Entrance fee.) On the other side of the fence lies **Bushy Park**, part of the palace gardens, and a great place for picnicking.

The larger part of the official gardens spreads east of the palace. William III dug the **Long Water**, which is separated from the palace by the **Great Fountain Garden**, with trees designed in the shape of cones. The young **Woodland Garden**, planted in the mid-twentieth century, constitutes most of the eastern park.

Outside the palace grounds is **Hampton Green**, with seventeenth- and eighteenth-century houses built by those who wanted to live in close proximity to the monarch.

LONDON

Windsor and Eton College — A Royal Retreat

Windsor Castle has served as the second residence of the kings of England for over 900 consecutive years. While the palaces of the kings inside London have been successively built and destroyed, Windsor Castle has remained, towering proudly over the environs, a symbol of the continuity and stability of the British monarchy. King George V gave this bond an official stamp in 1917 when he declared that the name of the Royal Family and its descendants would be Windsor.

You should give the trip to Windsor a full day, as this charming, picturesque town is located outside the boundaries of London. Trains leave from the British Rail stations at Paddington (change at Slough for the Central station in Windsor) and Waterloo (to the Riverside station in Windsor). The trains leave often and the trip takes less than an hour.

Begin the tour at the Central British Rail station in Windsor, where you will find one of the town's attractions: **Madame Tussaud's Royalty and Empire Exhibition**. (Open daily 9:30am-5:30pm, in winter until 4:30pm. Entrance fee. Tel. 0753-857837.) The train station in which the museum is located was specially renovated and enlarged in order to accommodate Queen Victoria's royal train during her Diamond Jubilee in 1897. The curators of the museum restored the train and memorialized the event with wax figures. The museum also has a theater presentation, "Sixty Glorious Years." The major events of Queen Victoria's reign are related by life-size figures from that period, with the aid of computer technology.

Go up to the old fortress that dominates the town. **Windsor Castle** is believed to be the largest castle of its kind in the world. The Saxon kings built themselves a palace in a place which was known as Old Windsor, but when William the Conqueror built New Windsor Castle high on a cliff top a few miles up the Thames, the older palace was abandoned and left to deteriorate. William built his fortress of wood, and Henry II rebuilt it with stone; Henry III and William III also added to and improved the fortifications. None of the later additions have detracted from its impressive medieval appearance.

The fortress has three sections: the Lower Ward, the Middle Ward, and the Upper Ward. (Precincts open daily, Jan.-March and late Oct.-Dec. 10am-4:15pm; April and Sept.-late Oct. 10am-

LONDON

WINDSOR AND ETON COLLEGE

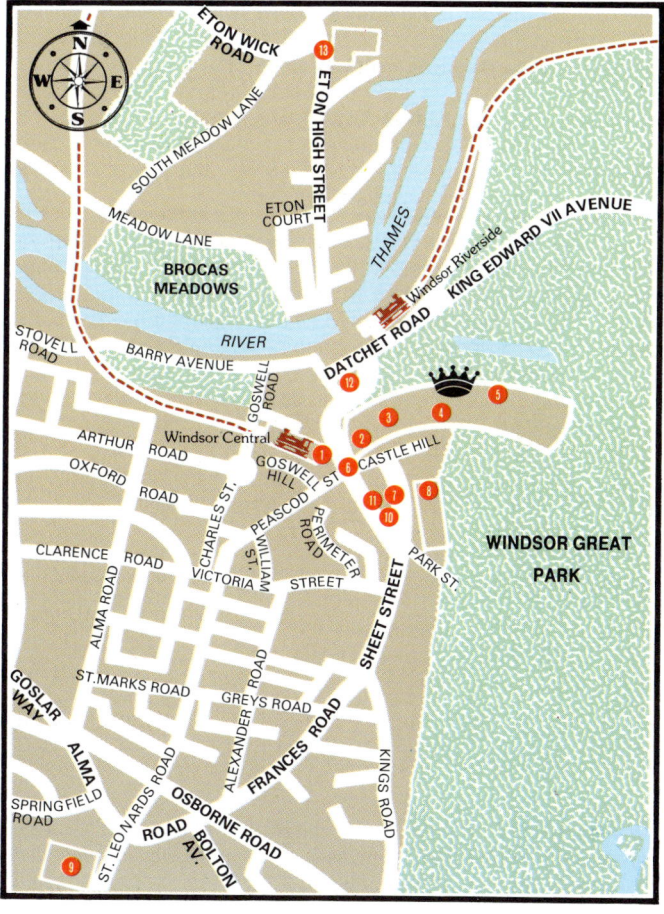

Index
1. Madame Tussaud's Royalty and Empire Exhibition
2. Windsor Castle
3. St. George's Chapel
4. Round Tower
5. State Apartments
6. Queen Victoria statue
7. Church Lane
8. Royal Mews Exhibition
9. Household Cavalry Museum
10. St. John the Baptist
11. Guildhall
12. Theatre Royal, Windsor
13. Eton College

LONDON

5:15pm; May-Aug. 10am-7:15pm. Free entrance. Windsor Castle tel. 0753-868286.) Enter the **Lower Ward** through Henry VIII's Gateway. On the left are parade grounds, where the *Changing of the Guard* ceremony takes place Mon.-Sat. at 11am. Opposite you is the gate leading to the **Horseshoe Cloister**, with attractive fifteenth-century brick houses. In the northwest corner of the fortress is the thirteenth-century **Curfew Tower**, which contains an awesome medieval dungeon. The eight bells in the tower chime every three hours, starting at midnight. Next to the tower is a row of buildings belonging to the Military Knights of Windsor.

In the center of the Lower ward is **St. George's Chapel**, one of the most beautiful chapels built in the late Gothic style. (Open Mon.-Sat.10:45am-4pm, Sun. 2-4pm, in winter until 3:45pm. Entrance fee.) Edward IV began building it in 1475 as a chapel for the Order of the Garter. This is the most important and highest order of Knighthood in the kingdom, founded in 1348 by Edward III. Legend says that the name was derived from an incident that occurred when a lady dropped her garter. King Edward retrieved it for her, admonishing the laughing bystanders, "Shame to him who thinks ill of it." These words became the motto of the order, whose banners decorate the inner area of the chapel. Several monarchs of England are buried here.

East of St. George's is the **Dean's Cloister**, bordered by the **Albert Memorial Chapel**. (Open Mon.-Sat. 10am-1pm and 2-3:45pm. Free entrance.) This chapel was intended as a burial place for several kings, including Henry VI, Henry VII, and Henry VIII. Such intentions were never realized. After Henry VIII's death in 1547, the chapel was unused until Queen Victoria renovated it in memory of Prince Albert after he died in 1861. He, too, is not buried here, but is entombed with the Queen in the nearby Windsor Home Park.

The **Middle Ward** is dominated by the **Round Tower**, which in days of yore was surrounded by a moat of its own. Built by Henry II in the twelfth century, it was intended to be the stronghold of the castle.

Go out onto the **North Terrace**, to the left of the Round Tower. The breathtaking view overlooks the Thames Valley and Eton College. In this area, on the way to the State Apartments, there are few exhibits worth visiting. **Queen Mary's Dolls' House**, designed by Sir Edwin Lutyens in 1923, is on display, along with a collection of the queen's dolls in the next room (Hours vary throughout the year. On average, open April-Oct., Mon.-Sat. 10:30am-5pm; May-Oct., Sun. 1:30-5pm; Nov.-March, Mon.-Sat. 10:30-5pm, closed Sun. Call for exact hours. Entrance fee.) It is only fitting that a queen's doll house should look like the house of the queen herself, and this one does, from

LONDON

the reception rooms to the servants' quarters. The contents of the house were made with special workmanship and precision to scale: miniature books, furniture, utensils, and even miniature oil paintings. In another hall next the Dolls' House is the **Exhibition of Drawings**. (Hours vary. On average same as for Dolls' House. Call for exact hours. Entrance fee.) From the queen's collections, these drawings are by the old masters, including Leonardo da Vinci and Holbein.

Next to this hall is the entrance to the **State Apartments** of the queen, in the **Upper Ward**. (Hours vary. On average, open May and July-Oct., Mon.-Sat. 10:30am-5pm, Sun. 1:30-5pm. Jan-mid-March and Nov., Mon.-Sat. 10:30am-3pm, closed Sun. Closed mid-March-early May, most of June and Dec. and whenever the queen is in residence. Call for exact hours. Entrance fee.) Inside the rooms are marvelous treasures: delicate china, knights' armor, ceilings decorated by great artists such as Antonio Verrio and Grinling Gibbons, and masterpieces by Rubens, Van Dyck, Lawrence, Holbein, Canaletto, Hogarth, Reynolds, and many others. The ceremonies and celebrations of the Order of the Garter are held in the elegant **St. George's Hall**. The rest of the Upper Ward contains private apartments and is not open to the public. South of Windsor Castle lies **Windsor Great Park**, covering some 2,000 acres. Once a hunting ground for the kings, the park is now divided into several parts. The section closest to the palace is closed to visitors as is **Frogmore Gardens**, where the mausoleum of Queen Victoria and Prince Albert is located. (The gardens are open by the queen's special permission on the first Wed. and Thur. of May. The mausoleum is also open on the Wed. closest to May 24, Queen Victoria's birthday.)

Stretching for some three miles south from the castle is the **Long Walk**. This tree-lined boulevard along the western edge of the park, closed to cars, was originally laid by Charles II in 1685 and later replanted in 1945. The Long Walk leads to the statue of a **Copper Horse**, mounted by George III.

In the southern part of the park is an artificial lake, the **Virginia Water**. Standing on the side of the lake are **The Ruins**, ancient Roman ruins, imported from Libya by George IV in the nineteenth century. On the northern shore lie the **Valley Gardens**, famous for the flowering rhododendrons and azaleas. Next to them is the enchanting **Savill Gardens**, planted in 1932 by Sir Eric Savill, who was deputy director of the park. The garden is noted for its myriad of colors, all year round, created by the clever layout of the plants. (Valley Gardens open daily throughout the year. Savill Gardens open March-Oct., daily 10am-6pm or dusk. Entrance fee.)

On the southwestern side of the park is Windsor Safari Park, filled with wild animals such as lions, elephants, and giraffes. (Open daily,

*L*ONDON

Windsor Castle

10am-5:45pm; in winter, until one hour before dusk. Entrance fee. Tel. 0753-869847.) Attractions include an aquarium, which presents dolphin and whale performances, a parrot show, a demonstration by birds of prey, a butterfly collection, tropical plants, and more. There are also snack bars, and a special bus for those without a vehicle who wish to tour the safari.

Exit Windsor Castle from where you entered Henry VIII's Gateway. Opposite the gate stands the **statue of Queen Victoria**, placed here at her Diamond Jubilee in 1897. Tour the paved medieval streets of the town. On Church Street you will find some interesting sixteenth- and seventeenth- century buildings. Continue to **Church Lane**, location of the Engine House, once occupied by Windsor's fire engine and now the site of a local restaurant, Benson's.

On St. Albans Street is the **Royal Mews Exhibition**. (Open May-Sept., daily 10:30am-3pm; Oct.-April, Mon.-Sat. 10:30am-3pm, closed Sun. Entrance fee. Tel. 0573-868286.) The stables house many of the horses and carriages still in use by the Royal Family. Harnesses and other related accessories are displayed.

From this street you can turn left onto Park Street, the continuation of the park's Long Walk, lined with handsome Georgian houses. Straight ahead lies Sheet Street, which is also lined with lovely buildings. To the left Sheet Street becomes Frances Road, which leads to St. Leonards Road. Located here is the **Household Cavalry Museum**, which shows personal items and equipment used by the monarchs' guard from the time of Charles II to the present. (Open

LONDON

Mon.-Fri. 10am-1pm and 2-5pm. Free entrance. Tel. 0753-868222, ext. 203.)

To the north of Park Street is High Street; turn right. On the right is **St. John the Baptist**, parish church of Windsor, which was built in the nineteenth century in place of the original Norman church. Inside is a Brass Rubbing Centre. (Open March to October, Mon.-Sat. 10am-5pm.) At the top of the street, standing alone, is the graceful **Guildhall**. Its construction began in 1687 and was completed twenty years later by Sir Christopher Wren, who designed the delicate pillars on the front. Statues of Queen Anne and her husband, Prince George of Denmark, decorate the building. (Closed to the public.)

From the castle walk down Thames Street, a commercial center with some charming tourist shops. At the bottom is the **Theatre Royal, Windsor**, built in 1793. The embankment along the river is a good spot for a rest.

Complete the tour of Windsor at **Eton College**, located north of the Thames. Anyone the slightest bit familiar with English society knows that the name Eton, more than any other status symbol, represents the height of British aristocracy and prestige. This is why many members of the nobility, high society, and those who are just plain rich spare no effort to see that their children are accepted to this school. Founded in 1440 by King Henry VI in order to provide free education and lodging to 70 poor scholars, it was only in the seventeenth century that the institution became fashionable among the aristocracy. There are now 1,200 students paying full tuition, and another 70 or so who are entitled to study here on the basis of their ability alone. Among Eton's graduates are many notable figures in literature, art and politics, including some twenty prime ministers.

When you tour the grounds of the college during the academic year, you can see the students walking around in their traditional uniform, with striped long-tail coats. The buildings include the original building — the Lower School built in 1443, the Upper School, built in the seventeenth century and the exquisite fifteenth-century Gothic Chapel. The Museum of Eton Life shows an exhibit of the college's 500-year history. (Open during the academic year daily 2-5pm; Apr.-Sept., 10:30am-5pm. Entrance fee. Tel. 0753-863593.)

South of Windsor you will find the Ascot horse race tracks, as well as a towering hill called **Runnymede**, where King John signed the Magna Carta in 1215. The Magna Carta Memorial, donated by the United States Association of Attorneys in 1957, and a monument erected in 1965 in memory of US President John F. Kennedy, are located on the hill. At the top is a monument in honor of the 20,455 victims of the air force of the Commonwelath whose place of burial is unknown.

*L*_ONDON_

London Under the Night Lights

When night falls and the City begins to slumber, its six thousand inhabitants are left alone after the day's hundreds of thousands of visitors. Now the West End comes to life, and masses flood the entertainment centers located west of the City of London.

The tour of London at night includes popular entertainment spots, combined with a look at those sights that seem to take on a different character under the flood lights.

Start at **Piccadilly Circus**. The flashing neon lights electrify the night, particularly on national holidays when the square is filled with thousands of people celebrating.

Continue east toward **Leicester Square**, the center of London's film world. The cinemas here show the newest, hottest films on the market. The square virtually overflows with young people, from whom you can learn the latest and wildest fashion trends.

Walk south from Leicester Square toward **Trafalgar Square**. Nelson's Column, the National Gallery, and the other buildings in the area all glow with light. At Christmas time a large evergreen decorated with flickering lights is placed in the middle of the square, and masses of people gather to sing Christmas carols, warming hearts on cold winter nights.

Leave Trafalgar Square to the south and walk down along **Whitehall** which is abandoned at this hour. The huge stone halls, the homes of the British government, seem stark and lonely, awaiting the light of the new day. Pass the **Cenotaph** memorial to the victims of the world wars, and you will come to Parliament Square.

In front of you, like an image from a medieval tale, stand the **Houses of Parliament**. The yellowish light shed on the neo-Gothic buildings adds to their mysterious air. The Big Ben clock is also lit at this hour. If the light at its top is shining, it is a sign that one of the Houses of Parliament is holding a late-night session.

Turn east and cross **Westminster Bridge**. The Thames River sparkles with reflections of the city lights. On the other side of the river, the impressive **County Hall** faces you. Stroll along the Albert Embankment, enjoying the view of the city lights across the river.

To the north, further up the embankment, you will come to the **South Bank Arts Centre**. This area, with the Royal Festival Hall, the National Theatre, and the National Film Theatre side by side,

LONDON

bustles with activity much of the day, and reaches its peak in the evening hours. Here, the crowning jewel of London's West End, you can enjoy the best concerts, plays, and films.

Walk onto **Waterloo Bridge**, named for the famous 1815 battle, fought between the British and allied army and the French led by Napoleon. In this battle Napoleon was severely defeated, a defeat that led to his downfall. The bridge will remind film-lovers of the movie of the same name, in which Vivian Leigh meets her lover here on a night during the World War II Blitz. Cross the bridge back to the northern bank. The lighted building in front of you is **Somerset House**. Walk down Lancaster Place to the busy Strand, with its flashing neon lights announcing its many theaters.

Complete your night tour at the center of London's nightlife, which in recent years has gained increasing popularity. The **Covent Garden** area is filled with restaurants, pubs, theaters, opera houses, and a myriad of little alleyways still lit with nineteenth-century gas lamps.

*L*ONDON

LONDON UNDER THE NIGHT LIGHTS

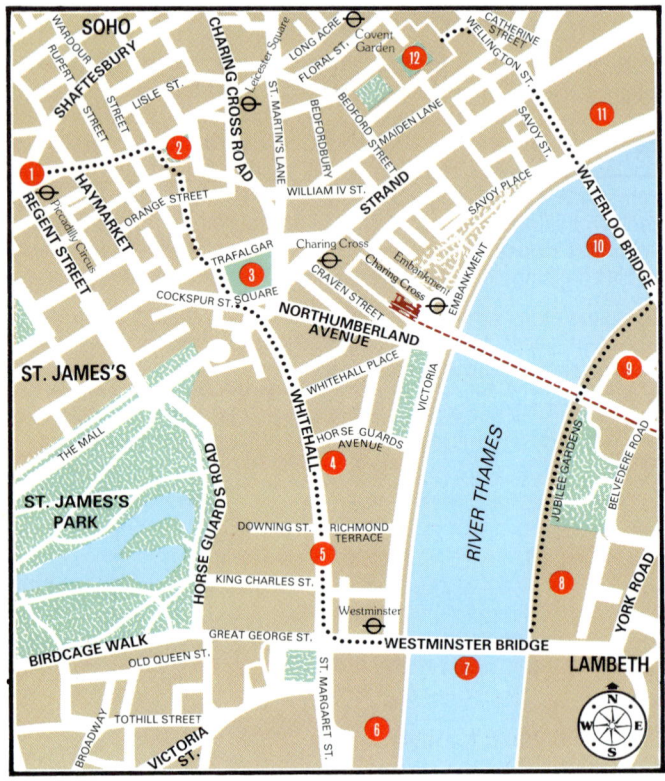

Index
1. Piccadilly Circus
2. Leicester Square
3. Trafalgar Square
4. Whitehall
5. Cenotaph
6. Houses of Parliament
7. Westminster Bridge
8. County Hall
9. South Bank Arts Centre
10. Waterloo Bridge
11. Somerset House
12. Covent Garden

*L*ONDON

An Umbrella for Two

London in the rain is an experience engraved in the memory of most of its visitors, regardless of the season in which they came. If you arrive in the city on a sunny day, take advantage of the good weather. But since the average is ten days of precipitation a month in London, chances are high that rain will fall sometime during your visit. We therefore offer a few suggestions for pleasant and relatively dry activities for a rainy day.

London boasts numerous and varied **museums**, most of which contain exhibits that you can spend hours viewing, a perfect pastime on a wet afternoon. Most have relatively inexpensive restaurants, so that you get a package deal including nourishment for both body and spirit under one roof. We recommend the following museums:

British Museum (see "Bloomsbury — The Home of Writers and Poets")
National Gallery (see "St. James's and Buckingham Palace — The Royal District")
Tate Gallery (see "Whitehall and Westminster — Stronghold of the Regime")

The following four museums are right next to one another, so that you can combine them into one tour (see "Knightsbridge and Kensington — Shops and Museums"):

Victoria and Albert Museum
Science Museum
Natural History Museum
Geological Museum

Another possibility is to arrange your tour to include visits to **indoor sights**. Recommended for this purpose is part of the tour of the City. Start at **St. Paul's Cathedral** and continue to the **Museum of London**. Finish the tour at the **Barbican Centre for Arts and Conferences**, which offers the visitor rotating exhibits, a library, afternoon concerts, a café, and much more (see "The City of London — The Ancient Heart").

Make this a **shopping day**. At the large *Brent Cross Shopping Centre* you can visit branches of all the important chains and two department stores, without ever setting foot outside (see "Where to Shop for What"). You can also immerse yourself in one of the large department stores in the center of London, such as *Harrods* or *Selfridges*, where you can wander to your hearts content without fear of getting caught in a downpour.

*L*ONDON

London for Children

London is a city for the entire family, with plenty of terrific recreation and entertainment for children. Below is a selection of some of the city's treasures. Parents looking through this guide may well find other sights that will interest their children.

Taking Them Out
For the following mobile activities, see "Getting to Know the City" for complete details.

A tour on a double-decker bus: A special experience that no child would want to miss. Travel on the urban routes and look at the city from the top deck. When the weather is fair you can enjoy a circle tour on a sightseeing bus with an open upper deck.

A sail on the river: A natural choice on a nice day. There are two piers in central London where boats sail to a number of destinations.

Canal sailing: This fun and relaxing activity can be enjoyed both within and outside of London. Within the city you can sail from Little Venice to Regent's Park and the London Zoo.

Canal trips outside of London can be taken all through England (see "Excursions — A Sail on the Canals and Waterways of England").

Favorite Attractions
Changing of the Guard, Buckingham Palace: This grand ceremonial event takes place daily in the summer and every other day in the winter. The colorful uniforms, the fur hats, and the sound of the band make this ceremony a daily festivity, attended by tourists from around the world (see "St. James and Buckingham Palace — The Royal District").

London Zoo: Thousands of different kinds of mammals, reptiles, birds, and insects, among them some very rare species, are gathered in an area of a few dozen acres. A visit to the zoo can be a treat for all ages (see "Regent's Park — The First Garden Suburb").

London Brass Rubbing Centre: Here a child can make his own picture of a knight or a lady using the paper and wax pencils provided for a moderate price. Even the novice can turn out impressive pictures, and the experience is fun for young and old alike. The London Centre is located at St. James's Church (see

LONDON

"Mayfair — The Life of the Aristrocracy"). There are also Brass Rubbing Centres located at All Hallows-by-the-Tower (see "The City of London — The Ancient Heart"), Westminster Abbey (see "Whitehall and Westminster — Stronghold of the Regime"), and St. John the Baptist Church (See "Windsor and Eton College — A Royal Retreat").

London Transport Museum: Carriages, buses, trains, cars, and engines are displayed in a colorful and interesting exhibit (see "Adelphi and Covent Garden — The World of Dickens and the World of Theater").

HMS Belfast: This British warship from World War II, permanently anchored opposite the Tower of London, is preserved just as it was during active duty. Children can wander between the deck and the bridge, and can inspect the armaments. The visit is not recommended for very small children or older people who have difficulty maneuvering steps and ladders (see "Southwark — The City South of the River").

Madame Tussaud's Wax Museum and the London Planetarium: The well-known museum is filled with famous characters, and is frequently updated, making it possible for every child to identify his or her favorite rock and sports stars. The planetarium next door presents hourly astronomical shows (see "Regent's Park — The First Garden Suburb").

Guiness World of Records: A selection of records from the famous book are presented in a multimedia program combining sounds narration, reconstruction, and pictures (see "Soho — Bohemian Chic").

Light Fantastic Gallery of Holography: These incredible three-dimensional pictures, photographed with a special technique, make for a fascinating exhibition (see "Adelphi and Covent Garden — The World of Dickens and the World of Theater").

Museum of Mankind: Rotating exhibits feature many cultures and peoples, past and present (see "Mayfair — The Life of the Aristocracy").

Science Museum: The history of science along with the miracles of today's technology are presented in overwhelming and intriguing exhibits, many involving participation with push buttons and levers. The biggest attraction is the Exploration of Space exhibit — highly recommended (see "Knightsbridge and Kensington — Shops and Museums").

Natural History Museum: Ever seen a life-size skeleton of a dinosaur? In this museum you will, together with hundreds of others amazing objects from the world of nature (see "Knightsbridge and Kensington — Shops and Museums").

*L*ONDON

Geological Museum: The solar system, the structure of the earth, a simulated earthquake, a fabulous collection of gems, a fascinating collection of fossils — all these and more turn a visit to this museum into a unique experience (see "Knightsbridge and Kensington — Shops and Museums").

RAF Museum, **Battle of Britain Museum**, and **Bomber Command Museum**, in Hendon: For those who love flying, these three museums cover all aspects of the British air force. The first exhibits planes from the two world wars; the second is devoted exclusively to the Battle over Britain in World War II; the last contains all types of bombers, including the most recent models (see "Hampstead — An Artist's Retreat").

Bethnal Green Museum of Childhood: For children and for the young at heart. An abundance of exhibits, most of them of toys, from tin soldiers to doll houses, from model theaters to children's costumes, all located in one pleasant building (see "The East End — An Immigrant's Haven, a Seaman's History").

Thames Barrier Visitors Centre: The huge dam across the Thames is a unique engineering achievement, and can be reached by boat. The Centre features an audio-visual presentation and other related exhibits (see "Greenwich — A Different Time").

*L*ONDON

In the Lap of Nature — Parks and Gardens

There is nothing more beautiful than an English garden in bloom. The yellow carpets of daffodils are dotted with patches of red, pink, orange, and purple flowers, and the rhododendron, magnolia,and cherry trees bring new life to the surroundings with their festive blossoms. The English lawn is always green, and the deliberate disorder of many gardens creates a wild, enchanting, and mysterious mass of foliage. Few cities in the world can compete with London in its variety and beauty of royal and public parks and gardens.

Take advantage of your first sunny day, pack some food in a picnic hamper or knapsack, and set out to enjoy one of London's many garden paradises.

Royal Parks

The **royal parks** are so called because they are the private property of the Royal Family. In fact, although most of the royal parks are now open to the pulbic, they are still officially the property of the Crown.

St. James's Park

A lovely spot in the very heart of the city, St. James's Park is named for a medieval hospice for leprous girls that was located here before the grounds were purchased by King Henry VIII. There is no park more worthy of a royal affiliation. The oldest of the royal parks, St. James's is surrounded on all sides by palaces: Whitehall Palace, of which only the Banqueting House remains; St. James's Palace, built by Henry VIII and still the official residence of the monarchs of England; and Buckingham Palace, home address of the Royal Family.

The park is also close to various important government buildings, including the nearby Houses of Parliament and the Treasury. The official residence of the Prime Minister, 10 Downing Street, is a stone's throw away from the park.

A huge lake stretches across the centre of the park. Ducks, pelicans, and other water fowl are a main attraction here. You will probably find them resting in the shade of the trees on Duck Island by the edge of the lake at the eastern end of the park.

LONDON

The park is most beautiful in April and May, when the daffodils bloom, and in autumn during September and October. (Open daily 5am-midnight. Tel. 930-1793. St. James's Park or Charing Cross underground stations.)

Green Park

Located between Piccadilly Street and Buckingham Palace, this is indeed the greenest of London's parks, as it name suggests. With the exception of a few wild flowers, only grass and trees grow here. It is said that the park was once planted with flowerbeds, but when the wife of King Charles II saw him pick a bouquet for one of his mistresses, she angrily ordered that all the flowers in the park be pulled out, and so it has remained flowerless. (Open daily 5am-midnight. Tel. 930-1793. Green Park underground station.)

Richmond Park

This is the largest of the royal parks, spreading over an area of more than 2,500 acres. Charles I demarcated it in 1637 as an exclusive hunting area for royalty, and to this day it is dominated by flocks of meandering deer. Charles's enjoyment of the vast stretches of hunting ground was cut short by his execution in 1649. The park was given to the public shortly thereafter.

The park is ideal for picnics and nature hikes all year round. In May and June, when the rhododendrons bloom, it is a special treat. (Open dawn-dusk. Tel. 948-3209. Richmond underground station.)

For information on other royal parks, see the following chapters:

Hyde Park and Kensington Gardens: see "Hyde Park and Kensington Gardens — Oasis in the City."
Regent's Park: see "Regent's Park — The First Garden Suburb."
Greenwich Park: see "Greenwich — A Different Time."
Hampton Court and Bushy Park: see "Hampton Court — The Majesty of Kings."

Public Parks

In addition to the royal parks, London has other parks and green areas that are public property.

Hampstead Heath

A green paradise, Hampstead Heath lies on a tall hill in the north of London. Some 800 acres of grassy lawns, an unkempt grove, paths, lakes, and beds of flowers all serve to create one of the most enchanting and popular recreational sites in the city, and it is an all-time favorite of city residents. Two picturesque neighborhoods border the Heath: **Hampstead Village** to the southwest, and **Highgate** to the east.

At the top of **Parliament Hill**, located on the eastern side of the Heath, there is a spectacular view of the city; on a clear day you can see the enormous dome of St. Paul's Cathedral in the distance. On Sunday the hill is covered with kite-flyers, joggers, strollers, and swimmers jumping into the cold water of the small lakes at the foot of the hill.

In the northern part of the Heath on Hampstead Lane is **Kenwood House**, one of the most beautiful and interesting of London's mansions. The house was purchased by the Earl of Mansfield in 1754, and was enlarged for him by architect Robert Adam. In 1925 the house was bought by Lord Iveagh and bequeathed to the state. The art collection here includes works by Rembrandt, Rubens, Frans Hals, Vermeer, Turner, Gainsborough, and others. Chamber concerts are held inside, and in the summer open-air concerts are offered to the public. (Open daily, Apr.-Sept. 10am-7pm; Oct., Feb., and March until 5pm, Nov.-Jan. until 4pm. Free entrance. Tel. 348-1286. Hampstead underground station.)

Holland Park

The landscape at Holland Park is a mosaic of wild groves, cultivated lawns, and cheerful flower beds. Peacocks walk proudly about among flocks of geese here. The best season for a visit is in the spring. (Open 7am-dusk. Holland Park underground station.)

Until the mid 1900s the park was a private garden adjacent to the **Holland House** mansion. The house was built by John Thorpe in 1607 in the Tudor style. In the eighteenth and nineteenth centuries the third Baron of Holland made it a popular meeting place for important politicians, writers, and artists. Bombing during the Second World War severely damaged the house, leaving only its eastern wing, now part of the King George VI Memorial Hostel. In the summer there are plays and concerts here.

Battersea Park

This pleasant 200-acre park, also known as Battersea Fields, is situated on the southern side of the Thames in Chelsea. Once a popular location for illegal business affairs, it became infamous for the duel held here in 1829 between the Duke of Wellington and Lord Winchelsea. In 1853 the park was opened and an artificial lake was later added to the grounds. Among its treasures are a sub-tropical garden, a garden of wild flowers, flocks of deer at pasture, and the Japanese Peace Pagoda, erected in 1985. The

LONDON

The lake at St. James's Park

park offers children a playground and a small zoo. (Open 7:30am-dusk. Tel. 871-7530. Sloane Square underground station, then bus 19 to the park.)

Syon Park

One of the most charming parks in Greater London, this became the first botanical center in the kingdom in the sixteenth century. Its present form is based on the wonderful plan by the eighteenth-century parks designer, "Capability" Brown.

A special feature of the park is the **Great Conservatory**, a huge structure of metal and glass, and the first of this type in the world. The building, which was designed by Charles Fowler from 1821-1827, served as the inspiration for the construction of the Crystal Palace built in 1851 for the Great Exhibiton. Inside is an aviary, an aquarium, and a fine private collection of tropical plants. (Open daily, April-Sept. 10am-6pm, Oct.-March 10am-dusk. Entrance Fee. Tel. 560-0882. Gunnersby underground station, then buses 237, 267 to Brent Lea Gate in Brentford.)

The **Syon House and Gardens** are owned by the Duke of Northumberland, who still resides here. This stately mansion was constructed in 1415 and remodeled in 1762 by Robert Adam. The interior is exquisitely designed and furnished, with a splendid anteroom covered by a beautiful gilded ceiling. The adjoining gardens were first sculpted by "Capability" Brown during the time Adam was working on the house. The breathtaking rose garden

*L*ONDON

stretches for approximately six acres from the house. (House open Easter-Sept., noon-5pm. Sun.-Thurs. and in Oct. on Sun. only. Entrance fee. Garden open daily from 10am-6pm. Entrance fee. Combined ticket available. Tel. 560-0881.)

The **British Heritage Motor Museum** is also on the grounds of the park. The museum rotates a collection of 250 various prototype and early British-make cars dating from the late nineteenth century until today. (Open April-Sept., daily 10am-5:30pm; Oct.-March 10am-4pm. Entrance fee. Tel. 560-1378.)

Wimbledon Common

This expansive park, covering over 1,100 acres, has a bit of everything: a wild forest, lawns, golf courses and sports fields, long riding trails, and lakes. The windmill standing in the center, **Wimbledon Windmill**, was erected in 1817 and has been renovated and converted into a small museum depicting the history of windmilling. (Open April-Oct., Sat. and Sun. 2-5pm. Entrance fee. Tel. 788-7655. Southfields underground station, Wimbledon British Rail station.)

Overlooking the Centre Court on Church Road is the **Wimbledon Lawn Tennis Museum**, a treat for tennis-lovers. The museum's displays explore the history of lawn tennis, including tennis fashion and equipment. (Open Tues.-Sat. 11am-5pm, Sun. 2-5pm. Closed Sat.-Sun. prior to the championship and the middle Sun. of the championship. Entrance fee. Tel. 946-6131.)

Next to the park is **Wimbledon Village**, a large suburb with picturesque seventeenth-century buildings and old English pubs.

Crystal Palace Park

This 100-acre park earned its fame from the building that was moved here in 1854. The **Crystal Palace**, a huge hall of iron and glass, was designed by Sir Joseph Paxton for the Great Exhibition held in Hyde Park in 1851. Its construction served as a statement on the use of modern building materials. The palace was disassembled at the end of the fair in order to be moved to this park, which was specially designed to receive it. In 1936 the Crystal Palace went up in flames. Its ruins were removed from the site; you can now see its foundations close to the parking lot. (Open daily 8am-dusk. Free entrance. Tel. 778-7148. Crystal Palace British Rail station.)

Inside the park is the **National Sports Centre**, with various athletic facilities, including a modern sports stadium and an Olympic-size swimming pool. (Open daily. Membership fee. Tel. 778-0131.) You can go boating on one of the artificial lakes with islands. On one of the islands you will suddenly encounter huge figures of prehistoric creatures, the last remnants of the Great Exhibition.

Kew Botanical Gardens: see "Kew Gardens and Richmond — From the Finest of Parks to the Finest of Villages."

LONDON

"Musts"

There are many things to see and do in London, and one could easily spend several weeks touring the city. For those whose time is limited, however, there are certain sights which are "musts" for any visitor. Each sight mentioned here is explained in greater detail in the section dealing with that area. The list is presented in order of importance (to the extent that this is possible).

Houses of Parliament: The stronghold of British government. Particularly well-known is the Big Ben clock tower. Parliament Sq., SW1. House of Commons, tel. 219-4273. House of Lords, tel. 219-3107. Westminster underground station. (See "Whitehall and Westminster — Stronghold of the Regime.")

Westminster Abbey: One of the most important churches in England, with beautiful Gothic architecture. Coronations for most of the English monarchs of the last nine centuries have been held here. Nave, aisles, precinct open daily 8am-6pm, Wed. until 8pm. Free entrance. Ambulatory, transepts, chapels open Mon.-Fri. 9am-4:45pm, Sat. 9am-2:45pm and 3:45-5:45pm. Entrance fee. Parliament Square, SW1. Tel. 222-5152. Westminster underground station. (See "Whitehall and Westminster — Stronghold of the Regime.")

St. Paul's Cathedral: Most impressive church in the City, designed by Sir Christopher Wren. Its dome can be seen rising above the City for miles around. Open daily 7:30am-6pm, until 5pm in winter. Free entrance. Ambulatory, Crypt, and Whispering Gallery open 10am-4:15pm. Entrance fee. EC4. Tel. 248-2705. St. Paul's underground station. (See "The City of London — The Ancient Heart.")

British Museum: Houses one of the largest and most important archaeological collections in the world. Open Mon.-Sat. 10am-5pm, Sun. 2-6pm. Free entrance. Great Russell St., WC1. Tel. 636-1555. Tottenham Court Road underground station. (See "Bloomsbury — The Home of Writers and Poets.")

National Gallery: Contains one of the most comprehensive collections of European art, including all major schools of painting from the Middle Ages to the present day. Open Mon.-Sat. 10am-6pm, Sun. 2-6pm. Free entrance. Trafalgar Square, WC2. Tel. 839-3321. Charing Cross underground station. (See "St. James's and Buckingham Palace — The Royal District.")

Tower of London: The massive City fortress with sections dating to

Big Ben

*L*ONDON

The evening skyline of Whitehall and Westminster

the eleventh century. The **Crown Jewels** are housed in one of the towers here. Open March-Oct., Mon.-Sat. 9:30am-5pm, Sun. 2-5pm; Nov.-Feb., Mon.-Sat. 9:30am-4pm, closed Sun. EC3. Tel. 709-0765. Tower Hill underground station. (See "The City of London — The Ancient Heart.")

Trafalgar Square: Most central of London's squares. Site of the famous Nelson's Column, pigeons, and Christmas celebrations. Charing Cross underground station. (See "St. James's and Buckingham Palace — The Royal District.")

Piccadilly Circus: Traditional gathering place for youth under the Eros statue. Piccadilly Circus underground station. (See "Mayfair — The Life of Aristocracy.")

Tate Gallery: Contains a comprehensive collection of British painting from all periods, as well as a collection of international modern art. Open Mon.-Sat. 10am-5:50pm, Sun. 2-5:30pm. Free entrance. Millbank, SW1. Tel. 821-1313. Pimlico underground station. (See "Whitehall and Westminster — Stronghold of the Regime.")

Changing of the Guard at Buckingham Palace: This world-renowned ceremony takes place at 11:30 daily, in the summer and every other day in the winter, weather permitting. Green Park or Victoria underground station. (See "St. James's and Buckingham Palace — The Royal District.")

Victoria and Albert Museum: Contains rich collections of crafts and art from all corners of the world. Open Mon.-Thur. and Sat.

*L*ONDON

10am-5:50pm, Sun. 2:30-5:50pm. Free entrance. Cromwell Rd., SW7. Tel. 589-6371. South Kensington underground station. (See "Knightsbridge and Kensington — Shops and Museums.")

Oxford Street: London's well-known and popular street for shopping. Marble Arch, Bond Street, Oxford Circus, or Tottenham Court Road underground stations. (See "Oxford Street and St. Marylebone — A Shopping Paradise.")

Covent Garden: A charming area in central London with restaurants, stores, theaters, and the like. Covent Garden underground station. (See "Adelphi and Covent Garden — The World of Dickens and the World of Theater.")

Highly Recommended

Kew Gardens: The most famous botanical gardens in the world. Open daily 9:30am-dusk. Entrance fee. Tel. 940-1171. Kew Gardens underground station. (See "Kew Gardens and Richmond — From the Finest of Parks to the Finest of Villages.")

Harrods: The world-famous department store, which claims to sell everything your heart could desire. Knightsbridge, SW1. Knightsbridge underground station (See "Knightsbridge and Kensington — Shops and Museums.")

Selfridges: Another famous department store, located on Oxford Street. Bond Street underground station. (See "Oxford Street and St. Marylebone — A Shopping Paradise.")

Leicester Square: The heart of the West End entertainment center, and a focus of attraction for London's youth. Leicester Square underground station. (See "Soho — Bohemian Chic.")

South Bank Arts Centre: Theaters, concert halls, a film center, and an art gallery, located in one complex on the river bank. Waterloo underground station. (See "Southwark — The City South of the River.")

Regent Street: Stretches between Piccadilly Circus and Oxford Circus stations and is famous for the stores lining both sides. Piccadilly Circus or Oxford Circus underground stations. (See "Mayfair — The Life of the Aristocracy.")

Barbican Centre for Arts and Conferences: The arts complex built in the City, with theater and concert halls, an exhibition center, and various cultural activities. Barbican underground station. (See "The City of London — The Ancient Heart.")

Whitehall: A street of government offices, running from Trafalgar Square in the north to Parliament Square in the south. Charing Cross or Westminster underground stations. (See "Whitehall and Westminster — Stronghold of the Regime.")

LONDON

Excursions

One can sink into London as into the depths of the sea, exploring it endlessly. There is no dispute that in size, richness, variety, and intensity it surpasses all other cities in England. Nevertheless, England boasts many other fascinating sights and cities. In this chapter we briefly review some of the places that can be visited from London in a day or half a day, by car or train.

For another kind of excursion, England's canals and waterways offer a delightful alternative to city sightseeing.

Oxford

Oxford can be reached from Paddington Station in London. Trains leave once an hour, and the trip takes approximately one hour.

Oxford is a famous, charming university town, a town of medieval spires, paved alleyways, hundreds of bicycles, incredible book stores, and more. Oxford has a long history, and mention of its name is found as far back as the tenth century, although definite references date to the twelfth century, when the university was established.

Oxford University, which began with groups of students gathering around important instructors, grew and developed in the Middle Ages and eventually was organized into separate colleges. The oldest is **University College**, which began in 1249. Since its establishment, Oxford University has been an intellectual center from which many of the leaders of English society have graduated. During the Reformation the university suffered greatly, and in 1672 it was legally changed to an Anglican institution. This law was repealed some 200 years later, in 1871. The most recent change took place in 1920 when women were admitted to the university.

The university dominates life in the town of Oxford, and therefore it also dominates the sights on this tour. Visit the largest and most impressive of the colleges, **Christ Church**, which was established by Cardinal Wolsey in 1525. Located here is the beautiful cathedral of Oxford. (Open Mon.-Sat. 9am-5pm., Sun. 1-5pm.) **Pembroke College**, attended by Samuel Johnson, and **Magdalen College**, which boasts Edward Gibbon, Oscar Wilde, and Edward VIII among its former students, as well as the other colleges, should also be visited.

LONDON

Several other places in Oxford are worth visiting. The **Bodleian Library**, founded in 1602, contains an enormous collection of books and old manuscripts, and receives a copy of every new book printed in the United Kingdom. (Open Mon.-Fri. 9am-6pm., Sat. 9am-12:30pm. Free entrance; fee for some sections. Broad St. Tel. 0865-277000.) The **Ashmolean Museum** has a large art and archeology collection. (Open Tues.-Sat. 10am-4pm., Sun. 2-4pm. Entrance fee. Beaumont St. Tel. 0865-278000.)

For a natural break there are the grassy banks of the Cherwell and Thames rivers, along with **Oxford Botanic Garden**. (Open Mon.-Sat. 8:30am-5pm., Sun. 10am-noon and 2-6pm. Free entrance. Tel. 0865-276920.)

North of Oxford is Oxfordshire county, dotted with picturesque villages.

Tourist Information Centre: St. Aldates, Oxford OX1 1DY. Tel. (0865) 726871. Open Mon.-Sat. 9am-5:30pm.

Stratford-upon-Avon

Stratford-upon-Avon can be reached from Euston Station in London, via Coventry, where you can take a bus the rest of the way. The trip takes approximately two hours. There is also a bus service from Oxford, a trip of an hour and twenty minutes.

With its old streets and lovely houses, Stratford-upon-Avon preserves the spirit of the past with grace. It is particularly famous as the place of birth of the great playwright, William Shakespeare, who was born here in 1504. The home in which he was born has been kept as a museum, **Shakespeare's Birthplace**. (Open April-Oct., Mon.-Sat. 9am-6pm, Sun. 10am-6pm; Nov.-March, Mon.-Sat. 9am-4:30pm, Sun. 1:30-4:30pm. Entrance fee. Henley St. Tel. 0789-204016.)

The **Royal Shakespeare Theatre** presents his work on a permanent basis in the town. (Box office tel. 0789-295623.) Tourist agencies in London offer a wide range of package deals that usually include a visit to the city, overnight accommodation, and a performance.

Tourist Information Centre: Judith Shakespeare's House, 1 High St., Stratford-upon-Avon, Warwickshire CV37 6AU. Tel. (0789) 293127. Open April-Sept., Mon.-Sat. 9am-5:30pm, Sun. 2-5pm; Oct.-March, Mon.-Sat. 10:30am-4:30pm, closed Sun.

Cambridge

Cambridge can be reached from the Liverpool Street or King's Cross Stations in London. Trains leave hourly. The trip takes an

*L*ONDON

hour from Liverpool and an hour and twenty minutes from King's Cross.

This is also a beautiful university city, located along the banks of the Cam River. There are those who claim that the university here was founded even before Oxford. In contrast to Oxford, the buildings of **Cambridge University** are not situated in a maze of narrow lanes, but in a spacious area by the river.

The university began to develop in the twelfth century, and gained its reputation when the Dutch humanist Erasmus arrived in 1510. The university is now composed of 31 colleges, housed in charming old buildings. Particularly noteworthy are **King's College**, with its fifteenth-century Gothic chapel, and **Trinity College**, which was attended by Sir Isaac Newton. The **Fitzwilliam Museum** contains an important art and antiquities collection. (Open Tues.-Sat. 10am-5pm, Sun. 2:15-5pm. Free entrance. Trumpington St. Tel. 0223-332900.)

Tourist Information Centre: Wheeler St., Cambridge CB2 3QB. Tel. (0223) 322640. Open April-Oct., Mon.-Fri. 9am-6pm, until 7pm July and August, Sat. 9am-5pm; Sun. open May-Sept. 10:30am-3:30pm; Nov.-March, Mon.-Fri. 9am-5:30pm, Sat. 9am-5pm, closed Sun.

Bath

Bath can be reached from Paddington Station in London. The trip takes an hour and a half.

Named for its famous bath houses, this is the only place in Britain that nature has blessed with hot springs. The springs were put to use as early as the first century A.D. when the Romans built a network of public bathhouses. These have been excavated and restored, and can be seen today.

In the eighteenth century, Bath became the most fashionable health spa in Britain; its growth and beauty are generally attributed to this period. The city is built on the banks of the Avon River, surrounded by rolling hills.

Bath is full of architectural gems, museums, and touring sights. The **Roman Baths Museum** is built around the hot springs that made the town famous. It is one of Britain's most impressive ancient Roman remains. (Open March-Oct., daily 9am-6pm, until 7pm in July and August; Nov.-Feb., Mon.-Sat. 9am-5pm, Sun. 10am-5pm. Entrance fee. Stoll St. Tel. 0225-461111.) Nearby is the **Bath Abbey**, built in the Perpendicular style, with a beautiful fan-vaulted ceiling.

The city is also noted for its eighteenth-century Palladian architecture and terrace houses, built by John Wood, Sr., and John Wood, Jr. Their work is exemplified in the Georgian City, a series

*L*_ONDON_

of buildings they designed. Most noteworthy is the **Royal Crescent**, the younger John Wood's most famous work of architecture. It is a curving row of some thirty houses. No. 1 has been fully restored as an eighteenth-century house. (Open March-Christmas, Tues.-Sat. 11am-5pm, Sun. 2-5pm. Entrance fee. Tel. 0225-28126.)

Robert Adam also has a fine piece of architecture here, the **Pulteney Bridge**. Dating to 1774, it is lined with shops and stretches over the Avon River. The embankment along the river is quite attractive.

Tourist Information Centre: Abbey Church Yard, Bath BA1 1LY. Tel. (0225) 462831. Open May-Sept., Mon.-Sat. 9:30am-7pm, Sun. 10am-4pm; Oct.-April, Mon.-Sat. 9:30am-5pm, closed Sun.

Stonehenge

Stonehenge is in the middle of the Salisbury Plain and can be reached only by car or guided tour. This famous prehistoric site is composed of two circles of megaliths, some of which are connected to one another by huge stone lintels. How these were raised is one of the great mysteries of Stonehenge. Two stages are apparent in the construction. The first is from the late Neolithic period (C. 1800 B.C.), when a ditch was dug, along with 56 pits containing human ashes. During this time the bluestones were brought to the site, presumably from Wales. The second stage was during the Early Bronze Age (1650-1500 B.C.), when huge sandstones were brought and arranged in a circle topped by the bluestones. The technical ability displayed in the site is unbelievably accurate.

It is not clear what the purpose of the site was, although it is thought that it was used for a ceremony or ritual. On the day of the summer solstice in June, the sun shines precisely above a single stone that stands outside of the circle; this has led some researchers to believe that Stonehenge was an ancient temple to the sun.

Contact the British Tourist Authority in London for information on guided tours to Stonehenge.

Canterbury

Canterbury can be reached from Victoria Station in London to Canterbury East Station, and from Charing Cross Station to Canterbury West Station. Trains leave once an hour, and the trip takes half an hour.

Canterbury is a charming medieval city, with lots of paved paths and quaint stores. A substantial part of its ancient city wall, composed of unworked flint stones, has been preserved. Canterbury is known

*L*ONDON

especially for its famous Gothic **cathedral**, where Archbishop Thomas Becket was murdered in 1170. (Open Mon.-Sat. 8:45am-7pm, until 5pm in winter, Sun. 12:30-2pm and for services. Free entrance. Tel. 0227-762862.)

Becket had a falling out with Henry II, who wanted to reduce Church power. He was murdered by the king's knights. Under public pressure Henry II repented and Becket was canonized. His tomb became a pilgrimage site, as described by Chaucer in the classic *Canterbury Tales*. The tomb was later pillaged and destroyed by Henry VIII. Buried here are King Henry IV and Edward the Black Prince, the son of Edward III, who gained this title after wearing a black suit of armor. The cathedral is particularly noted for its exquisite stained-glass windows and a fascinating **crypt**. (Open daily 10am-4:30pm.)

Various periods are represented in Canterbury. The **Roman Mosaic** is a fine example of a Roman pavement. (Open April-Sept., Mon.-Sat. 10am-1pm and 2-5pm, Oct.-March, Mon.-Sat. 2-4pm. Closing for repairs Christmas 1989. Located underneath the Long Market. Tel. 0227-452747.)

A **Norman Keep**, all that remains of a ruined fortress can be seen at the edge of town. At night it is illuminated by floodlights.

The Weavers, a renovated sixteenth-century weaver's house, has now been divided into a number of small shops featuring British crafts. A few restaurants are also located here.

The newest attraction in Canterbury is the **Pilgrims Way Centre**, a recreation of Chaucer's medieval England. This walk-through experience illustrates five of his *Tales* and is housed in an old church. (Open daily 9am-6pm. Entrance fee. St. Margaret's St. Tel. 0227-454888.)

Visitor Information Centre: 34 St. Margaret's St., Canterbury, Kent CT1 2TG. Tel. (0227) 766567. Open Mon.-Sat. 9:30am-6pm, until 5:30pm in winter, Sun. 10am-4pm, closed in winter.

Brighton

Brighton can be reached from Victoria Station in London. Trains leave hourly, and the trip takes an hour.

A vacation town on the beach of the British Channel, Brighton is famous for its **Royal Pavilion**. The exotic Pavilion, at one time a seaside palace of King George IV, was originally constructed as a small classical villa in 1787 by Henry Holland. It was reconstructed by John Nash from 1815-1822, with the exterior styled after Indian palaces. The splendid interior is overwhelmingly Chinese, although there are some furnishings and works of art on permanent loan

*L*ONDON

from the queen. The building is currently being restored and certain areas will be closed for two years, but it still open to visitors. (Open daily, June-Sept. 10am-6pm, Oct-May 10am-5pm. Entrance fee.)

If you seek the intoxication of ocean air, Brighton has developed vacation services and lovely long beaches.

Tourist Information Centre: Marlborough House, 54 Old Steine, Brighton, East Suffix BN1 1EQ. Tel. (0273) 23755 or 27560. Open Mon.-Sat., June-Sept. 9am-6pm, until 5pm Oct.-May; Sat., Easter-June 9am-12:30pm; Sun., July-Sept. 10am-6pm, Oct.-June closed.

West. St. Tourist Information Centre: open Easter-Sept., Wed.-Sun. 10am-6pm, Tues. 1pm-6pm.

A Sail on the Canals and Waterways of England

If you are tired of the crowds and bustle of London, or if you are interested in enjoying nature in a unique way, you should try traveling the canals and waterways of England.

The industrial revolution thrust the British Empire into the modern era in the early nineteenth century, creating industrial centers throughout the island. In order to transport raw materials and merchandise from one point to another, a network of narrow canals connecting the natural waterways was built to accommodate the barges carrying freight.

After improvements in land transportation, particularly in the twentieth century, the canals were abandoned. They remained neglected for a long period, until the initiative was taken to utilize them for recreation and vacations.

Today there are some 2000 miles of canals and waterways in Britain. The *British Waterways Board* maintains the canals and publishes maps and guides. (Located at Melbury House, Melbury Terrace, London NW1 6JX. Tel. (01) 262-6711.)

Numerous boat rental companies operate throughout Britain. Prices vary from one to another, and depend on the season. Rental fees are generally per boat, per week, although shorter periods are possible. There are self-skipper boats sleeping two to twelve, which include bedding, a small, fully-equipped kitchen, lavatories, and showers; some boats provide color televisions and other such amenities. Floating hotels are also available. Sleeping up to twelve, they come with a captain and crew as well as the standard conveniences.

Four main agencies represent the various boating companies.

*L*ONDON

U.K. Waterway Holidays Ltd.: Welton Hythe, Daventry, Northamptonshire NN11 5LG. Tel. (0327) 843773.
Blakes Holidays: Roxham, Norwich NR12 8DH. Tel. (06053) 2911.
Boat Enquiries: 45 Botley Rd., Oxford OX2 OPT. Tel. (0865) 727288.
Hoseasons Holidays Ltd.: Sunway House, Lowestoft, Norfolk NR32 3LT. Tel. (0502) 501010.

*L*ONDON

Making the Most of Your Stay

Wining and Dining

Restaurants

London is a cosmopolitan, dynamic city offering a wealth of restaurants of every type, color, and taste. You will find a wide selection of ethnic restaurants, pubs that serve traditional English food, and chains such as McDonald's.

Prices vary. You can satisfy yourself in a fast-food restaurant for £3, and you may pay £50 or more per guest in one of London's more prestigious enterprises. The quality of service also varies from place to place. Cordial service does not necessarily testify to good food, and vice versa.

In many restaurants you will be billed a cover charge, usually for the bread and butter that are not included on the menu, and perhaps also for entertainment. The cover charge may range from 15p to £3-£4, depending on the restaurant and its prices. Some restaurants may ask for a over charge of up to ten pounds in return for a show accompanying the meal.

Not all restaurants are licensed to serve wine at all hours — check in advance. Sometimes waiters will request that you order your wine first so that they are not forced to refuse you after the allowed hours.

The restaurants below have been classified into the following categories, based on prices per person:

    A — over £25
    B — up to £25
    C — up to £15
    D — up to £7

Reserve a table in advance at expensive restaurants. Most, but not all, honor credit cards. In pubs payment is usually in cash.

The range of restaurants in London is great. The following list is only a small, varied selection of quality eating and drinking establishments that are easily accessible to the hungry traveler.

Bon appetit!

LONDON

British
British food is not especially rich or exotic, but it is usually filling, nutritious, and reasonably priced.

A typical British breakfast consists of eggs and bacon, and sometimes sausage, accompanied by toast, butter and jam, and the inevitable cup of tea with milk. Lunch is usually light, as most people are at work and make do with fast food such as fish and chips. In the afternoon the British sit for tea, eating delicacies such as hot scones with cream or marmelade, and thin cucumber sandwiches. A typically British evening meal consists of steak and kidney pie, roast beef with Yorkshire pudding, cottage or shepherd's pie and steamed vegetables. Dessert might feature an English trifle or a rich custard.

Bates: 11 Henrietta St., WC2. Tel. 240-7600. Covent Garden underground station. (C) Limited selection of British food, with a French influence.
Plummers: 33 King St., WC2. Tel. 240-2534. Covent Garden underground station. (C) Pleasant atmosphere with good traditional English food.
Porters: 17 Henrietta St., WC2. Tel. 836-6466. Covent Garden underground station. (D) Typical British food. Courteous service.
Rules: 35 Maiden Lane, WC2. Tel. 836-5314. Covent Garden underground station. (B) Highly reputable since its establishment in 1798. Hearty meals, with roast beef from the trolley as a specialty.
Simpson's-in-the-Strand Grand Divan Tavern: 100 Strand, WC2. Tel. 836-9112. Charing Cross underground station. (B) An air of by-gone days. Very traditional kitchen.
The Printers Pie: 60 Fleet St., EC4. Tel. 353-8861. Blackfriars underground station. (C) The world of the Fleet Street newspaper industry is present here. Strictly British cuisine.
Ye Olde Cheshire Cheese: 145 Fleet St., EC4. Tel. 353-6170. Blackfriars underground station. (C) A pub on the ground floor and a restaurant upstairs. One of the oldest establishments in town, it predates the Great Fire. Go for the old English ambience and matching cuisine.
The Samuel Pepys: Brooks Wharf, 48 Upper Thames St., EC4. Tel. 248-3048. Blackfriars underground staiton. (C) On the river bank. Traditional English cuisine, featuring recipes from Pepys's time.
The Ritz: Piccadilly St., W1. Tel. 493-8181. Green Park underground station. (A) A must for afternoon tea. Luxurious and expensive.
Lockets: Marsham Court, Marsham St., SW1. Tel. 834-9552. St. James's Park underground station. (B) Pleasant atmosphere and fairly priced. A popular lunch stop for members of Parliament.

Chinese
Memories of China: 67-69 Ebury St., SW1. Tel. 730-7734/4276.

LONDON

Victoria underground station. (B) Features a variety of regional Chinese cuisine. A good value.

Mr. Kai of Mayfair: 65 South Audley St., W1. Tel. 493-8988. Bond St. underground station. (B) A nice selection specializing in Peking dishes. Somewhat pricey.

Kowloon: 21 Gerrard St., W1. Tel. 437-0148. Leicester Sq. underground station. (D) One of the first Chinese cake shops in Europe. Offers a wide variety of both sweet and savory cakes. Excellent food at very reasonable prices.

Fung Shing: 15 Lisle St., WC1. Tel. 437-1539. Leicester Sq. underground station. (C) Varied and tasty food, gourmet Cantonese.

Poons: 27 Lisle St., WC2. Tel. 437-4549. Leicester Sq. underground station. (C) Small and homey; very good food at reasonable prices.

Mr. Kong: 21 Lisle St., WC1. Tel. 437-7341. Leicester Sq. underground station. (D) Excellent Cantonese kitchen. Very good service.

Tiger Lee: 251 Old Brompton Rd., SW5. Tel. 370-2323/5970. Earl's Court underground station. (B) Excellent quality. Specializing in Cantonese fish dishes.

Indian

Sharuna: 107 Great Russell St., WC1. Tel. 636-5922. Tottenham Court Rd. underground station. (D) Vegetarian, self service.

Shan Restaurant: 200 Shaftesbury Ave., WC2. Tel. 240-3348. Covent Garden underground station. (D) Vegetarian cuisine with an emphasis on freshness. A good value.

Hare Krishna Curry House: 1 Hanway St., W1. Tel. 636-5262. Tottenham Court Rd. underground station. (D) Especially good vegetarian dishes.

Agra: 135-137 Whitfield St., W1. Tel. 387-8833. Warren St. underground station. (B) Pleasant atmosphere. Specializes in tandoori dishes.

Trusha: 11-12 Dean St., W1. Tel. 437-3559. Tottenham Corut Rd. underground station. (B) Tandoori cuisine. Charming surroundings and courteous service.

The Veeraswamy: 99 Regent St., W1. Tel. 734-1401. Piccadilly Circus underground station. (C) Imaginative regional menu. Overlooks Regent Street.

Kundan: 3 Horseferry Rd., SW1. Tel. 834-3434/3211. Victoria underground station. (C) Good service and delicious food in a spacious setting.

Shezan: 16-22 Cheval Place, off Montpelier St., SW7. Tel. 589-0314. Knightsbridge underground station. (B) Professional service and tastefully decorated. Dishes are delicately spiced.

Greek

Beotys: 79 St. Martin's Lane, WC2. Tel. 836-8768. Leicester Sq.

*L*ONDON

underground station. (C) Courteous service and good traditional Greek food.

Rodos: 59 St. Giles High St., WC2. Tel. 836-3177. Tottenham Court Rd. underground station. (C) Excellent cuisine at a reasonable price. Comfortable atmosphere.

Mykonos: 17 Frith St., W1. Tel. 437-3603 or 734-3011. Tottenham Court Rd. underground station. (D) Located at this site for more than forty years. Food continues to be inexpensive and delicious.

White Tower: 1 Percy St., W1. Tel. 636-8141. Tottenham Court Rd. underground station. (B) Professional service and a good variety of Greek and international dishes.

Portuguese

Ports: 11 Beauchamp Place, SW3. Tel. 581-3837. Knightsbridge underground station. (C) Very pleasant atmosphere. Exotic and varied cuisine with an extensive Portuguese wine list.

Spanish

Martinez: 25 Swallow St. W1. Tel. 734-5066. Piccadilly Circus underground station. (B) Long-standing with beautiful surroundings. Professional and courteous service.

Bar Escoba: 102 Old Brompton Rd., SW7. Tel. 373-2403. Gloucester Rd. underground station. (D) Delightful, lively atmosphere. Includes a good *tapas* bar.

Swiss

Chesa: 10 Wardour St., W1. Piccadilly Circus underground station. Tel. 734-1291. (C) The best of five Swiss restaurants in the Swiss Centre.

Eastern European

The Gay Hussar: 2 Greek St., W1. Tel. 437-0973. Tottenham Court Rd. underground station. (C) Excellent Hungarian food with an especially good fixed-price lunch menu.

Old Budapest: 6 Greek St., W1. Tel. 437-2006. Tottenham Court Rd. underground station. (C) Superb Hungarian restaurant with an "old world" atmosphere.

Luba's Bistro: 6 Yeoman's Row, SW3. Tel. 589-2950. Knightsbridge underground station. (C) Very popular. Delicious traditional Russian cuisine.

Daquise: 20 Thurloe St., SW7. Tel. 589-6117. South Kensington underground station. (D) Excellent Polish food.

Japanese

Fuji: 36-40 Brewer St., W1. Tel. 734-0957. Piccadilly Circus underground station. (A) Traditional, extremely varied Japanese cuisine. Tastefully decorated.

Ikeda: 30 Brook St., W1. Tel. 629-2730. Bond St. underground

station. (B) Charming restaurant. Excellent food and extremely good service.
Kitchen Yakitori: 12 Lancashire Court, off New Bond St., W1. Tel. 629-9984. Bond street underground station. (C) Pleasant and lively atmosphere. Good food at reasonable prices.
Miyama: 38 Clarges St., W1. Tel. 499-2443. Green Park underground station. (A) Especially plush and priced accordingly. Food is excellent and service is reasonable.
Suntory: 72-73 St. James's St., SW1. Tel. 409-0201. Green Park underground station. (B) Fine cuisine and courteous service.

Italian
Convent Garden Pasta Bar: 30 Henrietta St., WC2. Tel. 836-8396. Covent Garden underground station. (D) Several types of pasta and a variety of sauces. A very pleasant spot and well worth a visit.
Luigi's: 15 Tavistock St., WC2. Tel. 240-1795. Covent Garden underground station. (C) An Italian treat at reasonable prices. Popular among theater people.
Amalfi: 29-31 Old Compton St., W1. Tel. 437-7284, Leicester Sq. underground station. (C) Superb food. Reasonably priced.
Leoni's Quo Vadis: 26-29 Dean St., W1. Tel. 437-4809/9585. Leicester Sq. underground station. (B) In the heart of Soho. Professional service and good food.
Meridiana: 169 Fulham Rd., SW3. Tel. 589-8815. South Kensington underground station. (B) Good food. Elegant, with high prices.
Angelo's: Blackfriars Lane, EC4. Blackfriars underground station. (C) Lunch only. Good food and friendly service.

Middle Eastern
Omar Khayyam: Mitre House, 177 Regent St., W1. Tel. 437-3000. Oxford Circus underground station. (B) Traditional Middle Eastern cuisine served in large portions. Meals are accompanied by extensive entertainment, usually with a high cover charge.
Topkapi: 25 Marylebone High St., W1. Tel. 486-1872. Baker St. underground station. (C) Serving mainly Turkish cuisine. Courteous service.
Maroush II: 38 Beauchamp Place, SW3. Tel. 581-5434. Knightsbridge underground station. (B) Plush. Sensational food complemented by courteous service.

Jewish and Israeli
"Kosher" indicates that the restaurant is under rabbinical supervision.

Kosher Meat Restaurant: B'nai B'rith Hillel House, 1-2 Endsleigh St., WC1. Tel. 388-0801. Euston Sq. underground station. (D) Kosher. Self-service. Good for students on a tight budget.
Rubins: 39 Great Windmill St., W1. Tel. 437-8429. Piccadilly Circus

LONDON

underground station. (D) Fine Jewish cuisine. Pleasant atmosphere.
Bloom's: 90 Whitechapel High St., E1. Tel. 247-6001. Aldgate East underground station. (C) Kosher. The most famous Jewish restaurant in town.
The Nosherie: 12-13 Greville St., EC1. Tel. 242-1591. Chancery Lane underground station. (D) Excellent East European Jewish cuisine. Very reasonably priced.
Rothschilds: 8-10 Monkville Parade, Finchley Rd., Temple Fortune, NW11. Tel. 458-4750. Golders Green underground station. (C) Kosher Chinese. Reasonably priced good food.
B'Tay Avon: 853-855 Finchley Rd., NW11. Tel. 455-0692. Golders Green underground station. (D) Kosher. Vegetarian cuisine, run by the Jewish Vegetarian Society. Homey environment.
Falafel House: 95 Haverstock Hill, NW3. Tel. 722-6187. Chalk Farm underground station. (C) Typical Israeli cuisine.

North and Central American
Café Pacifico: 5 Langley St., WC2. Tel. 379-7728. Covent Garden underground station. (C) Reasonably priced Mexican-American cuisine.
Joe Allen: 13 Exeter St., WC2. Tel. 836-0651. Covent Garden underground station. (C) A wide variety of American dishes.
La Cucaracha: 12 Greek St., W1. Tel. 734-2253. Tottenham Court Rd. underground station. (C) Mexican food at a good value.
L.A. Café: 163 Knightsbridge, SW7. Tel. 589-7077. Knightsbridge underground station. (C) Food and atmosphere typically American.

American-style Pizza
Pizzeria chains are located throughout the city. Recommended are *Pizzaland* and *Deep Pan Pizza*. Check the telephone directory for the addresses and telephone numbers.

French
Boulestin: 1A Henrietta St., WC2. Tel. 836-7061. Covent Garden underground station. (B) Charming setting. Excellent, high-quality food.
Inigo Jones: 14 Garrick St., WC2. Tel. 836-6456. Covent Garden underground station. (A) High-quality nouvelle cuisine. Expensive, but a good value.
Au Jardin des Gourmets: 5 Greek St., W1. Tel. 437-1816. Tottenham Court Rd. underground station. (C) Reasonably priced superb food. Very pleasant.
Le Gavroche: 43 Upper Brook St., W1. Tel. 408-0881. Marble Arch underground station. (A) Highly recommended. Superb food and service.
Rue St. Jacques: 5 Charlotte St., W1. Tel. 637-0222. Goodge St. underground station. (A) Delicious, traditional cuisine in a beautiful setting.

*L*ONDON

Pubs

To many, pubs, or public houses, are as English as Buckingham Palace and afternoon tea. There are enough pubs in London to satisfy the most enthusiastic drinkers.

You might notice two separate entrance doors on the facade of some pubs, or double doors on others. Separate entrances were once common in London's pubs: the working class used one entrance, and seating area, and the middle class another. Double doors seen at other pubs have been installed to serve a reminder of this discriminatory tradition.

Beer, no doubt, is the drink that dominates the check-pads of waiters, waitresses, and bartenders in London's pubs. The novice drinker might be interested in understanding some beer basics. While there are hundreds of beer brands, London's pubs serve four distinct types of beer: *lager*, a traditional flavor; *bitter*, with a bitter taste; *guiness*, a strong black beer usually served lukewarm; and *Real Ale*, beer made the old fashioned way — with all natural ingredients. Real Ale is much stronger than most beers. It is not served in all pubs, yet you might find some that specialize in this type of brew.

Some pubs serve other alcoholic drinks and British food. Children under the age of 14 are not permitted in pubs and those under 18 are not served alcoholic beverages.

Although pub hours may vary, they are generally open Monday through Saturday, from 10am-11pm. On Sunday and holidays they are open from noon-3pm and from 7pm-10:30pm.

Check the weekly entertainment magazines for information on pub walks.

The following is a selection pubs worth a visit:

Center
Argyl-Arms: 18 Argyll St., WC1. A huge Victorian-style pub featuring lots of mirrors.
Baker and Oven: 10 Paddington St., W1. The pub's basement is now a restaurant that specializes in home-made pies baked in a Victorian oven.
Bunch of Grapes: 16 Shepherd Market, W1. Enjoy the colorful crowd and sit outside on a nice day. Not far from Piccadilly Circus.
De Hams: 11 Macclesfield St., W1. A Victorian pub close to Shaftesbury Ave. The walls are lined with paper money from all over the world.
Lamb and Flag: 33 Rose St., WC2. A small pub with oak paneling. Serves good beer and food. Near Covent Garden. Charles Dickens was a customer.

LONDON

Sun in Splendour: 7 Portobello Rd., W11. In the heart of Portobello Road Market. A charming location with a small garden. Excellent food.

Southwest

Admiral Codrington: 17 Mossop St., SW3. In Chelsea. Displays an interesting collection of jars. Use the patio on a sunny day. French cuisine.

Red Lion: 48 Parliament St., SW1. One of the few places to eat and drink in Whitehall.

Cockney Pride: 6 Jermyn St., SW1. A Cockney-style pub with live piano music. Near Piccadilly Circus.

Anchor: 1 Bankside, SE1. Enjoy the excellent restaurant and beautiful view of St. Paul's across the river. Expensive.

East

Orkens Inn by the Tower: St. Katharine's Way, E1. At St. Katharine's Dock, near the Tower of London.

George and Vulture: 3 Castle Court, EC3V. Opened its doors as an inn in 1175 and is one of the oldest pubs in the world. Daniel Defoe and Charles Dickens were customers here.

Mayflower: 117 Rotherhithe St., SE16. Located at the site where the pilgrims boarded the ship of the same name. The original pub was destroyed in World War II. The present one is decorated in keeping with its historical connection.

North

Holly Bush: 22 Holly Mount St. NW3. Established in 1796. Serves Real Ale.

Spaniards Inn: Spaniards Rd., Hampstead Heath NW3. A charming spot near the Heath with a rose garden and exotic birds.

King's Head: 115 Upper St., N1. A beautifully decorated pub with live music and a separate pub theater. Interesting clientele.

New Black Cup: 171 Camden High St., NW1. Stages cabaret shows.

Wine Bars

The wine bar is a combination of a pub and restaurant that features a wide selection of wine and beer. Prices vary and some can be expensive. Many provide the perfect atmosphere for a romantic evening. Wine bars are generally open the same hours as pubs.

Center

Brahms & Liszt: 19 Russell St., WC2. Popular Covent Garden location. Good wine-by-the-glass selection.

Cork & Bottle: 44-46 Cranpourne St., WC2. Extensive wine list and good food.

LONDON

Gordon's Wine Bar: 47 Villiers St., WC2. A historic atmosphere in a cellar location near Adelphi.

Southwest
The Ebury: 139 Ebury St., SW1. Dark green interior. Occasionally has live classical music.
Le Bouzy Rouge: 221 King's Rd., SW3. Intimate setting. Interesting international food, including Ethiopian dishes, with a more standard wine list.
The Archduke: Concert Hall Approach, SE1. Near the South Bank Arts Centre. Live jazz in the evenings.

East
El Vino: 47 Fleet St., EC4. Traditional establishment with a dress code. Good wine list.
The Pavilion: Finsbury Circus Gardens, EC2. Pleasant view of gardens in this city location.
Leadenhall Wine Bar: 27 Leadenhall Market, EC3. Elegant setting right next to the busy market. Attractive and expensive wine list.

North
Boos: 1 Glentworth St., NW1. Renovated basement setting with a friendly ambience.

London

Culture and Entertainment

After the sun sets, London's pulse begins to race and the electricity of the city's nightlife kicks on. Countless stage crews around the city, especially in the West End, prepare halls, back-drops, orchestra pits, and sets as culture-lovers flood the dozens of theaters, movie houses, auditoriums, and clubs.

The city offers a wealth of entertainment, whatever your pleasure, from theaters to operas, ballets, symphony concerts, to pop music performances, cabarets, and film.

When you arrive in London, you should buy one of the entertainment weeklies. *Time Out*, *What's on & Where to go*, and *City Limits* are published every Wednesday and are chock-full of information on the cultural life in the city, including theatrical productions, concerts, films, exhibitions, museums, walking tours, sports, and other events.

After midnight most public transportation stops, so you will most likely have to use a cab to move on.

Theater

West End Theater

London is replete with theaters. Many classical and world-famous productions begin their long tours as sure best-sellers on the central stages of the West End, the theater capital. Here the splendid theaters are adorned with domed ceilings, velvet seats, and plush carpets. West End theater goers dressed in their finest add to the overall posh ambience.

Some popular long running performances include *The Phantom of the Opera*, *Les Miserables*, *Cats*, and *Starlight Express*.

Tickets for the most popular plays, particularly musicals, may need to be purchased months in advance. If the production has been on stage for quite a while, you can buy tickets at an agency, but these are usually more expensive. Many of the theaters have matinées during the week, with less expensive seats. Another way to obtain tickets is to arrive at the theater an hour before the performance, and see if any tickets have been returned to the box office. You may also be assisted by your hotel concierge, who can give you ticket information. On Sunday there are usually no theater performances.

If you plan your trip to London several months in advance, your

LONDON

travel agent can help you purchase tickets, or you can order them from an agency, such as *Keith Prowse*, Banda House, Cambridge Grove, Hammersmith, W6. Tel. 741-7441.

While you are staying in the city, try your luck at the *Half-Price Ticket Booth*, sponsored by the Society of West End Theatres and located in Leicester Square. Here you can purchase any tickets remaining for the same day's performance at half the price. The booth is open Mon.-Sat. noon-2pm. for matinées, and 2:30-6:30pm for evening shows. The Ticket Booth can not be reached by telephone.

Fringe Theater

For a different kind of theater experience visit one of London's famous fringe theaters, which are spread all over the city, from ancient halls and houses to pubs. Fringe productions range from the conventional to the innovative, to the bold and audacious. Numerous highly successful productions start in London's fringe theaters, then move to the West End after they have gained critical acclaim and audience appeal.

Tickets for many fringe theater productions, which are relatively inexpensive and usually easier to obtain, even on the evening of the performance, can be purchased at the theater's box office or the central *Fringe Theatre Box Office*, Duke of York Theatre, St. Martin's Lane, WC2. Tel. 379-6002.

Pub Theater

Some fringe productions are performed in pubs, thus adding the pub atmosphere to the theater experience. This clever English innovation includes beer throughout and a dinner served before performances. During intermission or after the play, actors leave their makeshift stages and mingle with the audience (do not be surprised to discover famous actors among the cast). Prices for a combination package of dinner and theater are moderate.

Open-Air Theater

In Regent's Park there is an Open-Air Theater that stages performances during the summer, weather permitting. Consult the entertainment weeklies for more detailed information on this or other open-air theaters.

Shakespearean Theater

The *Royal Shakespeare Company* performs in the *Barbican Theatre* at the Barbican Centre, EC2. Box office tel. 628-8795. Moorgate or Barbican underground station. Shakespeare's plays, other classics, and newer performances are continually staged here, either by this company or by others. The company also runs a workshop theater in *The Pit* at the Barbican. You can also travel to Shakespeare's birthplace, Stratford-upon-Avon, to watch one of his

LONDON

plays at the *Royal Shakespeare Theatre*. Package tours, including travel, tickets, and accommodation, are available. Ask at any of the Tourist Information Centres.

Film

Most current popular films, both English and foreign, can be seen in London. Foreign films are usually shown in the original language with subtitles, or dubbed, in which case this is clearly indicated.

Standard classification of movies should be noted:

18 — admission for adults only, from age 18 and up
15 — admission from age 15 and up
PG — intended for general audiences, but likely to include parts unsuitable for small children
U — suitable for the entire family

Popular films are shown in the West End, usually several times a day, so you do not have to wait until the evening.

Old and new films, international screenings, and special previews can be seen at the *National Film Theatre* at the South Bank Arts Centre. To purchase a ticket you must join a members club. Temporary weekly membership is available for a nominal fee. Lectures by famous film directors are also given at the National Film Theatre. Tel. 928-3232. Waterloo or Embankment underground station.

Opera

There are two opera houses in London within a five minute's walk from one another:

Royal Opera House: Bow St., WC2, Covent Garden. Box office tel. 240-1066. Covent Garden underground station. Great productions of the best of the world's operas are performed at the Royal Opera House, which is also the home of the *Royal Ballet*. Tickets should be ordered in advance, otherwise they are almost impossible to obtain. Try your luck on the morning of the performance, or two hours before it is due to start.

London Coliseum: St. Martin's Lane, WC2, Covent Garden. Box office tel. 836-3161. Covent Garden underground station. The English National Opera presents operatic productions in the English language here in London's huge coliseum.

Ballet

In addition to the *Royal Ballet*, which performs at the Royal Opera House, there are several other highly regarded ballet companies

LONDON

in London. The _London Festival Ballet_ and the modern _Ballet Rambert_ generally perform together with visiting troupes from abroad at _Sadler's Wells Theatre_, Rosebery Ave., EC1. Box office tel. 278-8916. Angels underground station.

Classical Music

London has some five major symphony orchestras, the most famous being the _London Symphony Orchestra_, one of the best in the world. The orchestra performs in the _Barbican Concert Hall_ at the Barbican Centre, EC2. Tel. 588-1116. Moorgate or Barbican underground station.

Other chamber and symphony orchestras and smaller ensembles appear in the following halls:

Royal Albert Hall: Kensington Gore, SW7. Tel. 589-3203. Knightsbridge or South Kensington underground station. A wide variety of classical music performances are staged here, in addition to a host of other cultural events. The Henry Wood Promenade concert series is held here every summer from July to September. During the Promenade various concerts are performed at moderate prices. Tickets can be purchased at the box office before the concert. Half-price standing-room tickets are available as well.

Royal Festival Hall, Queen Elizabeth Hall, and _Purcell Room:_ Belvedere Rd., SE1. Tel. 928-0063. Waterloo or Embankment underground station. All three halls are housed in the South Bank Arts Centre and host pop and jazz performances as well as classicals.

Almeida Theatre: Almeida St., Islington, N1. Tel. 359-4404. Angel underground station. Situated in north London, the theater hosts chamber performances, cabarets, and various local and international festivals throughout the year.

Wigmore Hall: 36 Wigmore St., W1. Tel. 935-2141. Bond St. or Oxford Circus underground station. Wigmore Hall is noted for its chamber music, string quartet, and soloist performances.

Concerts are also held in numerous churches around the city, such as St. John's, Smith Sq., and St. Martin-in-the Fields. Some of the concerts are given in the afternoon. For more information, call Guildhall, tel. 606-3030 or check with any Tourist Information Centre.

Open-air concerts, generally held in the summer, are publicized in the entertainment weeklies mentioned above.

LONDON

Jazz, Rock, and Folk Music

London is a workshop of all kinds of music, from folk and country, to jazz, soul, reggae, and rock. All these rhythms come together to make London the capital of modern music, a city that attracts singers and groups from all over the world. Performances are held anywhere from dark, smoky clubs in Soho, to huge halls such as Wembley Arena. Check the entertainment journals, especially *Time Out*, to find out who is performing at the stadiums or hundreds of clubs, cabarets, and discos that shake the city. Performances of most popular singers are announced well in advance, but are usually sold out within a few days after tickets go on sale at the box office.

If you are interested in experiencing the music and club scene up close, the following list will be helpful:

Rock

A stop at one of the larger facilities has become a must for important entertainers.

Wembley Arena: Empire Way, Wembley, Middlesex. Tel. 902-8833. Wembley Park underground.
Hammersmith Odeon: Queen Caroline St., W6. Tel. 748-4081. Hammersmith underground.
Royal Albert Hall: Kensington Gore, SW7. Tel. 589-3203. Knightsbridge or South Kensington underground station.

Many groups and singers, mainly British, prefer performing in smaller halls and clubs, with a more intimate atmosphere. Each club has its own history and style that draws a different audience. Most are open until the small hours of the night. Here is a selection of a few such clubs:

Marquee: 90 Wardour St., W1. Tel. 437-6603. Piccadilly Circus underground station. One of the first rock clubs, in which many groups started in the '60s. Each evening two different groups perform.
Rock Garden: 6-7 The Piazza, Covent Garden, WC2. Tel. 240-3461. Covent Garden underground station. Rock and jazz performances each evening by two groups.
Limelight: 136 Shaftesbury Av., W1. Tel. 434-0572. Leicester Square underground station. Rock groups appear a few nights a week.
Dingwalls: Camden Lock, Camden High St., NW1. Tel. 267-4967. Chalk Farm or Camden Town underground station. One of the more famous music "institutions." Hosts famous names, both local and foreign. On Saturdays at noon there is a free jazz performance.
Camden Palace: 1A Camden High St., NW1. Tel. 387-0428. Camden Town or Mornington Crescent underground station. Each evening a different program. A large dance floor, sophisticated sound and light

London

systems, and a flashy audience are featured here. Restaurant and bar on the premises.

Electric Ballroom: 184 Camden High St., NW1. Tel. 435-9006. Camden Town underground station. A rock club during the week and disco on the weekend.

Jazz and Folk

Ronnie Scott's: 47 Frith St., W1. Tel. 439-0747. Tottenham Court Rd. underground station. Considered to be the best jazz club in town. House groups generally play, but sometimes there are guest performances of groups from other countries. It is advisable to phone in advance and check that the performance is not for members only.

100 Club: 100 Oxford St., W1. Tel. 636-0933. Tottenham Court Rd. underground station. Rock and classical jazz performances are held here.

Pizza Express: 10 Dean St., W1. Tel. 439-8722. Tottenham Court Rd. underground station. The jazz club is under the restaurant in the basement.

Town & Country Club: 9-17 Highgate Rd., NW5. Tel. 267-3334. Kentish Town underground station. A former cinema, hosts rock, jazz, and folk groups and singers from all over the world.

Discotheques

In London there are hundreds of discotheques. Some feature fantastic staging and computerized laser displays, special effects of light and smoke, and sophisticated sound systems. Others are more inconspicuously decorated and advertised. Many rock clubs turn into discotheques during the weekend, with live music. Call in advance to verify membership, dress requirements, and entrance fee. In some places women are granted free entrance on certain evenings.

Rheingold: 361 Oxford St., W1. Tel. 629-5343. Bond St. underground. A tourist haunt. Rich bar and buffet.

Studio La Valbonne: 62 Kingly St., W1. Tel. 439-7242. Oxford Circus or Piccadilly Circus underground station. Unusual stage design. Proper dress a must.

Les Elites: 253 Finchley Rd., NW3. Tel. 794-6628. Finchley Rd. underground station. A high-style club, in which everybody is dressed accordingly. Must be at least 23 years old to enter.

Purple Pussycat: 307 Finchley Rd., NW3. Tel. 794-2801. Finchley Rd. underground station. Attracts those between the ages of 20-35. Open on Sunday nights.

Gullivers: 11 Down St., W1. Tel. 499-0760. Hyde Park underground station. Soul music and foreign groups are featured here.

Empire Ballroom: Leicester Sq., WC2. Tel. 437-1446. Leicester Sq.

LONDON

underground station. Young and noisy. On Sunday afternoons the Ballroom becomes a skating disco.

Casinos

Casions adhere to a members-only policy, or require that you be accompanied by a member. It is also possible, in many places, to present your passport and purchase membership on the spot. It is not permissible to list casinos by name in guide books or other such publications. The reception desk at most hotels, however, should be able to provide you with the appropriate information. Check in advance for admittance regulations and dress code.

Sports

London, a sports capital, provides a wonderland of activity for the enthusiast. Several international sports events are held here annually, in addition to local events. English football (soccer) has drawn world-wide attention, both for its high quality and rambunctious audiences. Sports fans should check the papers for listings of sports activities. The city's many Tourist Information Centres can also help on this account. Tickets for sports events can be obtained in advance at *Keith Prowse*, Banda House, Cambridge Grove, Hammersmith, W6. Tel. 741-7441.

Football (Soccer)

England is the birthplace of football, the country from which the game spread, in various forms, to stadiums across the globe. English football teams have been and continue to be among the most successful in the world. As for the audiences, there is no more wild or uncontrollable a crowd. Much of the excitement associated with football occurs in the stadium bleachers: the singing, shouting, and spectator games are all part of the program. Unfortunately, much of the revelry too often turns dedicated fans into wild mobs that have been known to participate in dangerous riots.

London has quite a few football clubs, each representing a specific area of the city. The teams with the longest and most impressive records in the First League are Tottenham Hotspur (Spurs) and Arsenal, two bitter rivals. No football fan who comes to London should miss a competition between them. The football season starts in August and lasts until May. The games are usually held on Saturdays and Wednesdays.

The important games — the Football Association (FA) Cup Final and international games — are held in *Wembley Stadium* in Middlesex, which has 100,000 seats. It is a very modern and comfortable stadium, and watching a game there is a real experience. (tel. 902-8833).

*L*ONDON

You can obtain advance tickets for sports events by contacting team offices a few days before a game, or by contacting a ticket agency. It is best to buy tickets well in advance. If you have neglected buying your tickets until the last moment, go to the box office a few hours before the game and try to purchase them there. Beware of the scalpers who tell you that there are no more tickets at the box office.

There are almost always tickets available for half price in the standing area of the stadium. It is not recommended to enter this area, however, as this is where the most vicious of the fans stand, and it makes watching the game almost impossible.

Remember — if you are wearing a badge or the colors of a team, avoid entering the seating area of the rival team's fans.

The main football clubs are the following:

Arsenal F.C.: Highbury Stadium, Avenall Rd., N5. Tel. 359-0131.
Chelsea: Stamford Bridge, Fulham Rd., SW6. Tel. 385-5545.
Crystal Palace: Selhurst Park, Whitehorse Lane, SE25. Tel. 653-4462.
Queens Park Rangers: Loftus Rd., W12. Tel. 743-0262.
Tottenham Hotspur (Spurs): White Hart Lane, High Rd., N17. Tel. 808-1020.
West Ham United: Green St., Upton Park, E13. Tel. 472-2740.
Wimbeldon: 49 Durnsford Rd., SW19. Tel. 946-6311.

Rugby

Rugby is a rough and rugged game. Although not as sophisticated as American football, which traces its roots to Rugby, it is no less exciting and moves at a faster pace than its counterpart in the United States. London's professional rugby team plays on Sundays in *Fulham Stadium*, Craven Cottage, Stevenage Rd., SW6. Tel. 736-6561. Amateur games are played on Saturday afternoons from September to April at Twickenham Stadium, Whitten Rd., Twickenham. Tel. 892-9303.

Cricket

The popularity of this very British game has reached many playing fields across England, and the British Commonwealth countries as well.

The cricket season runs from April until September. More sophisticated matches can stretch for up to three days. The game is a bit complicated, but give it a go if you have the patience. Major games are held at two locations:

Lord's Cricket Ground, St. John Woods Rd., NW8. Tel. 289-1615.
The Oval, Kensington Rd., SE1. Tel. 735-4911.

LONDON

Tennis
London is famous for the Wimbledon Tennis Championship, held annually for two weeks during June and July at the *All England Club* in Wimbledon Park, Church Rd. Tickets for the championship on the Centre Court and Court 1 can be obtained by ballot only by writing to: All England Lawn Tennis Championship Club, Ballot Office, Church Rd., Wimbledon, SW1. During the championship, however, there will most likely be exciting matches under way in the other sixteen lawn courts, to which you can enter for a fee at the time of the match. The courts, surrounded by wooden benches, allow for easy access from one green to another.

Horse Races
Horse racing is as popular as the tennis championships. Those who feel like splurging can come to try their luck at a few of the large race tracks close to London. The prestigious competitions are held in Epsom, Sandown, and Ascot. Traditional racing competitions are held from May to November, while jumping competitions are held in the winter.

Rowing
The highlight of the rowing season focuses on the Oxford University and Cambridge University competition held annually on the Saturday before Easter. On this day, thousands of Londoners flock to the banks of the Thames, from Putney Bridge, where the competition starts, to Mortlake Anglican Boathouse at the finish line. You will be sure to see lots of London's old-timers converging to recount the events of past races.

For information on boat rentals, contact Mark Edwards, Constables Boathouse, 15 Thames St., Hampton, Middlesex, TW1-2EW. Tel. 941-4858.

*L*ONDON

Filling the Basket — Where to Shop for What

London is a veritable paradise for those who like to shop. The selection is enormous, the prices are often attractive, and ones appetite for spending usually increases with the offerings.

In the clothing chain stores prices are generally fixed, regardless of the area of the city in which the branch is located. There are big sales two to four times a year, usually with discounts of up to 50%. The major sales are after Christmas and in July.

In most stores you can obtain documents for the value-added tax (VAT) retail exemption (see "Practical Information — VAT and Retail Export"); it is worthwhile to ask before buying.

Bargains can be found mainly in the open-air markets and in unassuming stores. If you search hard enough, you are sure to come up with some great finds.

Department Stores

London's department stores are famous the world over; to some even more so than its palaces. *Harrods*, world renown, claims to offer anything you could ever imagine. There is no doubt that it is a thrilling experience to wander through London's many spectacular department stores. Most are designed in excellent taste, and some specialize in specific products. If you do not feel like buying, just look, examine, and enjoy yourself. The food and cosmetics displays are especially interesting. The following is a list of the largest and most well-known department stores.

Debenhams: 334-338 Oxford St., W1. Oxford Circus underground station. Mainly for clothes.
John Lewis: Oxford St., W1. Oxford Circus underground station. Specializes in clothing, household goods, and gifts. The owners claim that their prices are the lowest available, and are prepared to refund you for the difference if you prove otherwise.
Liberty: 210-222 Regent St., W1. Oxford Circus underground station. Highly regarded for their fine fabrics, known as "Liberty prints."
Selfridges: 400 Oxford St., W1. Marble Arch underground station. Mainly cosmetics, clothing, and food.
Marks & Spencer: 173 Oxford St., W1. Oxford Circus underground station. Clothing at good prices.
Simpson: 203 Piccadilly, W1. Piccadilly Circus underground station. Clothing.
Fortnum & Mason: 181 Piccadilly, W1. Green Park or Piccadilly

London

Circus underground station. Famous for its food section.

House of Fraser: 63 Kensington High St., W8. Kensington High St. underground station. Clothing and household items.

Army & Navy Stores: 105 Victoria St., SW1. St. James's Park underground station. Clothing.

Harrods: Knightsbridge, SW1. Knightsbridge underground station. Famous for having everything, particularly fine clothing and food. Widely known for its high prices.

Peter Jones: Sloane Square, SW1. Sloane Square underground station. Clothing, fabric, and household items. A part of the John Lewis group.

Harvey Nichols: Knightsbridge, SW1. Knightsbridge underground station. Clothing.

Shopping Malls and Commercial Centers

London is not yet abundant with American-style shopping malls. In fact, in London there are only two such malls worthy of a visit.

Brent Cross Shopping Centre: Brent Cross, NW4. Brent Cross underground station. The center is particularly popular, even though the selection at the branches there pales in comparison to the choices at the main stores downtown. There is a bus to the shopping center from the underground station. It is worth waiting for the bus rather than walking.

Wood Green Shopping City: High Road, N22. Wood Green or Turnpike Lane underground station.

Several stores, generally high-priced, can be found grouped together at the following locations:

Covent Garden, WC2. Covent Garden underground station.
Burlington Arcade, Piccadilly St., W1. Green Park or Piccadilly Circus underground station.
Knightsbridge, SW1. Knightsbridge underground station.
Bond Street, W1. Bond St. underground station.
Kensington Market: 49-53 Kensington High Street, W8. Kensington High Street underground station. Stores for young people.

Women's Fashion

Expensive Stores

Bond Street and Knightsbridge cater to the up-scale shopper. The establishments there definitely warrant a peek, even if you are not buying. They include shops of exclusive fashion designers, some of whom also have boutiques in *Harrods* and *Selfridges* department stores.

Saint Laurent: 113 New Bond St., W1. Bond St. underground station.

LONDON

Valentino: 160 New Bond St., W1. Bond St. underground station.
Cacharel: 103 New Bond St., W1. Bond St. underground station.
Ungaro: 153A New Bond St., W1. Bond St. underground station.
Guy Laroche: 33 Brook St., W1. Bond St. underground station.
Giorgio Armani: 123 New Bond St., W1. Bond St. underground station.
Chanel: 26 Old Bond St., W1. Green Park underground station.

Moderately-priced Stores

Merchandise in the following stores is not inexpensive, but is certainly within reach for many, and the quality of the products justify the expense. The major areas are Oxford Street, Covent Garden, and King's Road, which has always been the center for young fashion.

Benetton: 328 Oxford St., W1. Bond St. underground station. Check for branches throughout the city.
Austin Reed: 103-113 Regent St., W1. Piccadilly Circus underground station.
Connections: 12 James St., WC2. Covent Garden underground station.
Papier Mâché: 14 Endell St., WC2. Covent Garden underground station.
Laura Ashley: 256-258 Regent St., W1. Oxford Circus underground station. Check for branches throughout the city.
Stefanel: 15 South Molton St., W1. Bond St. underground station. Check for branches throughout the city.
Next: 160 Regent St., W1. Oxford Circus underground station.
Monsoon: 67 South Molton St., W1. Bond St. underground station.
Ashton's Designer Wear: 5 Gees Court, W1. Bond St. underground station.
Scottish Merchant: 16 New Row, WC2. Covent Garden underground station.
Fenwick of Bond Street: 63 New Bond St., W1. Bond St. underground station.
Koko: 4 Garrick St., WC2. Covent Garden underground station.
Beau Monde: 43 Lexington St., W1. Oxford Circus underground station.
Brown's: 23-27 South Molton St., W1. Bond St. underground station.
Dickins & Jones: 224-244 Regent St., W1. Oxford Circus underground station.

Inexpensive Stores

Next to Nothing: 129-131 Oxford St., W1. Oxford Circus underground station.
Top Shop / Top Man: In Peter Robinson, Oxford Circus, W1. Oxford Circus underground station.
C&A: 505 Oxford St., W1. Marble Arch underground station. Check

*L*ONDON

for other branches in town.
Marks & Spencer: 173 Oxford St., W1. Oxford Circus underground station. Check for other branches in town.
Littlewoods: 207 Oxford St., W1. Marble Arch underground station.
Chelsea Girl: 124 Kensington High St., W8. Kensington High St. underground station.

Large Sizes

Crispins: 28-39 Chiltern St., W1. Baker St. underground station.
Largesse Fashions: 84 Marylebone High St., W1. Baker St. underground station.

Men's Fashions

London has many stores that specialize in clothing for men. For ready-made clothing, you can try the men's departments in the large department stores. Any Londoner with the means, however, has his suits made to order by one of the elite tailors, most of whose shops are on Savile Row.

Connections for Men: 55-56 Long Acre, WC2. Covent Garden underground station.
Moss Bros.: 21-26 Bedford St., WC2. Covent Garden underground station. Here you can also rent formal wear for special occasions.
Cecil Gee: 47 Long Acre, WC2. Covent Garden underground station.
Austin Reed: 103-113 Regent St., W1. Oxford Circus underground station.
Cerruti 1881: 76 New Bond St., W1Y. Bond St. underground station.
Jaeger: 204 Regent St., W1. Oxford Circus underground station.
Top Shop / Top Man: In Peter Robinson, Oxford Circus, W1. Oxford Circus underground station.

Coffee and Tea

Tea has been Britain's national drink since the eighteenth century, and some of the firms that currently market tea and coffee were already established then. The most famous are the following:

Twining's: 216 Strand, WC2.
Tea House: 15A Neal St., WC2.
Angelucci: 23B Frith St., W1.
HR Higgins: 79 Duke St., W1.

Books

Dozens and dozens of book stores dot the entire city. Many new and used book stores are located in the Cecil Court, Charing Cross Rd. area, and on Great Russell St.

London

A small sample selection:

Foyles: 119 Charing Cross Rd., WC2. Claims to be the largest and most comprehensive book store in the world. Its chaotic atmosphere makes it fun for scavengers and a real frustration if you are looking for something specific.

Penguin Bookshop: 10 The Market, Covent Garden Piazza, WC2. Here you will find all the books on the market published by Penguin, in addition to books by other publishers.

Virago Book Shop: 34 Southampton St., WC2. This highly regarded book store owned by a feminist publishing house offers a wide selection of books on many topics as well as feminist literature.

Probsthain and Co. Oriental Booksellers: 41 Great Russell St., WC1, Probsthain's specializes in Oriental literature (from Asia in particular), with a plentiful selection for those interested.

Dillons the Bookstore: 82 Gower St., WC1. This was once one of the largest book stores in the world, although its moment of glory has faded.

Art Bilbiographic: 37 Great Russell St., WC1. Here the shelves are stocked with an excellent selection of literature on the arts, with a special emphasis on late nineteenth-century material.

Electric Appliances
Most of these stores are located in the Tottenham Court Road area.

Photography
The following stores are also concentrated around Tottenham Court Rd.:

Keith Johnson Photographic: 11 Great Marlborough St., W1.
City Camera Exchange: 43 Strutton Ground, SW1, with branches in other parts of the city as well.

Toys
Of a wide selection, two are particularly recommended:

Hamleys: 188-196 Regent St., W1. Hamleys is considered the largest toy store in the world, and is a very popular attraction for many.
Toys-R-Us: 78-80 High St., N22. An enormous structure, this is the place for visitors to north London who knows what they are looking for. The toys are shelved and inaccessible, but the selection is large and the prices are attractive. Next to the Brent Cross Shopping Centre.

Household Furnishings and Kitchen Appliances
There are a number of large and well-known stores stocked with

LONDON

household items, such as *Habitat* on Tottenham Court Rd., W1, and the *John Lewis* department store on Oxford St. The following are also worth a visit:

Next Interiors: 160 Regent St., W1.
Laura Ashley Decorator Showroom: 71-73 Lower Sloane St., SW1.
The Design Centre, 28 Haymarket, SW1. An interesting modern British design. The Centre sells items recommended by the British Design Council and stores information on thousands of British-made products.
Reject China Shops: 33-35 Beauchamp Place, SW3. The three shops located here sell seconds twice a year and discounted firsts the rest of the year.
Garrard: 112 Regent St., W1. Established in the eighteenth century, many members of the Royal Family come to purchase sterling and cutlery.
Authentics: 42 Shelton St., WC2. Carries a chic, stylish selection of furniture and household accessories.

Cosmetics

Two chains compete for the title in cosmetics and health-related items: *Boots the Chemist*, in the Brent Cross Shopping Centre, 137-139 High Rd., N22, and *Underwoods*, 7 Strand, WC1. The cosmetics and perfume departments in the large department stores, such as *Selfridges*, *Harrods*, and *Debenhams*, are particularly exclusive. *The Body Shop*, 32 Great Marlborough St. W1, is a popular chain for natural cosmetics at affordable prices. Check the telephone directory for addresses of branches throughout the city.

Jewelry

A particularly large selection of jewelry stores are located on Oxford Street.

In the *Burlington Arcade* and on Bond Street you will find exclusive jewelers, such as *Cartier*, 175 New Bond St., W1. It is also worth visiting the *London Diamond Centre*, 10 Hanover St., W1.

Records

Virgin Megastore: 14-16 Oxford St., W1.
HMV: 363 Oxford St., W1.
Tower Records: 1 Piccadilly Circus, W1.
Smithers and Leigh: 527-531 Oxford St., W1.
Cheapo Cheapo: 53 Rupert St., W1. Especially good for classical works.
The Music Discount Centre: 29 Rathbone Place, W1.

For jazz enthusiasts:

Ray's Jazz: 180 Shaftesbury Avenue, WC2..
58 Dean Street Records: 58 Dean St., W1.

*L*ONDON

Open-air Markets

London's open-air markets are as popular as its museums. A visit to a market in London is a fun experience for any tourist, and you are guaranteed not to leave empty-handed. But watch out for modern-day Artful Dodgers, who might leave you with empty pockets.

The following are the most important markets:

Covent Garden Market: The Piazza, Covent Garden, WC2. Covent Garden underground station. The market is one of London's liveliest. A variety of hand-crafted knickknacks and souvenirs are displayed during most of the week. On Monday antiques are sold. The market is well stocked with cafés and permanently installed shops. (Open Mon.-Sat. 9am-5pm.)

Jubilee Market: WC2. Covent Garden underground station. Jubilee, bordering the Covent Garden Piazza, operates as a general market during most of the week, selling houseold items and other odds and ends. On Mondays, when the market here merges with the antiques market at Covent Garden, stalls are filled with second-hand clothing, bric-a-brac, and some interesting antiques. (Antiques market open Mon. 9am-5pm, general market open Tues.-Sat. 9am-5pm.)

Portobello Road Market: Portobello Rd., W11. Notting Hill Gate or Ladbroke Grove underground station. The market is most highly regarded for its fine, expensive antiques. If you are interested, come on Fri. or Sat. when reputable dealers trade. Other stalls selling discounted clothing and crafts are also sold then. The rest of the week stands are filled with fruits and vegetables and some clothing. (Antiques market open Fri. 5am-3pm, Sat. 8am-5pm, fruit and vegetable market open Mon.-Wed., Fri.-Sat. 8am-5pm, Thurs. 8am-1pm.)

Berwick Street Market: Berwick St., W1. Oxford Circus or Piccadilly Circus underground station. This is Soho's colorful vegetable market, where you will find stands filled with other food items. (Open Mon.-Sat. 9am-5pm.)

Petticoat Lane: Middlesex St., E1. Aldgate, Aldgate East or Liverpool St. underground station. This is one of the oldest and most popular Sunday markets in London. New garments and fashion accessories are the main attraction here. Other textiles and some electronics are also sold. (Open Sun. 9am-2pm.)

Leadenhall Market: Whittington Ave. near Gracechurch St., EC3. Bank underground station. If you are in the central part of the city be sure to visit Leadenhall market. The exclusive shops in this charming food market carry delicacies, meat, fish, poultry, cheeses and wine. (Open Mon.-Fri. 7am-3pm.)

London

Leather Lane Market: EC1. Chancery Lane underground station. The market caters to your every need: from fruits and vegetables to plants, fashion accessories to household accessories, hardware to underwear, and more. (Open Mon.-Fri. noon-3pm.)

Camden Lock Market: Camden High St., NW1. Camden Town or Chalk Farm underground station. This charming shopping area is particularly popular among young Londoners. The open-air market on Sat. and Sun. is filled with antiques, crafts, jewelry, clothing and the like. Home-made food stalls can also be found here. (Open Sat.-Sun.)

Camden Passage: N1. Angel underground station. Camden Passage is a busy and highly regarded antiques market. The antiques shops situated around the market make the area a real treat for collectors. In order to find bargains you should arrive early. (Open Wed. and Sat. 8:30am-3pm.)

Greenwich Market: Greenwich High Rd. and Covered Market Square. SE10. British Rail to New Gate Cross and bus no. 117, or a direct bus to Greenwich. This popular antiques, crafts, and second-hand market is open on the weekend. The quality of the merchandise here is better than what is found in most markets. Antique and second-hand clothing are well represented. There is also a fruit and vegetable market that operates during the week. (Antiques market open Sat.-Sun. 9am-5pm, fruit and vegetable market open Mon.-Fri. 9am-5pm.)

New Caledonian Market (Bermondsey Market): Tower Bridge Rd., SE1. London Bridge underground station. London's prosperous antiques market opens only once a week, at the crack of dawn. This is the most popular market for dealers and experienced collectors. Treasure hunters should rise early to be there for the bargains. (Open Fri. 4:30am-noon.)

Auction Houses

London is the hub of auction house activity. Some houses are world renowned and do business in five continents. In both the large auction houses and in the smaller neighborhood establishments, a wide variety of goods are offered, from antique coins and old shoes to vintage cars and legendary treasures. The prices vary to match the goods.

If you are interested in purchasing goods, it is advisable to obtain a catalog of the auction in advance. Items are also usually displayed the day before the auction.

Even if you do not intend to buy the Duchess of Windsor's jewels or Elton John's glasses, attending a London auction is a unique experience.

*L*_ONDON_

Tension fills the air, and the auctioneer closes deals at top speed.

Information on the sales can be found in *The Times* and *The Daily Telegraph* newspapers.

The most important auction houses are the following:

Bonham's Montpelier Galleries: Montpelier St., SW7. Tel. 584-9161. The smallest of the four. Specializes in antiques, furniture, and art objects.
Christies: 8 King St. SW1. Tel. 839-9060. A wide variety of objects, some very attractively priced. There is also a branch at 85 Old Brompton Rd., South Kensington, SW7. Tel. 581-7611.
Phillips: Blenstock House, 7 Blenheim St. W1. Tel. 629-6602. A huge selection of art objects, collectors items, pictures, antiques, etc.
Sotheby's: 34-35 New Bond St., W1. Tel. 493-8080. The largest and most famous auction house in the world. Specializes in art objects, antiques, cars, and a variety of collectors items from all over the world. Do not feel inhibited by the name, as there are items for every pocket.

*L*ONDON

Important Addresses and Phone Numbers

Emergencies

Ambulance, fire-fighters, and police (free from all telephones): Tel. 999.

Automobile breakdown (24-hour-a-day): Automobile Association (AA) breakdown service. Tel. 954-7373. Royal Automobile Club breakdown service Tel. 839-7050.

Lost items in taxis: Metropolitan Police Lost Property Office, 15 Penton St., NW1. (Telephone inquiries not accepted.)

Lost items in underground trains or buses: London Transport Lost Property Office, 200 Baker St., NW1. (Telephone inquiries not accepted.)

General

Intra-city public transportation information (24-hour-a-day): Tel 222-1234.

Babysitters: Childminders, tel. 935-2049 or 935-4386.

Operator for addresses and telephone numbers: Tel. 142 for information in London; tel. 192 for information outside of London.

Operator for collect calls and international exchanges: Tel. 100.

Talking clock (time): Tel. 123.

Weather forecast: Tel. 246-8091.

London for Children: Tel. 246-8007.

Sports: Tel. 246-8020.

Tourism in Britain: Tel. 730-3488.

Daily Telegraph Information: Tel. 353-4252.

Heathrow Airport: Terminal 1: Tel. 745-7002
Terminal 2: Tel. 745-7115
Terminal 3: Tel. 745-7412

Gatwick Airport: Tel. 0293-28822

Luton Airport: Tel. 0582-36061

LONDON

Stansted Airport: Tel. 0279-502380

London City Airport: Tel. 474-5555

Embassies and High Commissions

Australian High Commission: Australia House, Strand, WC2. Tel. 438-8000.

Canadian High Commission: Canada House, Trafalgar Square, SW1. Tel. 629-9492.

Irish Embassy: 17 Grosvener Place, SW1. Tel. 235-2171.

New Zealand High Commission: New Zealand House, 80 Haymarket, SW1. Tel. 930-8422.

United States of America Embassy: 24 Grosvener Square, W1. Tel. 499-9000.

*I*NDEX

A

Admiralty Arch	96
Admiralty House	84
Albany Court Yard	108
Albany House	108
Albert Bridge	148
Albert Embankment	200
Albert Memorial	144
Almeida Theatre	236
Ambassadors' Court	101
Apothecaries Hall	50
Apsley House	134
Arthur Middleton	82
Ascot	199
Athenaeum	104

B

Bank of England	60
Bankside	156
Banqueting House	83
Barbican	56
Barbican Centre for Arts and Conferences	57
Bath	219
Battersea Park	209
Baynard Castle	52
BBC	128
Beating the Retreat	84
Bedford Square	120
Berkeley Square	109
Berwick Street Market	248
Big Ben	92
Blackfriar Pub	50
Blackfriars Bridge	50
Bloomsbury Square	121
Blue Ball Yard	102
Bodleian Library (Oxford)	218
Bond Street	109
Brass Rubbing Centre (All Hallows-by-the-Tower)	64
Brass Rubbing Centre (St. James's Church)	204
Brass Rubbing Centre (St. John the Baptist Church)	199
Brass Rubbing Centre (Westminster Abbey)	89
Bridewell Prison	73
Brighton	221
British Design Centre	104
British Library	121
British Telecom Tower	128
Brook's	102
Buckingham Palace	97
Burlington Arcade	108
Burlington House	108

C

Cabinet War Rooms	85
Cadogan Pier	148
Café Royal	111
Cambridge	218
Cambridge Circus	116
Cambridge University	219
Camden Lock Market	249
Camden Passage	249
Canterbury	220
Carlton Club	101
Carlton House Terrace	96
Carlyle's House	149
Cecil Court	113
Cenotaph	85
Central Criminal Court (Old Bailey)	73
Charbonnet et Walker	109
Charing Cross	83
Cheapside	57
Chelsea Palace	148
Chelsea Physic Garden	148
Chinatown	115
Chiswick House	188
Christies	250
Churches and Chapels	
Albert Memorial Chapel	196
All Hallows-by-the-Tower	64
Brompton Oratory	141
Chapel Royal	100
Chelsea Old Church	149
Christ Church	56
Christ Church (Oxford)	217
Christ Church (Spitalfields)	163
Church of St. James	107
Danish Church	130
French Protestant Church	117
Notre Dame de France	113
Queen's Chapel	100

253

INDEX

St. Andrew-by-the-Wardrobe..................52
St. Ann and St. Agnes Church.....................56
St. Anne's..........................116
St. Bartholomew the Great.........74
St. Benet's.........................52
St. Botolph Aldgate............161
St. Botolph-without-Aldersgate.......................56
St. Brides Church...............73
St. Clement Danes Church......69
St. Dunstan-in-the-West Church.............................72
St. George's Chapel (Windsor)..........................196
St. Giles Cripplegate..........57
St. Giles-in-the-Fields......118
St. John's (Smith Square)......93
St. John the Baptist..........199
St. Lawrence Jewry..............57
St. Luke's Church...............149
St. Margaret's Church..........85
St. Martin-in-the-Fields......95
St. Martin-within-Ludgate......73
St. Mary-le-Bow.................58
St. Mary-le-Strand..............77
St. Mary's Catholic Church....171
St. Michael's Church............61
St. Pancras Church.............123
St. Patrick's Church...........117
St. Paul's Cathedral............52
St. Paul's Church...............81
St. Sepulchre-without-Newgate..........................73
St. Stephen Walbrook............60
Savoy Chapel....................77
Southwark Cathedral...........153
Temple Church...................71
Westminster Abbey..............85
Westminster Cathedral..........99
Citadel..........................96
Clarence House.................101
Cleopatra's Needle..............75
Clink Prison...................156
Cock Tavern.....................72
Coliseum........................82
College of Arms.................52
Commonwealth Institute........144
County Hall....................160
Courtauld Institute of Art....127
Covent Garden Market..........248
Covent Garden Plaza.............79

Criterion Theatre..............105
Crown Jewels....................65
Crystal Palace.................210
Crystal Palace Park............211
Cutty Sark.....................176

D
Duke of York's Column...........96
Duke of York's Headquarters....................145

E
Eros statue....................105
Eton College...................199

F
Faraday Building................52
Fenton House...................171
Fitzroy Square.................129
Flamsteed House................180
Flask Walk.....................173
Fleet Prison....................73
Fleet Street....................72
Floris.........................102
Fortnum & Mason................108
Foyles.........................117
Freedom Press Bookshop........164
French House...................116
Frogmore Gardens...............197

G
Garrard........................111
George Inn.....................153
Gipsy Moth IV..................176
Globe Theatre..................156
Golden Square..................116
Goodwin's Court.................82
Gordon Square..................121
Gordon's Wine Bar...............75
Gower Street...................124
Grave of the Unknown Warrior..........................88
Gray's Inn......................67
Great Conservatory.............210
Green Park.....................208
Greenwich Foot Tunnel.........176
Greenwich Market...............249
Greenwich Park.................180
Guildhall.......................57
Guildhall (Windsor)............199
Guildhall Library...............57
Guiness World of Records......112

254

INDEX

H
Ham House 185
Hamleys 111
Hampstead Heath 169
Hampstead Village 209
Hampton Court Palace 189
Hampton Green 193
Harrods 140
Hatchard's 107
Her Majesty's Theatre 104
Highgate 172
HMS Belfast 152
Hogarth House 188
Holland House 209
Holland Park 209
Horse Guards 84
House, Foreign, and Commonwealth Offices 84
House of St. Barnabas 117
Houses of Parliament 91

I
Inner Temple 71
Inns of the Chancery 67
Institute of Contemporary Art 96
Isle of Dogs 176

J
Jack Straw's Castle 172
Jewel House 65
Jewel Tower 92
John Wesley's Chapel and House 66
Jubilee Gardens 160
Jubilee Market 80

K
Keats House 172
Kensington Palace 137
Kenwood House 209
Kew Gardens 216
Kew Palace 184
Kew Royal Botanic Gardens 183
Kew Village 185
King's College (Cambridge) 219
King's Cross train station 123
King's Road 145

L
Lamb and Flag 81
Lambeth Palace 160
Lancaster House 101
Leadenhall Market 61

Leather Lane Market 248
Leicester Square 112
Light Fantastic, the World Centre of Holography 112
Lincoln's Inn 68
Lincoln's Inn Fields 68
Linley Sambourne House 144
Little Venice 131
Lloyd's of London 61
Lobb 102
Lock 102
London Brass Rubbing Centre 107
London Bridge 61
London Diamond Centre 111
London Dock 166
London Dungeon 153
London Experience, The 112
London International Financial Futures Exchange 60
London Library 103
London Planetarium 133
London Silver Vaults 68
London Stock Exchange 61
London University 121
London Zoo 131

M
Magna Carta Memorial 199
Mansion House 60
Marble Arch 134
Marble Hill House 185
Markets, Open-air 248
Mall, The 96
Marlborough House 100
Meridian Building 181
Mermaid Theatre 50
Michelin House 150
Middle Temple 71
Middlesex Crown Court (Middlesex Guildhall) 85
Ministry of Defence 84
Monument 63
Museums and Galleries
    Abbey Trearure Museum 91
    Ashmolean Museum (Oxford) 218
    Battle of Britain Museum 173
    Bear Gardens Museum 156
    Bethnal Green Museum of Childhood 165
    Bomber Command Museum 173

INDEX

British Heritage Motor Museum ... 211
British Museum ... 120
Clock Museum ... 57
Courtauld Institute Galleries ... 121
Dickens House Museum ... 124
Eton Life, Museum of ... 199
Fitzwilliam Museum (Cambridge) ... 219
Flaxman Gallery ... 124
Geffrye Museum ... 165
Geological Museum ... 205
Hayward Gallery ... 157
Historic Ships Collection ... 166
Household Cavalry Museum ... 198
Hunterian Museum ... 68
IBA Broadcasting Gallery ... 140
Imperial War Museum ... 160
Instruments, Museum of ... 143
Jewish Museum ... 121
Kew Bridge Engines and Water Supply Museum ... 185
Le Fevre Gallery ... 109
Light Fantastic Gallery of Holography ... 80
London, Museum of ... 56
London Transport Museum ... 79
Madame Tussaud's Royalty and Empire Exhibition ... 194
Madame Tussaud's Wax Museum ... 132
Mankind, Museum of ... 109
National Army Museum ... 147
National Gallery ... 95
National Maritime Museum ... 179
National Museum of Labour History ... 168
National Portrait Gallery ... 113
National Postal Museum ... 56
Natural History Museum ... 141
Percival David Foundation of Chinese Art ... 121
Petrie Museum ... 124
Pollock's Toy Museum ... 128
Queen's Gallery ... 97
RAF Museum ... 173
Ranger's House ... 180
Roman Baths Museum (Bath) ... 219
Royal Fusiliers Museum ... 65
Royal Mews Exhibition ... 198
Science Museum ... 143
Serpentine Gallery ... 136
Shakespeare's Birthplace ... 218
Sir John Soane's Museum ... 68
Tate Gallery ... 93
Theatre Museum ... 79
Thomas Coram Foundation for Children ... 124
Tradescart Museum of Garden History ... 160
Victoria and Albert Museum ... 141
Wallace Collection ... 127
Wellcome Museum of the History of Medicine ... 123
Wellington Museum ... 134
Whitechapel Art Gallery ... 164
Wimbledon Lawn Tennis Museum ... 211
Wimbledon Windmill ... 211

N

National Film Theatre ... 157
National Sports Centre ... 211
National Theatre ... 157
Naval and Military Club ... 109
Neal Street ... 81
Nelson's Column ... 95
New Caledonian Market (Bermondsey Market) ... 249
Newgate Prison ... 73

O

Old Admiralty ... 84
Old Bailey (Central Criminal Court) ... 73
Old Compton Street ... 116
Old Curiosity Shop, The ... 68
Old Deer Park ... 185
Old Royal Observatory ... 180
Old War Office ... 84
Oxford ... 217
Oxford Botanic Garden ... 218
Oxford University ... 217

P

Palace Theatre ... 116
Pall Mall ... 104
Parliament ... 26,
Parliament Hill ... 209
Parliament Square ... 85
Paternoster Square ... 56
Paxton & Whitefield ... 103
Pencraft ... 61

INDEX

Penhaligon's..77
Petticoat Lane market.............................162
Piccadilly...107
Piccadilly Arcade.....................................108
Piccadilly Circus......................................105
Placentia Palace......................................177
Port of London...157
Portman Square.......................................127
Portobello Road Market..........................138
Prince Henry's Room................................72
Public Record Office.................................69
Puddle Dock...50
Pulteney Bridge (Bath)............................220
Purcell Room..236

Q

Quadrant, The..111
Queen Anne's Gate.................................100
Queen's Cottage......................................184
Queen Elizabeth Hall...............................236
Queen Victoria Memorial..........................97
Queen Victoria (statue of)......................198
Queen's Chapel.......................................100
Queen's House (Greenwich)..................179

R

Ranelagh Gardens..................................146
Regent Street...107
Richmond...183
Rippon..116
Ritz, The...109
Roman Fortress...56
Royal Academy of Arts...........................108
Royal Albert Hall.....................................143
Royal Arcade...109
Royal College of Music...........................143
Royal College of Physicians..................130
Royal College of Surgeons......................68
Royal Court Theatre................................145
Royal Courts of Justice............................69
Royal Crescent (Bath).............................220
Royal Exchange..60
Royal Festival Hall..................................157
Royal Hospital, Chelsea.........................145
Royal Institute of Painters
in Water Colors.......................................107
Royal Mews..97
Royal Naval College................................177
Royal Opera Arcade................................103
Royal Opera House...................................87
Royal Pavilion (Brighton)........................221
Royal Shakespeare Theatre...................218
Royal Society of Arts................................76

Rule's Restaurant......................................77
Russell Square..121
Runnymede..199

S

Sadler's Wells Theatre............................236
St. Alban Tower..57
St. Bartholomew's Hospital......................74
St. James's Park.....................................207
St. James's Square.................................103
St. Katharine's Dock...............................165
St. Mary Overy Dock...............................156
St. Pancras Chambers............................123
St. Paul's Cathedral..................................52
St. Stephen's Tavern................................85
St. Thomas's
Old Operating Theatre............................153
Savile Row...111
Savill Gardens...197
Savoy Theatre..77
Scottish Office...84
Selfridges...125
Seven Stars, The.......................................69
Shepherd Market.....................................109
Shipwrights Arms....................................152
Simpson's-in-the-Strand...........................77
Sion College..73
Smithfield...74
Smithfield Central Market.........................74
Smith Square...92
Soho Square..117
Somerset House..77
Sotheby's...250
South Bank..157
South Bank Arts Centre..........................157
Spanish and Portuguese
Synagogue...161
Speakers' Corner....................................136
Spencer House..101
Spitalfields Market..................................163
Staple Inn...67
Stonehenge..220
Strand...77
Stratford-upon-Avon................................218
Sweetings...59
Syon Park...210

T

Tavistock Square.....................................121
Temple Bar Monument..............................69
Temple of Mithras......................................58
Ten Downing Street..................................84

257

INDEX

Thames Barrier
and Visitors Centre ... 181
Thames River ... 18
Theatre Royal, Drury Lane ... 77
Theatre Royal, Haymarket ... 104
Theatre Royal, Windsor ... 199
Time Life Building ... 109
Tower Bridge ... 151
Tower Hill ... 64
Tower of London ... 64
Town of Ramsgate ... 167
Trafalgar Square ... 95
Trafalgar Tavern ... 181
Travellers ... 104
Trocadero ... 112
Trooping the Colour ... 84
Trumper's ... 109
Turnbull & Asser ... 102
Twinings ... 69
Tyburn Memorial ... 134

U
Unilever House ... 73
University College ... 124

V
Valley Gardens ... 197
Vanbrugh Castle ... 181
Victoria Embankment ... 73
Victoria Tower ... 92
Victoria Tower Gardens ... 93

W
Waterloo Bridge ... 157
Waterloo Place ... 103
Welsh Office ... 84
Wembley Arena ... 237
Wembley Stadium ... 239
Westminster Bridge ... 200
Westminster Hall ... 92
Westminster Palace ... 92
Whitechapel ... 161
White's ... 102
White Tower ... 64
Whitechapel Bell Foundry ... 164
Whitehall ... 84
Whitehall Palace ... 83
Wigmore Hall ... 236
Wig & Pen Club, The ... 69
Wimbledon Common ... 211
Wimbledon Village ... 211
Windsor Castle ... 194
Windsor Great Park ... 197
Windsor Home Park ... 196
Windsor Safari Park ... 197
Winfield House ... 131
Woodhouse & Son ... 69

Y
Yacht Tavern, The ... 181
Ye Olde Cheshire Cheese ... 72
Yeoman Warders ... 65
York House ... 75
York Water Gate ... 75

NOTES

NOTES

Notes

Notes

QUESTIONNAIRE

In our efforts to keep up with the pace and pulse of London, we kindly ask your cooperation in sharing with us any information which you may have as well as your comments. We would greatly appreciate your completing and returning the following questionnaire. Feel free to add additional pages. A complimentary copy of the next edition will be sent to you should any of your suggestions be included.

Our many thanks!

To: Inbal Travel Information (1983) Ltd.
P.O.B. 39090
Tel Aviv 61390
Israel

Name: _____

Address: _____

_____

Occupation: _____

Date of visit: _____

_____

Purpose of trip (vacation, business, etc.): _____

_____

_____

Comments/Information: _____

_____
_____
_____
_____
_____
_____
_____
_____
_____
_____
_____
_____
_____
_____
_____
_____

L/9/1

INBAL Travel Information Ltd.
P.O.B. 39090 Tel Aviv
ISRAEL 61390